Abraham Lincoln

The Quest for Immortality

Abraham Lincoln

The Quest for Immortality

by

Dwight G. Anderson

Alfred A. Knopf

NEW YORK   1982

THIS IS A BORZOI BOOK
PUBLISHED BY ALFRED A. KNOPF, INC.

Copyright © 1982 by Dwight G. Anderson
All rights reserved under International and Pan-American Copyright
Conventions. Published in the United States by Alfred A. Knopf, Inc., New York,
and simultaneously in Canada by Random House of Canada Limited, Toronto.
Distributed by Random House, Inc., New York.

LIBRARY OF CONGRESS CATALOGING IN PUBLICATION DATA
Anderson, Dwight G.
Abraham Lincoln, the quest for immortality.
Includes bibliographical references and index.
1. Lincoln, Abraham, 1809–1865. 2. Weems, M. L.
(Mason Locke), 1759–1825. Life of George Washington.
3. Washington, George, 1732–1799. 4. Presidents—
United States—Biography. I. Title.
E457.2.A58 1982   973.7'092'4   81-13738
ISBN 0-394-49173-4   AACR2

Manufactured in the United States of America
First Edition

To fathers and sons:
Norman, Gale, Derek, Dore, Fritz

Contents

Acknowledgments

Most of what is important in my knowledge of American political culture I have learned from Norman Jacobson, including many of the perspectives developed in this work. Nancy Scott Anderson has not only assisted me with much of the research, but has made invaluable contributions to the analysis by her unerring grasp of essentials. I am especially grateful, also, to Michael Paul Rogin, who gave me a thoughtful critique of an earlier version of the manuscript and offered assistance in finding my publisher.

Henry Nash Smith, Charles Andrain, and Harlin Lewin have read portions of the manuscript and made valuable suggestions for its improvement. Jules Karlin first introduced me to the subject of Lincoln and was very generous in his support of my earlier academic efforts. Louis Hartz and Hannah Arendt, though I have known neither personally, have influenced my thinking about American politics in ways that cannot be adequately acknowledged in footnotes.

Finally, I wish to thank Henry Janssen, who has contributed to whatever merit this work may have in ways that he could not fully appreciate.

D.G.A.

Abraham Lincoln

The Quest for Immortality

Lincoln's Quest
and the Quest for Lincoln

. . . men should utter nothing for which they would not willingly be responsible through time and in eternity.

—A. Lincoln, 1862

More books have been written about Abraham Lincoln than any other figure in American history. Why another? Both prudence and modesty would seem to require an artful evasion of that question. The tradition of Lincoln scholarship in the United States is an old, active, and honorable one; by now, one would have to assume, all the questions about Lincoln have been raised and answered many times over. Yet, as the author of a recent study has observed,[1] the fundamental question about Lincoln, though vividly defined by an early biographer, has not been answered satisfactorily. Writing about Lincoln in 1893, John T. Morse, Jr., said, ". . . we cannot evade the insoluble problem of two men—two lives —one following the other with no visible link of connection between them; . . . physically one creature, morally and mentally two beings."[2] This book attempts to resolve the problem of the "two Lincolns"—the unprincipled politician versus the presidential god, the man versus the myth—by providing an explanation which confounds the categories of the two Lincolns, while restoring what Morse described as that "most singular life which many have been content to regard as an unsolved enigma." The result will, I hope, be not only a better understanding of the man, but a fuller appreciation of his impact on American political culture.

Both schools of thought about Lincoln—the one which sees him primarily as an ambitious, unscrupulous politician, as well as the one which views him as a moral exemplar and god—have noted Lincoln's inaccessibility; both have admitted there is something about him which defies analysis and have struggled to define that missing link mentioned by Morse. William Herndon, for example, a representative of the former viewpoint, wrote in an 1887 letter, "Probably except in his scrapes, Lincoln never poured out his soul to any mortal creature at anytime and on no subject. He was the most secretive—reticent—shut-mouthed man that ever existed." As a result, Herndon believed, "You had to *guess* at the man after years of acquaintance, and then you must look long and keenly before you *guessed,* or you would make an ass of yourself."[3] In the face of Lincoln's inaccessibility, many other writers have followed Herndon's advice, although, like Herndon, they have not always avoided the consequences of bad guessing.

No one has formulated the problem with greater force or precision than Woodrow Wilson, a spokesman for the reverential school, on the occasion of his acceptance of Lincoln's birthplace as a national memorial. In a speech that is as revealing about Wilson as it is about Lincoln, he said:

> I have read many biographies of Lincoln; I have sought out with the greatest interest the many intimate stories that are told of him, the narratives of nearby friends, the sketches at close quarters . . . but I have nowhere found a real intimate of Lincoln's. I nowhere get the impression in any narrative or reminiscence that the writer had in fact penetrated to the heart of his mystery, or that any man could penetrate to the heart of it. That brooding spirit had no real familiars. I get the impression that it never spoke out in complete self-revelation, and that it could not reveal itself completely to anyone. It was a very lonely spirit that looked out from underneath those shaggy brows and comprehended men without fully communing with them, as if, in spite of all its genial efforts at comradeship, it dwelt apart, saw its visions of duty where no man looked on. There is a very holy and very terrible isolation for the conscience of every man who seeks to read the destiny in affairs for others as well as for himself, for a nation as well as for individuals. That privacy no man can intrude upon. That lonely search of the spirit for the right perhaps no man can assist. This strange child of the cabin kept company with invisible things, was born into no intimacy but that of its own silently assembling and deploying thoughts.[4]

By depersonalizing his metaphor of the "brooding spirit" Wilson added stylistic force to his assertion that Lincoln was a man apart, outside the mundane order of things, seeing his visions of duty in lonely isolation from other men. Such a picture of Lincoln has been greatly enhanced more recently by the critic Edmund Wilson's "discovery" of Lincoln's 1838 address before the Springfield Lyceum. Calling attention to the portion of the Lyceum Address in which Lincoln seemed to project himself into the very Caesarian role against which he warned his audience, Edmund Wilson argued that Lincoln saw himself as a heroic figure from the very beginning of his public career: ambitiously seizing the opportunity presented by sectional conflict over slavery, "he created himself as a poetic figure, and he thus imposed himself on the nation."[5]

But Lincoln was both more and less mysterious than the two Wilsons depict him; he was both more and less candid about himself than Herndon believed. He was more mysterious because the Lyceum Address was prophetic not only of Lincoln's ambition, but of his specific presidential actions in founding a new constitutional order; less because the Lyceum Address was heavily indebted to Parson Weems's biography of George Washington.[6] Indeed, Weems's book provides the visible link connecting the two Lincolns, for Weems offered two contradictory models of political action which roughly correspond to the two dominant images of Lincoln in American history. The contradictory nature of these two models would seem to lend credence to the "two Lincolns" concept. However, the manner in which Lincoln followed these models suggests a confutation of the conventional wisdom about Lincoln's dual career: actually it was the virtuous Lincoln who was the ambitious Whig politician, and it was the demonic Lincoln who was founder of the political religion in which he was the leading exemplary figure.

That Lincoln the god and Lincoln the ambitious politician can both be traced to a single source further suggests that he was both more and less candid about himself than Herndon and others have realized. Lincoln usually said what he meant, and always meant what he said, but this meaning was not readily available to those who interpreted him without the key provided by Weems's book.

In presenting his life of Washington, an ersatz epic "with curious anecdotes equally honorable to himself and exemplary to his young countrymen," Weems offered a model of virtue to his readers which the young Lincoln attempted to follow carefully. It was a model which promised success to those who emulated Washington's virtues: honesty, industry, religious devotion, patriotism, and self-control of "malignant" passions. However, by including in his book the full text of Washington's Farewell Address, Weems was also presenting an alternative model of political success: that of a "cunning, ambitious, unprincipled" man who would seek greatness "on the ruins of public liberty"—the figure against whom Washington warned in his valedictory. That Lincoln followed both models sequentially—one upholding the advice of the father of his country, the other destructive of it—is an indication not only of the inadequacy of the "two Lincolns" concept; it is also evidence of how Lincoln's personal psychology became intertwined with the political history of the nation.

Weems's account of Washington's career is a story of family conflict and fratricide from which emerged a new basis of legitimacy for both himself and his countrymen. Depicting the Revolution as a civil war which began as a dispute over family birthrights and ended in permanent dissolution of the family, Weems presents Washington as the paternal founder of a new family regenerated through violence and the blessings of God. Washington's paternal authority, which depended in part on his renunciation of a crown at the war's conclusion, is embodied in the Farewell Address—an excellent summary of Federalist political thought— which Weems introduces as "the solicitude of a father for his children" whom he was about to leave to themselves. Much of the remainder of the book is devoted to the embellishment of Washington's advice in which Weems emphasizes the need for obedience to the law and preservation of the Union; constant vigilance to the dangers posed by ambitious, unprincipled men; and the establishment of "true religion." All these themes found their way into Lincoln's Lyceum Address.

Weems's book, which Lincoln read repeatedly as a youth, gave him more than an intellectual legacy; it also provided him with an imaginary father to replace the natural father whom he disdained.

Lincoln was a good son: he did emulate Washington's character as described by Weems, and remained formally committed, through his early years, to upholding Washington's advice and example. Even the Lyceum Address, in which Lincoln seemed to identify himself with an ambitious tyrant and proposed the establishment of a political religion to augment the Constitution, concluded with a paean to Washington. Lincoln's filial piety, however, was extinguished by the public reaction to his 1848 Mexican War speech in the House of Representatives, a speech in which he rebuked Polk's war policies as failing to meet Washingtonian standards of virtue. Lincoln had hoped the speech would attract national attention to himself as a virtuous leader. After it was ignored in Washington and widely ridiculed in Illinois, Lincoln entered a prolonged period of despondency from which he would not recover until 1854. When he finally emerged from this moratorium, he did so with a revolutionary vengeance, identifying himself not with Washington, the father of his country, but with Jefferson, the revolutionary son. By aligning his personal resentments against constitutional fathers with the injustice of Negro slavery, Lincoln discovered in the Declaration of Independence a means of liberation for both himself and the slave.

The liberation of Lincoln's "malignant" passions of hate and revenge was necessarily restrained by his election to the presidency. But though he attempted to reconcile his newly acquired obligations to the Constitution with his prior commitment to the Declaration, he was unable to do so. Two themes from his Lyceum Address provided him with a presidential agenda that was revolutionary in content: the establishment of a political religion and the re-creation of the Revolutionary community of 1776. Waging fratricidal war on the basis of divine authority, Lincoln succeeded in reestablishing the covenant of 1776. He thus effected a fusion of piety and politics in which the Civil War could be viewed as divine punishment for the nation's sins. His political religion drew not only upon Old Testament sources; it also anticipated the conventions of the New. Through his interpretation of the meaning of the war, as set forth especially in the Gettysburg Address, Lincoln succeeded in joining the constitutional order to a Christian immortality of sacrificial death and rebirth.[7] His theology connected death, the punishment for sin, to the promise of political redemption and everlasting life. As the founder of a new Union, Lincoln not only took Washington's place as the father of his country, but indirectly provided an ideological rationale by which the United States could become lawgiver to the world. This view of Lincoln's presidential purpose as informed by Weems's mythopoeic reading of American history challenges widely accepted views of American political culture and the role of the presidency in that culture.

Modern interpreters of United States history have been divided over whether to emphasize conflict or consensus as the central feature of the American past. The historiography of the Progressives in the early part of the century, which stressed the prominence of social conflict, was displaced at midcentury by a pluralist social science which emphasized the pervasiveness of a political consensus. This pluralist orthodoxy was undermined, in its turn, both by actual events of the 1960s and '70s and by a withering critique of pluralist assumptions developed during the same period. The result is an unresolved paradox: the United States is a nation which apparently combines a high degree of political stability with a high degree of domestic violence, conflict, and rebellion. In other words, a crisis of legitimacy has been seen as recurrently endemic to the institutions of national governance, despite the success of the central government in enforcing constitutional order.[8]

Recent scholarship suggests that neither conflict nor consensus in the United States has been understood very well by these dominant modes of analysis. Progressive historians and their followers have not been able adequately to explain the Revolution, the Constitution, or the Civil War simply in terms of the clash of economic forces; pluralist social scientists have not come to grips with the compulsive, irrational dimensions of a national politics which they have seen as essentially rational and pragmatic. Closer attention to the actual historical language of American politics has lately offered an alternative analysis which collapses conflict and consensus into a single category so as to clarify them both. On the basis of what political actors say about themselves, it is possible to conclude that Americans have experienced formative events in their history as a species of family and generational conflict in which the passions of familial strife are rooted in fraternal bonds, and acts of symbolic parricide are accompanied by acceptance of a providential destiny.[9] The recognition of these familial dimensions of eighteenth- and nineteenth-century American politics provides a better means of understanding both the nature and the intensity of much American conflict, as well as a fuller appreciation of the emotional and religious dynamics which support the consensus. Such a perspective also helps to explain the historical inadequacy of constitutional liberalism as a source of political legitimacy.

In a sense, the creation of the United States in 1789 was contingent upon a moral hiatus which lay at the center of the Constitution. Paradoxically, the existence of that hiatus rendered the legitimacy of the new order tenuous. The founders of 1789 had no clearly defined concept of political obligation beyond the revolutionary act of constitution-making itself—an act the Constitution was explicitly designed to bring to an end. Thus, having no intrinsic moral legitimacy, the Constitution's authority rested largely upon an instrumental legitimacy (i.e., the politics of interest) and whatever extrinsic moral authority it could borrow from the religious sphere and from the reputations of the founders themselves. This moral lacuna fostered a utilitarianism that made it possible to construct and hold together the Union on the basis of compromise over slavery; at the same time it created a vacuum that was filled immediately by a civic religion which embodied the major elements of American Puritanism. Thus when the legitimacy of the Constitution was challenged by Southern secession, the issue at stake was not simply the meaning of a rational-legal order, but which side had the blessing of the national deity. The crucible provided by the Southern insurrection forced American liberalism to return to its origins, where it discovered not a cerebral agreement on social ends, but a religious absolutism and fanaticism.

By waging fratricidal war against religious heresy, and winning it on the terms he did, Lincoln not only proved that the Union had God on its side, he also established a rite of political regeneration which was to be followed by subsequent presidents. Just as Lincoln found his legitimacy in triumphing over Washington by reenacting the Revolution and refounding the Constitution, so would his successors in office measure their achievements against Lincoln's. And just as Lincoln interpreted the Civil War as a reenactment of the Revolution leading to the refoundation of constitutional authority, so too would his more ambitious successors seek historical greatness by similarly interpreting subsequent American wars, leading to a refoundation of authority in some external form—in the League of Nations, in the United Nations, and elsewhere in the world. Lincoln's quest thus has implications not only for the study of the political culture in general, but for the study of the presidency in particular.

Students of the presidency have disagreed about whether the Constitution is a guarantee of presidential power, with skeptics arguing that presidential "powers" do not ensure real political influence.[10] It is usually taken for granted that the Constitution is a guarantee of legitimacy. Actually, the Constitution guarantees power more than it does legitimacy. Although a president may be effectively limited by the conflicting demands of his various constituencies, requiring him to modify policy objectives accordingly, he nevertheless remains commander in chief. Whatever his strengths and weaknesses as a politician, he has the power to render constitutional definitions of legitimacy irrelevant. An incumbent president has the power to create his own legitimacy, and in this respect his most important constituency becomes not those who put him in office or support his policies, but the ghosts of his dead predecessors which serve as a reminder of past glory.[11] The most compelling ghosts are those of presidents who established their legitimacy in violation of the Constitution.

Presidential studies in the post-Nixon period have tried to come to grips with the problem of presidential action that is of dubious constitutionality by embracing the concept of prerogative. A recent text even argues that presidential power consists primarily of prerogative power.[12] But what is prerogative power? The Constitution does not mention it and the *Federalist* does not discuss it. Prerogative is a legal abstraction borrowed from the seventeenth-century thought of John Locke, and used to describe presidential assertions of power which may or may not be constitutional, but which are later sustained by public support. The difficulty with this approach is that such an abstraction misses entirely the cultural meaning of such assertions of power. Presidents who seek to gain access to the Revolution and re-found the Constitution in some form are not following John Locke, though they are harking back to the role of the seventeenth-century executive. Rather they are following Lincoln, making of the presidency the very elective kingship which the Antifederalist opponents of the Constitution feared it might become; and, armed with an unofficial state religion, also provided by Lincoln, they have been able to sustain imperial ambitions. The invitation to establish presidential legitimacy, however, does not guarantee success, as both Lyndon Johnson and Richard Nixon have served to prove. The result has been an office restored to its constitutional proportions, but with a diminished capacity to act upon the general will of the American people.

Finally, a note on methodology: The principal focus of this study is the interrelationship between Lincoln's psychology and the dominant cultural and political forces of his time, but it does not employ clinical language or methods. These were not deemed necessary, because Lincoln was a man with an unusually coherent and logical mind, who not only resolved the cultural conflicts he experienced, but resolved them on a grand scale, and even provided his own self-analysis in the process. "In times like the present," he said in 1862, "men should utter nothing for which they would not willingly be responsible through time and in eternity."[13] This is an extremely exacting standard for the use of language, but it is a standard which Lincoln met extraordinarily well throughout his life, and the effect is that both the intended meaning of his words and his unintended lapses are easy to recognize. The major task of this investigation has been to assemble Lincoln's self-analysis from its various sources and present it in a coherent form so that the reverberations between his individual life history and the history of the nation can be more readily understood.

Although not strictly clinical in approach, the form given here to Lincoln and his times necessarily has psychoanalytic implications. Indeed, the definition of the subject matter is dependent upon Freud's theory of the origins of monotheism and Erik Erikson's study of Martin Luther.[14] This investigation also offers confirmation for a recently proposed revision of Freud: that more important than the Oedipus complex to the myth and psychology of the hero is the theme of triumphing over death.[15] For Lincoln's quest for immortality was rooted in a profound anxiety about death which had both personal and political dimensions, and which revealed itself in his premonitions and his dreams, his poetry and his public speeches. The main purpose here is neither to confirm nor to deny any particular social science theory or historical interpretation; it is rather to make sense out of Lincoln's role as a political actor and thereby contribute to the understanding of his influence on American political culture. Given the eclectic method, the conclusions are likely to please neither traditional Lincoln scholars nor psycho-historians. As Lincoln said in renewing his political career at Peoria in 1854, " 'Fools rush in where angels fear to tread.' "

1

The Inheritance of the Fathers: Parson Weems and Washington's Farewell Address

PRESIDENT WITHOUT A NAME

. . . without a name, perhaps without a reason why I should have a name, there has fallen upon me a task such as did not rest even upon the Father of his country. . . .

—A. Lincoln, 1861

In his address to the New Jersey senate on February 21, 1861, Abraham Lincoln recalled that "away back in my childhood, the earliest days of my being able to read, I got hold of a small book . . . 'Weem's [*sic*] Life of Washington.' I remember all the accounts there given of the battle fields and the struggles for the liberties of the country. . . ."[1] Lincoln might have also remembered it was in this little book that he had first encountered Washington's Farewell Address, which, according to Parson Weems, the nation out of "filial piety" had come to call *"his Legacy."* It was presented to the readers, said Weems, in the knowledge

> . . . that they will all read it with the feelings of children reading the last letter of a once-loved father now in his grave. And who knows but it may check for a while that fatal flame of discord which has destroyed all the once GLORIOUS REPUBLICS OF ANTIQUITY, and here now at length in the United States has caught upon the last republic that's left on the face of the earth.[2]

It is quite likely that Lincoln did recall Washington's advice to posterity on this occasion. For Lincoln's earliest reading occurred at a relatively late age (fourteen), and Weems's *Life of Washington,* parts of which he had committed to memory, was one of the few books available to him as a youth—perhaps the only book he had personally owned. As he told the New Jersey legislators, "you all know, for you have all been boys, how these early impressions last longer than any others."[3] At the moment he addressed the New Jersey Senate, on the eve of Washington's birthday, the "fatal flame of discord" against which Washington (through Weems) had warned threatened the Union with permanent dissolution, a result which Lincoln had already resolved must not be permitted to occur, even at the cost of armed conflict. In remembering Weems's *Washington* and his accounts of Revolutionary battles, Lincoln found in Washington's advice an appropriate statement of his own presidential purpose. "I am exceedingly anxious," he said, "that this Union, the Constitution, and the liberties of the people shall be perpetuated in accordance with the original idea for which that struggle was made. . . ."[4]

If Lincoln did recall his own earlier encounter with Washington's advice, it was not out of "filial piety" that he invoked that legacy. As he made his way from Springfield to assume the presidency, he knew that his election to office was inextricably bound up with the fraternal strife against which Washington had warned. As he talked his way across the country to Washington, D.C., he was restating themes first articulated twenty-three years earlier in a speech to the Springfield Lyceum, a speech in which Lincoln had warned his audience against a tyrant who might gain power under conditions of civil strife, and had proposed the establishment of a political religion to augment the constitutional settlement of 1789. It was a speech heavily indebted to Parson Weems's *Life of Washington,* and can best be understood as a direct response—in some respects, even as a rebuttal—to Washington's Farewell Address.

There can be no doubt that Washington was much on Lincoln's mind as he made his journey east. With seeming clairvoyance, he told his friends as he left Springfield: "I now leave, not knowing when or whether ever I may return, with a task before me greater than that which rested upon Washington. Without the assistance of that Divine Being who ever attended him, I cannot succeed. With that assistance, I cannot fail."[5] Repeating this thought before the Ohio legislature, two days later, in an extemporaneous speech which was more revealing of his own anxiety and perplexity, Lincoln admitted:

> I cannot but know what you all know, that without a name, perhaps without a reason why I should have a name, there has fallen upon me a task such as did not rest even upon the Father of his country, and so feeling I cannot but turn and look for the support without which it will be impossible for me to perform that great task. I turn, then, and look to the American people and to that God who has never forsaken them.[6]

Since seven Southern states had seceded by the time Lincoln took office in March, such statements could be seen as appropriate expressions of humility in the face of the great obstacles which would immediately confront his administration. Lincoln did give the impression that he was proceeding with considerable caution, if not timidity; he had waged no campaign in 1860 (unlike Douglas), and had made no public statements between the time of his election and his departure from Springfield. When he did begin to speak out, he did so warily and reluctantly, claiming that his silence was the result of wanting to adapt his policies to changing events. On several occasions he even denied that secession was a genuine crisis, calling it artificial and harmless. Invariably, he made a point of disparaging his own importance by asserting that the various receptions given him as his train moved across the country were not intended for him personally, but for the office he temporarily and accidentally held. He repeatedly revealed his inner anguish, the result of feelings of his own unworthiness and illegitimacy.

Lincoln's public reticence, however, did not reflect a lack of private resolve; nor were his professions of humility an accurate indication of his own self-assessment. The Inaugural Address, which removed all doubt about his willingness to use force in defense of the Union, had been drafted in January, and, as delivered in March, remained substantially unchanged. At the same

time that Lincoln was displaying indecisiveness about his response to secession, he was also formulating and beginning to
articulate a theology appropriate to the political religion for
which he had proclaimed a need in his 1838 address to the
Springfield Lyceum. It was a theology which assumed that the
Constitution was not yet sacred but could become so by the taking of a revolutionary pledge in its behalf, implying that constitutional regeneration could occur only on the basis of blood sacrifice. Furthermore, even as Lincoln openly admitted his
self-doubts about his abilities, he was also warning the people
against his own possible wickedness, apparently seeing something of himself in the malevolent genius he had depicted in the
Lyceum Address, a tyrant who would tear down the government
and its laws in order to gratify his own ambition.

It was not simply out of uncertainty, much less humility or filial
piety, that Lincoln invoked the name of Washington and echoed
his advice as he made his journey to the capital. Lincoln's task was
"greater" not only because he faced an unprecedented situation,
but also because his ambitions rivaled those of the founders of
1789. Unlike Washington, he could not rely upon a reputation as
revolutionary hero to afford him the kind of authority he would
require for accomplishing that task. For if a man "without a name,
perhaps without a reason . . . [to] have a name" were to realize such
ambitions, he would have to draw upon a kind of authority which
was not dependent upon the characteristics of an individual for its
effectiveness. In comparing himself with Washington, therefore, it
was no mere coincidence or casual rhetorical gesture that Lincoln
also appealed for the assistance of that "Divine Being who ever
attended" Washington, that "God who has never forsaken" the
American people. Washington too had once been a man without
a name and, according to Parson Weems, had achieved a new
legitimacy for himself and his countrymen through a civil war and
the divine blessing which accompanied participation in that war.
This would also be Lincoln's way of establishing authority. By
repudiating Washington's paternal counsels, but by following his
example, Lincoln would take Washington's place as the father of
his country.

POLITICS AND FAMILIAL STRIFE: THE FIRST CIVIL WAR

The Americans are the sons, not the bastards of England.
　　　　　　　　　　　　　　　　　—Lord Chatham, 1773

. . . I ardently wish that these spurious, unworthy sons of Britain could feel the iron rod of a Spanish inquisitor. . . .
　　　　　　　　　　　　　　　　　—Martin Howard Jr., 1765

No two persons have had a greater influence on securing George Washington's place in the American pantheon than Mason Locke Weems and Abraham Lincoln. Through publication of his *The Life of George Washington; with Curious Anecdotes Equally Honorable to Himself and Exemplary to His Young Countrymen,* one of the most widely read books of the early nineteenth century, Weems became the first architect of the Washington legend as Revolutionary hero and father of his country. By establishing his birthday as a national holiday, to be marked by public readings of the Farewell Address, Lincoln helped to guarantee Washington's deification. These two forms of tribute are connected, for it was Weems's Washington whom Lincoln both emulated and deified, and finally, by ceremonial apotheosis, elevated to divine rank.

The creator of a model of the ideal American, Parson Weems was himself an extraordinary indigenous type. He was ordained for the Anglican ministry by the Archbishop of Canterbury, but fashioned for himself a career which combined the saving of souls with the selling of books. Traveling by wagon between New York and Georgia for some thirty years, Weems hawked his wares as the occasion and circumstances demanded, dispensing not only printed matter but songs and sermons as well. Writer and printer of his own edifying pamphlets, he was also a publisher's agent and a shrewd market analyst who had a keen sense of the public's mood and taste. If he was "an amiable and energetic charlatan,"[7] as one interpreter describes him, there nevertheless was nothing fraudulent about his perception of what Americans wanted to believe about themselves as a nation and its leadership.

Weems was born in Maryland in 1759, the youngest of nineteen children, and was studying in England at the time of the Revolution. With the end of the war, he found himself in an awkward predicament. He wanted to be ordained in the Anglican church, but as an American citizen he could not take the required oath of allegiance to the British crown. A way out of his dilemma was apparently discovered for him by American representatives abroad, Adams and Franklin, and he was duly ordained an Anglican priest in 1784. Upon his return to the United States, Weems served as rector of two different parishes (neither of which was Mount Vernon, as he later claimed) and simultaneously launched his career as a bookseller. In 1794 he became an agent for the Philadelphia publisher Mathew Carey, a profitable relationship for both of them which eventually produced Weems's life of Washington under Carey's imprint.

As early as 1797, Weems was certain that there existed a rich and untapped market for tales of American heroes produced in cheap editions. "Experience has taught me," he wrote to Carey, "that small, i.e. quarter of dollar books, on subjects calculated to *strike* the Popular Curiosity, printed in very large numbers and properly *distributed*, w^d prove an immense revenue to the prudent and industrious Undertakers." Weems was at work on just such a volume about Washington when the latter died unexpectedly in December 1799. Certain of the additional demand for his book created by Washington's death, Weems became exuberant about his project. He told Carey: "I have something to whisper in your lug. Washington, you know is gone! Millions are gaping to read something about him. I am very nearly prim^d and cock^d for 'em."[8]

At first, Carey was apparently unresponsive, requiring Weems to find other printers for his 80-page pamphlet; but eventually it began to appear under his auspices and sold very well. In 1806 Carey issued a new edition, completely rewritten, which included for the first time the story of the cherry tree, as well as the tale of the cabbage seed which his father had sown so that the sprouting plants would spell out the letters of the boy's name ("To startle

George with a lively sense of his Maker," said Weems). Then in 1808—the year before Lincoln's birth—Weems substantially revised and expanded the text from 80 to 228 pages in what was to become its final form, including additional historical material and new anecdotes. Among the latter was an account of Washington's mother's prophetic dream in which she saw George, then five years old, extinguish a fire which had started on the eastern side of their new house's roof. (Afterward George told her, "Well, Ma! now if you and the family will but consent, we can make a far better roof than this ever was; a roof of such a quality, that, if well kept together, it will last for ever; but if you take it apart, you will make the house ten thousand times worse than it was before.") This edition also contained the full text of the Farewell Address, presented to readers as the "solicitude of a father for his children, over whom he had long watched, but was about to leave to themselves."[9]

The book was a best seller for its time. According to one estimate, more than 50,000 copies were sold within a decade of its first publication.[10] Weems, however, was still not satisfied with it. He repeatedly urged Carey to let him enlarge and embellish it or to bring out an "elegant edition" at three or four dollars a copy. "You have a great deal of money lying in the bones of old George," Weems wrote to Carey in 1809, "if you will but exert yourself to extract it."[11] But Carey apparently was not interested in further excavation and continued to reprint the same edition. Weems had no recourse but to accept this policy, since, much to his regret, he had sold Carey the copyright. Thus, although the book was in its twenty-ninth "edition" at the time of Weems's death in 1825, there were no further changes in the text after 1808. By 1925 the book had achieved its eightieth printing.

Weems's book is best known for its whimsical anecdotes about Washington. There were not only the stories of the cherry tree, the cabbage-seed, and Mary Washington's dream, but also tales of George as a schoolboy whose word was accepted as law among his friends, of a gifted young athlete who could throw a stone across the Rappahannock, of a brave warrior who could not be killed by a bullet though fired upon seventeen times. All these and more found their way into the literature on Washington and became an enduring part of his heroic legend. Perhaps the book's appeal can be best understood in terms of its epic effect: the fusion of fact and fancy in which minor events are exaggerated to heroic proportions for the edification and emulation of present and future generations.

Despite Weems's moralizing tone and fanciful approach to the historical record, his book—as its most recent editor points out—is not altogether unreliable. Many of the stories about Washington turn out to be true in fact or at least plausible. Moreover, Weems did succeed in capturing some essential truths about his protagonist which were confirmed by subsequent biographers. What is even more surprising and important is the accuracy of Weems's interpretation of the American Revolution and his assessment of the basis of constitutional legitimacy in the United States. His ersatz epic form and extravagant language were appropriate to express the passions and anxieties of the politics of familial strife. Despite the many instances in which the author's mythopoeic purpose superseded empirical accuracy, the book is nevertheless a surprisingly dependable guide to the Revolution and the Constitution. Through his mythical, didactic approach to American history, Weems provided a vision of revolutionary fraternity and constitutional salvation which was to be realized by his avid reader Abraham Lincoln.

Weems depicted the Revolution as a family quarrel which began as a dispute among the sons over birthrights and ended in fratricide and permanent dissolution of the family. It was fomented by greedy elder sons (the British ministry), who were envious of their younger brothers (the Americans) and thus attempted to alienate the affections of their mother (England) and succeeded in corrupting the father (the king). As loving and dutiful children the Americans petitioned the parent state for recognition of their rights as equal members of the family, but to no avail. Although they received the support of many of their British brethren (Whigs), the power-maddened ministry could not be dissuaded from its course of reducing the colonies to slavery. Determined to protect their liberty (a birthright) from the ravages of this ministerial attack, the colonists reluctantly took up arms. The results were civil war, dismemberment of the imperial family, and independence for the American sons, which eventually led to the reestablishment of paternal authority.

According to Weems's account, the year 1763 opened with "peculiar brightness" for Britain and her colonies.[12] United by "love and mutual helpfulness" and together enjoying a measure of economic comfort seldom seen among nations, American hearts leaped for joy at the mention of old England, "as at the name of a great and venerable mother" who felt "an equal transport at thoughts of us." Darkening clouds of ministerial intrigue soon changed that happy scene. Upon conclusion of the French and Indian War, returning British officers conveyed the impression that their American brothers lived in great affluence. From that time on, Weems asserted, the British ministry began to look upon the Americans "with an evil eye," determined to make them bear part of the costs of empire. This policy was undertaken, however, not to acknowledge the colonists as "Sons of Britons," equally free and independent as those in England: "Oh no! . . . We were not to be treated as *brothers,* but as *slaves!* over whom an unconditional right was claimed to tax and take our property at pleasure!!!"

So the plunder of the colonies began. "When a king wants money for his own pride, or for his hungry relations, and when his ministers want stakes for their gaming tables, or demand necklaces for their strumpets, they *will* have it. . . ." But the sons of Columbia, according to Weems, had enjoyed the "sweets of Liberty and Property" too long to part with them tamely. As soon as the Stamp Act had passed, the people rose up against it as one man. Old grudges and differences were put aside and people rushed into patriotic societies. Every man looked to his fellow as a brother, and ". . . their looks on each other were as lightnings in a parched forest—the sacred fire kindled and ran from end to end of the continent." Aided by the Whig opposition in England, who denounced the Stamp Act as contrary to British freedom, the colonists forced the ministry to abandon its nefarious scheme—at least temporarily.

With the repeal of the Stamp Act, Weems claimed, many cherished the hope that the former golden days would return. But those days were gone forever. "Government had shown the cloven foot—and America had taken a fright . . ." which only the kindliest of treatment could alleviate. The ministry, however, was in no mood for kindness. Long accustomed to viewing Americans as a pack of convicts whom British ships had saved from the gallows, they were doubly embarrassed at having been forced to yield to American demands, and determined to have revenge.

Such an opportunity presented itself in 1773 when the ministry ordered collection of the taxes on tea. Once again, said Weems, the colonies caught fire and the "old flame of '64 was completely rekindled throughout the continent." But even in the midst of their outrage, he said, the colonies never lost sight of the respect due the mother country. Their numerous petitions to the King, Parliament, and the people of Britain ". . . all breathe the full spirit of dutiful children, and of loving brothers." In terms "most modest and pathetic" they state the extreme injustice, barbarity, and unconstitutionality of such measures, which, unless repealed, would lead to civil war.

At this point Weems interrupted his narrative to quote extensively from a speech by Chatham. The old statesman was brought to the House of Lords from his sickbed, willing to expend his dying breath in order to warn the country against the disastrous consequences of its imperial course. Trembling with age and infirmity, Chatham told the assembled peerage that they must not only repeal the colonial tax laws, but declare that they have no right to enact such taxes. The basis of this recommendation, according to Weems, was Chatham's belief that the Americans were native sons of Britain, lovers of liberty and their mother country who were "ready, as her *children,* to *give* her *every thing;* but, as her *slaves, nothing.* " Thus he urged solidarity between the English Whigs and their colonial brethren, and beseeched the lords to remove the troops from Boston in order to avert bloodshed.

By Weems's reckoning, such a speech should have been sufficient to "stop the career of the maddest politicians," but it fell on deaf ears in a government bent on American subjugation. Massachusetts was singled out for special punishment as a reprisal for the destruction of English tea. Still, the colonies would not submit. The ministerial attack on Boston liberties was considered as an attack on the whole, and a general congress was convened in Philadelphia to deliberate the common interest. In September

1774 this "most unkingly" body published a "bill of rights" in which the delegates repeated "their loyalty and love to the mother country," but also asserted that by the laws of nature, the principles of the British constitution, and their own several charters, they had rights to liberty and were determined, at the risk of everything short of their *"eternal salvation,"* to defend and transmit these rights to their posterity.

The British ministry still ignored colonial claims and persisted in its belligerent course by sending troop reinforcements to Boston. Finally, on April 19, 1775—"the fatal day marked out by mysterious heaven, for tearing away the stout infant colonies from the long-loved paps of the old mother country"—violence erupted at Lexington. Civil war had begun. The mother country was goaded by the ministry so "as to make her *run riot* over her own children, and crush thousands of them into their bloody graves." From this point on "LIBERTY, heaven-born goddess, was to be bought for blood."

Weems's discussion of the signing of the Declaration of Independence, with the countryside already awash in fraternal bloodshed, appeared as something of an afterthought. Yet despite the actual warfare, the colonists were still reluctant to formalize their separation. It was Samuel Chase who "first taught the startled vaults of Congress-hall to re-echo the name of Independence." After listing the many instances of ministerial violation of American rights—"on all of which George the Third, the *expected father of his people,* had looked with a *most unfatherly calmness"*—Chase declared he owed no allegiance to the King of England. Upon hearing mention of independence, said Weems, many in Congress trembled and "felt the pang which nature feels when the soul and body are parting." Nevertheless, convinced that the "wounds of deadly hate" had pierced too deep for reconciliation, the Declaration was duly framed and adopted.

Events on the battlefield received an even more dramatic treatment. Facing Lord Howe's army of 40,000 seasoned troops with a band of 3,000 men who lacked even basic supplies, Washington was forced to retreat during the summer and fall of 1776 from Long Island to New York to New Jersey and finally into Pennsylvania. As Howe's army overran the countryside, the Hessians under his command despoiled property and abused women, causing such alarm that thousands of Americans rushed to take an oath of allegiance to the British. It appeared, said Weems, that this "apostacy" would soon spread throughout Pennsylvania and New Jersey, for it seemed to most people that "the cause of liberty was a *gone cause.*" But "Jehovah, the God of Hosts" was with Washington, Weems assured his reader, and Washington not only kept up his own spirits, but cheered those of his disheartened comrades. At last an opportunity to strike a retaliatory blow against the enemy presented itself at Trenton, New Jersey. It was Weems's account of this battle and the "great hardships" endured by Washington and his troops which Lincoln said "fixed themselves on my memory more than any single revolutionary event."[13]

As Weems set the order of battle, Howe had stationed 4,000 men on the eastern bank of the Delaware in Trenton, Bordentown, and Burlington, and then returned with his main army to New York for Christmas celebration. Suspecting that the remaining troops would not be observing Christmas like "good Christians," but would instead "be drinking and hopping like fools," Washington decided to launch a surprise attack from his position on the Delaware's western bank. He divided his forces into three groups, with generals Ewing and Cadwallader to lead the assault on Bordentown and Burlington, reserving for himself the heavier charge at Trenton. The plan was frustrated, however, when the first two groups were unable to cross the river. Unaware of this failure, Washington and "his little forlorn hope," as Weems characterized them, pressed on through a heavy storm, finally reaching the river. They embarked immediately, and after five hours of "infinite toil and danger" succeeded in crossing it. The remainder of Weems's account deserves to be quoted at length:

> Forming the line they renewed their march. *Pale,* and slowly moving along the neighbouring hills was seen, (by Fancy's eye) the weeping GENIUS OF LIBERTY. Driven from the rest of the world, she had fled to the wild woods of America, as to an assured asylum of rest.—Here she fondly hoped, through long unfailing time, to see her children pursuing their cheerful toils, *unstarved* and *uncrushed* by the INHUMAN FEW. But alas! the *inhuman few,* with fleets and

armies, had pursued her flight! Her *sons* had gathered around her, but they had failed—some, on their bloody beds: others, dispersed; all desponding. *One little band alone* remained! and, now, resolved to bleed or to defend, were in rapid march to face *her foes. Pale* and in tears, with eyes often lifted to Heaven, she moved along with her children to witness perhaps the last conflict.

Thus it was, with the fate of world liberty hanging in the balance, that Washington and his beleaguered band prepared to meet the enemy at Trenton. Initially the soldiers quavered at the sight of the large enemy encampment, said Weems, but Washington was like a lion among his cubs—"stately and terrible," with the eager wish for battle flushed over his burning face. His presence inspired the men and they dove fearlessly into battle. Caught unprepared, the Hessians were no match for the Americans. A thousand prisoners were captured and immediately marched to Philadelphia, where their appearance caused patriots to weep with joy.

In victory, Washington was both generous and forgiving. Following the *"divine policy of doing good for evil,"* said Weems, he offered the captured Hessians the opportunity to quit their British employers and join the Americans, which they did. Such was Washington's policy: "It melted down his iron enemies into golden friends." And so ended the battle of Trenton.

When Lincoln recalled Weems's account of this battle as he addressed the New Jersey Senate on February 21, 1861, he was not merely making a politician's polite obeisance to local tradition. At that moment he saw himself in much the same way as Weems had pictured Washington at Trenton: embattled and alone, perhaps the despondent nation's last representative of the genius of liberty, ready to give up his own life, and, if need be, those of his fellow citizens as well, for the sake of preserving a revolutionary ideal. Lincoln was also about to embark on a course which in his mind involved a reenactment of the first civil war, the Revolution of 1776: severance of the bonds of an inherited political union and a fraternal bloodletting which would lead to the reestablishment of constitutional authority and the creation of a new fraternal union. That Lincoln's presidential purpose was informed by

Weems's reading of history is perhaps less startling if it is understood that in many respects Weems's interpretations were essentially correct.

It would be useless to submit Weems's account of the period 1763–76 to close empirical scrutiny. He gave little attention to economic factors, and virtually ignored the constitutional debates which so dominated Anglo-American relations. There were major lapses in his chronology. He assumed there was a uniformity of opinion among the colonists and overlooked the differences between American radicals and their Whig supporters in England. He wove together fanciful vignettes of his own creation with the ponderous rhetoric of eighteenth-century speeches, presuming to improve upon the original as he saw fit. Where words failed him, he made punctuation suffice. Yet despite all these and other eccentricities, Weems did succeed in presenting a picture of the Revolution which, until lately, has been ignored by historians and which in some respects may be superior to more sophisticated formulations.

Recent scholarship has supported Weems's assumption that political authority was experienced in both England and the colonies as a form of familial authority.[14] After 1688, divine-rights theory, which had justified the patriarchal absolutism of the monarch, was modified by John Locke's contractual model of authority, but the analogy of state to family remained intact. By 1750, images of the Lockean family, in which paternal authority was based on reason and experience rather than force and will, were widely used to explain and justify political institutions. Thus, political writers of the period commonly made the assumption that imperial relations should conform to the parent-child relationship of the Lockean family, one in which it was presumed that children had natural rights and did not owe unlimited obedience to their parents. It was the widespread acceptance of this familial analogy on both sides of the Atlantic which helped to define the language of imperial debate and ultimately of the Revolution itself.

The king's paternal authority was readily acknowledged by the colonies; protestations of filial loyalty and devotion to him abound in the Revolutionary tracts, and were being made repeatedly as late as 1776. The image of England as mother also found easy acceptance in colonial political writings, and as such became the focus for expressions of affection, reverence, and gratitude. After 1763, however, with the passage by Parliament of various revenue and trade measures, the Tea Act, and finally, the "Intolerable Acts," acceptance of the king's paternal authority became tainted by fears of patriarchal tyranny, and filial affection for the mother was replaced by rage and bitterness. The officials most commonly identified as responsible for this transformation in colonial attitudes were, as Weems correctly suggested, the king's ministers.

Bernard Bailyn has shown that the ideology of the American Revolution was fully formed as early as the 1730s by a group of English opposition writers, on both the left and the right, who were alarmed at the threat of ministerial influence in corrupting the constitution and violating liberty. This group of writers, whom Bailyn described as "coffeehouse radicals and opposition politicians, spokesmen for . . . the disaffected," gave expression to a configuration of ideas and anxieties which, he argued, shaped the mind of the Revolutionary generation and formed the basis of its political culture.[15] For when American radicals became convinced in the 1760s and 1770s that they were faced with a deliberate conspiracy by the crown's ministry and its deputies to overthrow the British constitution and to destroy their rights as Englishmen, they had been well prepared both to perceive the dangers and to analyze the causes of this course of events. By that time the English opposition version of politics had become "the ordinary presumption of informed Americans,"[16] and, as such, provided an ideological legacy for revolutionary action.

What made this opposition version of politics so persuasive was that the Glorious Revolution, with its many guarantees against arbitrary executive power, had never been fully extended to the colonies. This factor, when combined with peculiarities inherent in the structure of colonial politics, created an explosive situation. On the one hand, colonial executives had legal powers which far exceeded those exercised by the crown in England, including veto over legislation, power to dissolve legislative assemblies, and power to appoint and dismiss the judiciary; but on the other, they lacked the effective means of exercising this power, because colonial governors were denied decision-making autonomy as well as control over patronage and other kinds of influence by which the executive managed politics in England.[17] As a result, when the crown attempted to tighten imperial controls after the French and Indian War, it seemed obvious that paternal authority was reverting to patriarchal despotism. The connecting link between opposition politics and familial authority was provided not simply by the fear of a ruthless father, but by the psychology of fraternal resentment. In this respect, Weems's portrayal of the Revolution was precisely correct.

Colonial pamphleteers expressed fear and outrage at the prospect of parental domination, but they reserved their harshest language for the older brothers in the imperial family, the favorites of the realm, who were thought to be responsible for policy. Indeed, the most common explanation for the causes of American grievances, according to Bailyn, was the existence of "an overruling arbitrary power, which absolutely controls the King, Lords, and Commons," and which was composed of the king's "ministers and favorites" who made their "despotic will" the authority of the nation.[18] These men, described variously as "pimps and parasites," "court locusts," "state jobbers," and a "corrupt and prostituted ministry," were seen as having gained the king's ear for their detestable schemes of reducing the colonies to slavery by whispering about divine right and by deceiving the British people about their motives. These motives were also characterized variously, but almost always in ways which denoted dissoluteness: greed, envy, profligacy, licentiousness. Weems's descriptions and explanations accurately reflected those given at the time.[19]

Of more significance than the literal accuracy of Weems's descriptions is the faithfulness with which he reflected the emotional turmoil of the British-American conflict. For Weems as well as for the participants, it was an excruciating family fight made the more painful by the convoluted ambivalence of the passions involved: contempt concealed admiration; resentment, approbation; anger, affection. Weems intimated what was also often implied by the Revolutionary tracts without being fully articulated—that the imperial dispute was a clash between the first or favored sons of the crown and mother England on one side, and their illegitimate American offspring on the other. He hinted at a significant refinement in the familial interpretation of eighteenth-century Anglo-American political conflict, as seen from the point of view of the American radical: it was a battle over family birthrights, influenced and supported by spokesmen for disaffected outsiders in England, intensified by the humiliation of supercilious treatment at the hands of colonial administrators, and resolved (at least temporarily) by the violence of a civil war from which emerged the basis of a new legitimacy, a regenerative republican world view. What Weems suggested—and there is much evidence to support him—was that the psychology of American republicanism was rooted in an unspoken but deeply felt sense of American bastardy. He also provided a model of regeneration through civil war which led to the reestablishment of paternal authority.

Americans, of course, never accepted recognition of their status as illegitimate sons of Britain; rather, it was thrust upon them over their objections, wheedling, and threats, until finally their unacknowledged ignominy became transformed into a doctrine of virtue, the basis for their declaration of independence. Nevertheless, poorly concealed within the many protestations of loyalty and dutifulness which marked the colonial petitions to the parent state was a shrillness of tone which betrayed anxiety and outrage that their legitimacy had been called into question. The Americans, many Revolutionary tracts said in effect, are not only loving and obedient children, but the *most* loving, the *most* obedient in the family—not only good Englishmen, but the best, and most jealous of their heritage. Why then, it was asked, did not the king intercede in their behalf and restore fraternal harmony to the imperial family by ending the discriminatory treatment?

At the same time these uneasy supplications were coupled with an implicit threat, apparently based upon a defensive pride in illegitimacy itself: the colonies were happily dependent upon the parent state, but not too dependent. Deprived of parental support, they had carved out an existence in a hostile environment by their own efforts, and thus, unlike their less adventuresome British brethren, were fathers of themselves and independent from the beginning.

Perhaps the most obvious indication of colonial anxiety is the fact that such pleadings and protests were made at all. There would seem to be an extraordinary degree of unreality to proclaiming one's undying filial devotion at the very moment it appears one's family birthrights are being taken away.

This sense of unreality beclouded a decade of colonial disputation. When Jefferson concluded his "Summary View of the Rights of British America" (1774) with an appeal to the king to "establish fraternal love and harmony through the whole empire" by interposing himself between his quarreling subjects, he spoke with a "manly firmness,"[20] but his assumptions were not much different from those of Stephen Hopkins and James Otis ten years earlier. Hopkins, in a widely acclaimed pamphlet of 1764, argued (as did Jefferson later) that British subjects in America had equal rights with those in Britain, and that they did not enjoy those rights as a privilege or a favor but "possess them as an inherent indefeasible right." As did Jefferson, Hopkins said that many colonies had been planted at the planters' own expense, rather than England's, and were "left to the protection of Heaven and their own efforts."[21] Both Jefferson and Hopkins assumed that crown policy must be based on some misunderstanding—Hopkins thought it was jealousy—which could be cleared up, if only the right argument were presented or the proper manner of expression found. For his part, Hopkins adopted those "expressions of servility" rejected by Jefferson, but his conclusion reflected the same anxious concern that Americans be accepted as legitimate members of the empire. The colonies, he wrote,

> have honestly obeyed every royal command, and cheerfully submitted to every constitutional law; . . . have never been troublesome or expensive to the mother country; have kept due order, . . . and in every relation, have demeaned themselves as loyal, as dutiful, and as faithful subjects ought; and that no kingdom or state hath, or ever had, colonies more quiet, more obedient, or more profitable, than these have ever been.[22]

Some writers came close to acknowledging American illegitimacy without actually doing so. In drawing his "filial pen" to vindicate the mother country, Martin Howard, Jr., referring to the opponents of the Stamp Act, said, ". . . I ardently wish that these spurious, unworthy sons of Britain could feel the iron rod of a

Spanish inquisitor. . . ."[23] On the opposite side, Richard Bland took note of the fact that "Acts of Parliament made in England without naming the foreign Plantations will not bind them." Thus the colonies were legal nonentities unless specifically mentioned by Parliament—the same legal status as bastards in inheritance settlements. Bland also thought that various acts of trade which imposed severer restrictions on the colonies than England "constituted an *unnatural* Difference between Men under the same Allegiance, born equally free, and entitled to the same civil Rights."[24]

Some of the same implications can be seen even more clearly in the writings of William Hicks. Quoting approvingly from Chatham's speech mentioned by Weems, in which that peer said that "the Americans are the sons, not the bastards of England," Hicks then proceeded to demonstrate how they were nevertheless being treated as bastards—and dangerous bastards at that. He explained crown policy as follows: "A jealous fear, that, from the natural advantages which we possess, we may, in some future age, rival our envious brethren in strength and riches, has urged them to exercise a piece of Ottoman policy, by strangling us in our infancy."[25] Presumably, the policy to which he referred was that of murdering the offspring of concubines in order to preserve the direct bloodlines of the Ottoman throne.

The colonists, however, did not experience their "bastardy" simply as a theoretical abstraction, or as diffuse anxiety about their collective status within the empire. Their reaction also had a very immediate personal dimension which took the ambivalent form of both an intense attraction for and repulsion against all things British, especially the power and prestige represented by the royal governor. Owing to the absence of a stable class structure, and the presence of a patronage system which made colonial appointments dependent upon the exigencies of domestic politics in England, the colonial administration was never fully integrated into American society; indeed, it was widely perceived as an external threat to colonial liberties. At the same time the royal governor, as Gordon Wood has shown, became the principal arbiter of political influence and cultural refinement, and thus the focal point for colonial aspirations and dissatisfactions.[26] As a result, a social paradox was created which mirrored the ambivalence of American attitudes: colonists deeply respected the class distinctions of British society, perhaps coveting symbols of status even more than the English themselves because they were outsiders; yet they also reacted to British displays of superiority with bitter resentment and hatred. The tensions created by this paradox were what John Adams called "the secret Springs of this surprising Revolution."[27]

Americans dreamed of recovering the virtue of the ancient republics while witnessing, with both disgust and envy, the corruption and degeneracy of the British constitution. From abroad, John Dickinson wrote of his mortifying humiliation at his treatment by the British, admitting that since he could not attract the admiration of mankind, the pride which urged him to seek it prevented him from giving it to others—although he still "could not forbear looking on them [the corrupt nobility] with veneration."[28] At home, many sensed that avenues of political advancement were being closed to them, and were outraged at the abuse of power by which royal sycophants were given positions over their betters. Charles Carroll expressed fears that "all power might center in *one family*" and that offices of government "like a precious jewel will be handed down from *father* to *son*." A South Carolinian wrote, "None of us, when we grow old, can expect the honors of the State. . . ." John Adams saw the Stamp Act as a personal rebuke: "I have groped in dark obscurity, till of late, and had but just become known, and gained a small degree of Reputation, when this execrable Project was set on foot for my Ruin. . . ."[29] George Washington was repeatedly denied the commission in the regular British army he so desperately wanted, and repeatedly humiliated by the royal officers who showed only contempt for their American counterparts.[30] Republicanism, with its promise of a public forum open to merit and excellence, with its emphasis upon simplicity, frugality, temperance, and industriousness, and its strictures against luxury, cultural refinement, inherited status—values which corresponded closely to actual conditions in America—had a potent and nearly universal appeal.

Implicit in Weems's conception of the Revolution is an answer to the historians' question of why there was a sudden and complete transition to republicanism in 1776.[31] The personal resentments of the colonists, Weems suggested, together with a deep sense of moral outrage at British corruption, combined to produce a political creed which transformed the illegitimate sons of Britain into the saviors of world liberty. An important step in this transformation occurred when American bastardy was denied by renouncing the family connection with the British. As Thomas Paine wrote in *Common Sense,* "Europe, and not England, is the parent country of America"; moreover, the king, he said, was not a father, but the "Pharaoh of England," an unfeeling "wretch" with the "pretended title of father of his people." At the same time, a new fraternal bond was created which celebrated the virtues of illegitimacy itself. As Paine pointed out, America had always served as an orphanage for Europe's rejected children, the refugees from its oppression: "This New World has been the asylum for the persecuted lovers of civil and religious liberty from *every part* of Europe" who fled "not from the tender embraces of the mother, but from the cruelty of the monster."[32] Thus, what the loyalist Joseph Galloway called the "spurious infant," the "ill-shapen diminutive brat, INDEPENDENCY,"[33] was born of truths self-evident to the disinherited sons of Europe, who then baptized their progeny with a mutual pledge of fraternal honor and republican virtue.

The key events in this transformation of illegitimate sons into exemplars for the world, as far as Weems was concerned, were, first, the war itself with its blood sacrifices for liberty, and secondly, the renunciation by Washington of the crown which was his for the taking at the war's conclusion. Both events represented republican virtue, the willingness to sacrifice private interests—even life itself —for the sake of the public good; and both were superintended by a divine presence. Thus both the war and Washington's renunciation of power reflected a new standard of legitimacy, one in which authority was disembodied from the father while retaining its paternal character in spiritual form.

Indeed, the ideal of republican thought—the harmonious integration of society on the basis of a public interest which transcends individual interests[34]—suggests a familial model of authority in which parental influence is felt but not seen. It was as if the republican brethren, by prior agreement, had pledged to forswear all paternal ambitions for themselves while at the same time mutually acceding to a kind of parental direction, perhaps one implanted by their guilt at having symbolically killed the king.[35] In committing themselves to support the idea of political equality, the signers of the Declaration of Independence placed "firm reliance on the protection of divine Providence."

Washington's postwar acts of self-denial were consistent with this commitment. But his renunciation of actual paternal power, which demonstrated his fraternal loyalty and republican virtue, as well as his reliance upon divine guidance, was but a prelude (according to Weems) to his becoming the father of his country. It was this model of fraternal forbearance which Lincoln would seemingly accept but actually reject as he prepared to take Washington's place at the seat of authority.

With the war over, Washington, by order of Congress, proceeded to disband the army. "Loving his soldiers as his children," said Weems, he trembled with anxiety at the unpleasant task that lay before him. How could he tell them, after all their suffering, that the country's poverty would require that they return home without pay? He was saved the pain of making this announcement when letters were circulated throughout the army informing the soldiers that an ungrateful Congress would not give them their money. These letters, according to Weems, urged the men to fight as bravely for their own rights as they had for the rights of others. Now is the time for redress, the letters said, "while you have weapons in your hands, the strength of an army to support you, and a beloved General at your head, ready to lead you to that justice which you owe yourselves. . . ."

The effect of such inflammatory recommendations on the soldiers was instantaneous and explosive. Rage swept through the camp and needed only a sign of approval from Washington to be translated into action: "Instantly with the fixed bayonets they would have hurled the hated Congress from their seats, and placed their beloved Washington on the throne of St. Tammany." At this point, Weems speculates, "the tempter flashed the dangerous diadem before the eyes of our Countryman! but religion at the same time, pointed him to the GREAT LOVER OF ORDER, holding up that crown in comparison of which diadems of kings are but dross." Having fought for liberty and won, Washington considered its blessings at hand.

Yet a little while, and America shall become the glory of the earth
—a nation of brothers, enjoying the golden reign of equal laws,
and rejoicing under their own vine and fig-tree, and no tyrant to
make them afraid. And shall these glorious prospects be darkened? shall they be darkened by WASHINGTON! shall he, ever friend
of his country, become her bitterest enemy, by fixing upon her
again the iron yoke of monarchy? shall he! the Father of his army,
become their assassin, by establishing a government that shall
swallow up their liberties for ever?

This thought, said Weems, filled his soul with horror. Therefore, instead of yielding to the wishes of his army, he bravely
opposed them; ". . . instead of drinking in, with traitorous smile,
the hosannas that would make him King, he darken[ed] his brow
of Parental displeasure at their impiety." Calling in his officers, he
reminded them that they had drawn their swords to defend their
country's liberty. Now, he said, having waded, "like Israel of old,
through a *Red Sea* of blood," having traveled through a "howling
wilderness of war," with the *"ark* of your country's liberties" in
camp, would they give themselves up for the "sordid *flesh-pots"* of
a few months' pay, and fall back into a worse "Egyptian bondage"?
No, said Washington, he trusted not. Having achieved great miracles in the past, a greater miracle remained to be achieved. "We
have had the glory to conquer our enemies," he said, "now for the
greater glory to conquer ourselves." Too often victorious armies
had trampled on their countries' liberties; "be it our nobler ambition, after sufferings unparalleled for our needy country, to return
cheerful, though pennyless, to our homes, and patiently wait the
rewards which her gratitude will, one day, assuredly bestow."
By so doing, Washington concluded, ". . . you shall display a spect-
acle of patriotism never seen before—you shall teach the delighted world, that men are capable of finding a heaven in noble
actions. . . ."

Republican virtue carried the day, and the troops obediently
and pennilessly, if not altogether cheerfully, returned home.
Washington likewise gave up his commission and returned to private life. Then suddenly he became "alarmed by the appearance
of an evil, which threatened to put an end to all his well-meant
labours for ever—this was the *beginning dissolution* of the federal

government!!" That "fair but flimsy fabric" had been put together
on the basis of "equal rights and mutual interests" with the pre-
supposition that the "good sense and virtue" of the nation would
be sufficient to guarantee its safety. " 'But alas!' said Washington,
'experience has shown that men, unless constrained, will seldom
do what is for their own good.' " As a result, he said, the America
which had won the admiration of Europe (with the hope that its
"fair example would regenerate the old world") was now, because
of its own internal disorder, becoming the object of abuse and
contempt. The only solution was to create "a power that may
command the full energies of the nation for defense from all its
enemies, and for supply of all its wants."

Weems paid slight attention to the process by which this new
energizing power was given constitutional form, except to imply
that it was done at Washington's behest. He gave little notice also
to Washington's presidency, in which various attempts were made
to compel people to do what was for their own good, except to
compare Washington to the Old Testament God who created
heaven and earth out of the void. But Weems did help to further
the ends of 1789 by according to Washington full status as the
father of his country; he also managed to suggest something important about the motives of the men who abandoned the republicanism of 1776 in favor of the paternalism of 1789 (reembodied,
as it were, in the form of Washington).

As Weems's account of both the troop dismissal and Washington's response to the "dissolution" of the government would
imply, what alarmed many Revolutionary notables in the 1780s
was that their newly won legitimacy, as represented by republican
ideals, was being threatened both from abroad and from within
their own society. They were concerned not only that republican
virtue was giving way to greed and immorality, as Washington's
answer to his troops would suggest, but that their fraternal union,
the symbol of their regeneration created for Europe's applause
and edification, was vulnerable to foreign contempt and intrigue
on one side, and internal subversion by a new group of disorderly
bastards (the "unworthy") on the other.[36] The paternal Union of
1789 was created to preserve the fraternal union of 1776. Washington's Farewell Address obscured this incongruity in the hoary

counsels of fatherly wisdom. When Weems concluded his interpretation of Washington's public life by reprinting the full text of this address, which he billed as the "solicitude of a father for his children," the "last letter of a once-loved father now in his grave," he was helping to establish Washington's paternal authority. At the same time he was also presenting an excellent summary of the contradictions of 1789 for which a perceptive and rebellious child, intent upon establishing his own legitimacy, could call his political fathers to account.

For Weems, Washington's advice to posterity (which will be more fully considered in the next section) was but a public expression of his own private virtues, and it was to his private virtues that Weems attributed Washington's public greatness. In the future, said Weems, when children asked, "What was it that raised Washington to such height[s] of glory?" they should be told that it was his talent guided by religion. And how did Washington come to be known by that "dearest and best of all appellations," the father of his country? It was the "natural fruit of that *benevolence* which he so carefully cultivated through life"; it was the result of his having controlled and conquered his "malignant passions."[37] "And what is it that raises a young man from poverty to wealth, from obscurity to never-dying fame?" Industry, replied Weems, "Oh! divine In dustry! queen mother of all our virtues and of all our blessings!" Finally, it was Washington's patriotism, his republican virtue and obedience to the law, as expressed in the Farewell Address, which distinguished his career.[38] Thus, Weems urged parents to place these virtues constantly before their children because, he said, in these "every youth may become a Washington." To children he offered the following advice:

> Young Reader! go thy way, think of Washington, and HOPE. Though humble thy birth, low thy fortune, and few thy friends, still think of Washington, and HOPE. Like him, honour thy God, and delight in glorious toil; then like him, "thou shalt stand before kings; thou shalt not stand before common men."[39]

Washington surely would have been pleased with the parson's embellishment of his advice. For as Weems suggested, Washington did urge his countrymen to cultivate the private virtues—to be religious; to be benevolent toward one another and other nations, avoiding factionalism and the spirit of party; to be industrious and frugal; and above all, to be obedient to the laws, guarding the Union jealously, avoiding innovations upon its principles, resisting opposition to its authority, and ever alert to the dangers of ambitious, unprincipled men who would overturn the established government. Such was Washington's counsel, but it was not a very accurate description of his career. A careful young reader might have noted that it was not by his virtues alone that Washington achieved his great stature, much less by following his own advice. When Washington stood before kings, he did so not as an obedient subject faithfully upholding the law, but as a defiant rebel engaged in acts of high treason; when Washington became father of his country, it was the result not simply of his religious devotion or benevolence toward his fellow man, but of his having committed fratricide and symbolic parricide.

The same would be true of Lincoln.

THE FAREWELL ADDRESS: PATERNAL AUTHORITY AND THE FOUNDING OF 1789

The very idea of the power and right of the people to establish government presupposes the duty of every individual to obey the established government.
—George Washington, 1796

Since 1862, on each anniversary of Washington's birthday, the words of the Farewell Address have been read to the Senate, and have been offered "as the unchallenged wisdom of the greatest of all Americans."[40] Whether it is Washington's wisdom or Lincoln's influence in establishing Washington's birthday as a national holiday that explains such a ritual, it would be difficult to find a single document which better summarizes the political thought of the founding fathers—or better captures the ambiguities which surrounded their agreement on fundamentals—than Washington's valedictory. In part, this is due to the fact that two of the most notable of American political thinkers—Madison and Hamilton—

directly contributed to the composition of the address.[41] But Washington's advice also succeeded in distilling from a decade of intellectual controversy and political discord recommendations which found widespread support among his Federalist contemporaries.

Washington opened his address with the announcement that he would not be a candidate for another term, stating that he had wanted to take this step four years earlier but that the "critical posture" of foreign affairs and the unanimous recommendations of his advisers had convinced him to abandon the idea. However, aware that the value of his services could only be temporary, he thought he would be able to quit the political scene without abandoning his sense of duty to the country. In looking forward to his retirement, he did not wish to leave public service without first acknowledging the debt of gratitude which he owed his country. If benefits have resulted from his service, Washington said, let it always be remembered as a praiseworthy and instructive example that my success has been dependent upon the "constancy of your support." This idea, he continued, would go with me to the grave

> as a strong incitement to unceasing vows that Heaven may con-
> tinue to you the choicest tokens of its beneficence; that your union
> and brotherly affection may be perpetual; that the free constitu-
> tion which is the work of your hands may be sacredly maintained;
> that its administration in every department may be stamped with
> wisdom and virtue; that, in fine, the happiness of the people of
> these states, under the auspices of liberty, may be made complete,
> by so careful a preservation and so prudent a use of this blessing,
> as will acquire to them the glory of recommending it to the ap-
> plause, the affection, and the adoption of every nation which is yet
> a stranger to it.[42]

Washington's implication that God's blessing was somehow dependent upon the constancy of the people's support for himself, and that a prudent use of this blessing would render the United States a model for the world, drew upon a tradition of thought which reached back to New England Puritanism, but which had also found secular expression during the Revolutionary period. Covenant theology had emerged in political tracts as the idea that the settlement of America had been part of a divine plan, the fulfillment of which gave the colonists a special identity.[43] Thus John Adams wrote that he always considered the settlement of America "as the opening of a grand scene and design in Providence for the illumination of the ignorant and the emancipation of the slavish part of mankind all over the earth."[44] Such an identity carried with it special obligations and dire consequences should the obligations be left unfulfilled. Again, Adams: "The people in America have now the best opportunity and the greatest trust in their hands that Providence ever committed to so small a number since the transgression of the first pair; if they betray their trust, their guilt will merit greater punishment than other nations have suffered and the indignation of Heaven."[45] Washington's usage of this idea did not threaten punishment so much as it promised rewards; but, as in most other cases when political leadership looked to heaven, it had one eye on the earthly tasks of establishing authority and unity.

These are the dominant concerns of the remainder of the Address. Presenting his advice as the "disinterested warnings of a parting friend," Washington proceeded to illustrate the possible uses of providential blessing by urging upon his countrymen a theory of history which was substantially exempt from mundane empirical constraints: "The unity of government, which constitutes you one people . . . is a main pillar in the edifice of your real independence, the support of your tranquility at home, your peace abroad; of your safety; of your prosperity; of that very liberty which you so highly prize."[46] The problem with this interpretation is that in fact the government did not unify the people; the unity of the people, such as it was, preceded the government, with its zenith occurring at the moment of revolution (1775–76) when there was virtually no government at all, but rather a spontaneous union which declared independence and established constitutions.[47]

Washington's assertion, which sprang from the desire to create a unity where none otherwise existed, points up a major paradox of Federalist political thought: At the same time that its authors celebrated the unity of the American people—their fraternal bonds, their common sociocultural characteristics, even their providential specialness—they also conjured up the specter of class conflict, internal civil war, and foreign intrigue as endangering the existence of society. One explanation for the paradox is that in the minds of the founders there were actually two unions —a sacred fraternal union of 1776 which was being jeopardized by hostile forces both from within and from without the society, and a contrived utilitarian Union of 1789, which was designed to protect against these threats in a paternal way, and to immortalize the fraternal bonds of 1776.

These distinctions were implicit in Washington's counsels. Without acknowledging any differences, he spoke of both "union and brotherly affection." He exhorted his countrymen to ". . . properly estimate the immense value of your national union to your collective and individual happiness . . . accustoming yourselves to think and speak of it as the palladium of your political safety and prosperity"; yet he also recognized the existence of a prior unity which would seemingly render such exhortations superfluous: ". . . you have the same religion, manners, habits, and political principles. You have, in a common cause, fought and triumphed together. The independence and liberty you possess are the work of joint councils, and joint efforts, of common dangers, sufferings, and successes." He warned that both the internal and external enemies of the country would attempt to weaken the people's attachment to the union, yet he also called those ties "sacred." In his view, the great advantage of union was that the states derive "an exemption from those broils and wars between themselves, which so frequently afflict neighbouring countries, not tied together by the same government; which their own rivalships alone would be sufficient to produce, but which opposite foreign alliances, attachments, and intrigues would stimulate and embitter"; yet he also believed that all parts of the country were bound together in an interdependent economic union of mutual self-interest.[48] One reason for this confusion is that Washington did not always distinguish between the "is" and the "ought," between his descriptions and his moral injunctions. It is clear that his purpose—and that of the authors of the *Federalist*—was less to delineate a preexistent political reality than to influence the creation of a new one.

Students of Federalist political thought have by no means been oblivious to these ambiguities and contradictions. Norman Jacobson has suggested that there were two varieties of political thought which contended for the allegiance of the American people in the late eighteenth century. One, which was notable for its expression of friendship and brotherhood, found institutional form for a brief time in the Articles of Confederation; the other, which was preoccupied with social order and procedural rationality, eventually triumphed, and its assumptions were reflected in the Constitution.[49] Writing from a different perspective, Gordon Wood has similarly concluded that the 1780s produced a separation between those who looked to republicanism as a forum for moral regeneration and those who relied upon mechanical, institutional contrivances as a substitute for moral virtue, a separation which ultimately distinguished the Antifederalists from the Federalists.[50]

Despite the validity of these insights, they should not obscure the degree to which the Federalists sought to reconcile the polarities of these two strands of political thought by attempting to drape the Constitution in the mantle of the Revolution. What was at stake for the authors of the Constitution was the preservation of their newly won model of fraternal legitimacy in the face of hostile forces, both internal and external, which they saw as threatening it. The irony is that their success in safeguarding their own legitimacy denied posterity access to any further legitimizing experience without violating the Constitution.

Foreign threats to Revolutionary legitimacy received the most candid public treatment. Indeed, Washington's Farewell Address, which accurately reflected long-standing Federalist fears of foreign domination, is best remembered in connection with foreign policy. The announcement that the United States considered itself outside the European system has so overshadowed the rest of the Address that Washington's advice has become virtually synonymous with his "great rule" that the nation should avoid foreign political connections. This is due in part to the circumstances which led up to the publication of the Address.

The French ministers to the United States had worked assiduously to bring about the defeat of Jay's Treaty, and had even reported to Paris that the American people were so opposed to their government that France should support them in overthrowing it.[51] If it was Washington's immediate purpose to tell a patronizing ally that the United States would not tolerate foreign interference in its internal affairs, he also wished to instruct his countrymen on the utility of their Union. Among the chief benefits of Union, according to its authors, was an institutional arrangement which could forestall such foreign intrigue and condescension. The promised result would be the preservation of a model of governance, which, as Hamilton had said earlier, could "vindicate the honor of the human race."[52]

The assertion that the honor of the human race was somehow at stake in the success of the Constitution was not merely a rhetorical exaggeration; it was an expression of the profound ambivalence in American attitudes toward Europe. As previously indicated, American republicanism was rooted in a deeply felt sense of illegitimacy. Revolutionary ideology, as expressed in the Declaration of Independence, made a credo of bastardy by transforming the vulnerabilities of illegitimacy into a regenerative world view. This awkward combination of unacknowledged ignominy and overstated virtue often produced unresolved contradictions in American attitudes toward the Old World. While absolutely rejecting European standards of legitimacy based upon patriarchy and inherited status, Americans simultaneously coveted the advantages of such a social order for themselves. As a nation, they insisted that they were embarked on a new and independent course, unprecedented in human history, but they also expected that their system of authority would receive, as Washington put it, "the applause, the affection, and the adoption of every nation which is yet a stranger to it." This was bastardy's compliment to its origins; no one paid the compliment more fully than did Alexander Hamilton—the child of unmarried parents himself—perhaps because no one experienced American bastardy more keenly than he.

Like other Federalists, Hamilton was convinced that only the adoption of the Constitution could save the new nation from European domination. Yet the anger and fear he expressed about dangers from abroad did not conceal the envy and admiration he felt for European greatness. Noting that philosophers had readily assumed that European power was traceable to the physical superiority of the European people, and had claimed that all species, including humans, "degenerate" in America—even that "dogs cease to bark" having breathed American air—Hamilton exhorted his countrymen to repudiate these arrogant pretensions:

> Let Americans disdain to be the instruments of European greatness! Let the thirteen states . . . concur in erecting one great American system superior to the control of all transatlantic force or influence and able to dictate the terms of the connection between the old and the new world![53]

In the fifteen years between the military victory at Yorktown and Washington's retirement from office, there was ample reason to fear humiliation in international affairs and scant evidence of American success in achieving autonomy, let alone the superiority Hamilton desired. During the 1780s, Great Britain ignored its obligations under the treaty of peace (1783) to evacuate its posts in the Northwest, while Spain refused to recognize American claims to the territory between the Ohio River and Florida, closing the Mississippi to American trade. Both the British and Spanish engaged in intrigue with the Indians and encouraged separatist movements in the Northwest and Southwest. Even the rulers of the Barbary States treated the new republic with contempt, seizing American ships and selling their crews as slaves.

Nor did the adoption of the Constitution automatically reverse this trend. Washington's anticipation in 1796 of a period "not far off " when the United States would be able to "defy material injury from external annoyance," a period when its neutrality would be "scrupulously respected" and belligerent nations would "not lightly hazard" American provocation, indicates the degree to which Federalist bravado failed to match realities in the 1790s. More accurate measures of the nation's international prestige during this period were Citizen Genêt's attempt to appeal, over the head of the government, directly to the American people for support of the French, and Jay's Treaty, by which the Americans abandoned many of their former claims against the British in exchange for little more than the promise of peace.

The actual vulnerabilities of the new nation fueled Federalist fears, which in turn produced a rhetoric that exaggerated both the protection offered by the Constitution and the dangers to be experienced without it. From the plausible assumption that only under a unified "national government" could the country avoid inviting foreign intrigue and wars, Jay and Hamilton proceeded to project onto the future of American states not so united the history of European conflict. Abstractly considered, not only do republics tend toward belligerency, Hamilton argued, but the particular conditions and conflicts of the American states would exacerbate this tendency. Disputes over Western territories and commercial competition would lead to martial strife. Recrimination over apportionment of the public debt and conflicting legal codes would cause breaches of moral obligation which again could lead to war.[54]

Moreover, once war came, some of the circumstances which distinguished America from Europe would render that war more destructive and predatory than a European conflict. The absence of disciplined armies and heavily fortified boundaries between the states would mean that attacks would be easy to mount but difficult to repel, that the populous states would overrun their less populous neighbors, with the results that always characterize the work of irregulars: plunder and devastation. Confronted with the possibility of constant war, Americans would then turn to standing armies as a means of enhancing their security. "Thus we should, in a very little time, see established in every part of this country the same engines of despotism which have been the scourge of the old world."[55]

By such phantasmagorical reasoning, which mixed fear and envy with dubious historical analysis and ideological purpose, Europe could serve the Federalists as a model both of calamities to be avoided and of advantages to be achieved through the Constitution. To mention but one example, England and Scotland divided were illustrative of the dangers inherent in disunity, and united they were indicative of the propensity of commercial nations for war. At the same time, Great Britain, in its insularity and unity, and with the modest military establishment appropriate to those conditions, was a model to be emulated by the united American states.[56] It was not a consistent argument, but it certainly was an ingenious one.

The ingenuity of the authors of the *Federalist* was perhaps never better demonstrated than in the ease with which they moved from the assumption that a virtually Hobbesian state of nature then existed among the states to the conclusion that a kind of Hobbesian solution was the only means of guaranteeing both the security and the liberty of the American people. At the Philadelphia Convention, Madison had argued against the view of Roger Sherman—a view widely, if not universally, held at the time—that while a national government could better guarantee external security and internal order, the happiness of the people—i.e., their liberty and civil rights —was better left in the hands of the states.[57] Sherman's assumption, based on the current reading of Montesquieu, was that only small states could enjoy republican government, and that if such states wanted the advantages of greater size, they could form a federation. Such a federal union, however, contributed nothing to republicanism; it merely increased the military strength of the member states. Did this mean, then, that the establishment of a strong national government automatically precluded republicanism? Were liberty and security unattainable under the same arrangement? Madison's resolution of this dilemma was so masterful and persuasive that he not only succeeded in redefining the meaning of republican government, and that of federalism,[58] but he also managed to lay on his political opponents, who represented the traditional federalist-republican point of view, the somewhat cumbersome burden of defending the antifederalist position.

Sherman had given Madison an opportunity for such a feat of theoretical manipulation by arguing that although ". . . people are more happy in small than large States," some states "may indeed be too small as Rhode Island, and thereby be too subject to faction." If that is the case, Madison responded, if small states are more subject to the oppression of faction than large states, should we not infer that any state subject to the abuses of faction is too small? And is it not true that even our largest states have suffered such abuses? Thus are we not thereby admonished to enlarge the sphere of government as far as possible as the only democratic defense against the inconveniences of democracies?[59]

Developing a line of reasoning he was to elaborate more fully in the *Federalist*, Madison then went on to say that all societies are divided into economic, political, and religious factions, and ". . . where a majority are united by a common interest or passion, the rights of the minority are in danger." The reason is that there is nothing to restrain them. Neither honesty, nor respect for character, nor conscience is adequate to check the passions and interests of men acting in the majority. Thus Madison concluded:

> that where a majority are united by a common sentiment and have an opportunity, the rights of the minor party become insecure. In a Republican Government the Majority if united have always an opportunity. The only remedy is to enlarge the sphere, and thereby divide the community into so great a number of interests and parties, that in the 1st place a majority will not be likely at the same moment to have a common interest separate from that of the whole or of the minority; and in the 2d place, that in case they should have such an interest, they may not be apt to unite in pursuit of it. It [is] incumbent on us then to try this remedy, and with that view to frame a republican system on such a scale and in such a form as will control all the evils which have been experienced.[60]

It was a powerful argument, and, as presented by the *Federalist* in somewhat more elaborate form, became the centerpiece of American constitutional theory. Madison's proposed remedy for republican ills was so ingenious that Antifederalists—easily dismissing the notion of an extended republic as appropriate for America—could not effectively refute the atomistic theory of society on which it rested. Antifederalist thinkers were obsessed with a fear of aristocracy and were convinced that the movement for strengthening the central government could only be an aristocratic conspiracy.[61] By denying the possibility of rule by a virtuous elite, opponents of the Constitution were unwittingly destroying the foundation of republican government, the assumption of social homogeneity.[62] As a result, Madison's conception of society as threatened by the unrestrained passions of a factious majority carried the day almost by default, and doubts about an extended republic were to be resolved, as Washington said, by experience: "Is there a doubt, whether a common government can embrace so large a sphere? Let experience solve it. To listen to mere speculation in such a case were criminal."[63]

Whether rooted in criminality or not, the appeal of Madison's speculations on an extended republic did have a practical aspect closely related to vice. As Gordon Wood has shown, what alarmed so many "men of reflection" in the 1780s, both those who later supported the Constitution and those who opposed it, was their perception of widespread social disorder—"the atmosphere of mistrust, the breakdown of authority, the increase of debt, the depravity of manners, and the decline of virtue."[64] It was not simply a matter of republican ideals giving way to greed and corruption, as many Revolutionary notables claimed, but also the appearance of "new" men everywhere, men "whose fathers they would have disdained to have sat with dogs of their flocks" in positions of wealth and power.[65] As a result, the authors of a doctrine which celebrated the condition of bastardy—the self-evident truth that all men are created equal—found their positions of authority challenged by a new group of disorderly bastards. The appeal of Madison's proposed constitution, for the Federalists, lay in part in its promise to protect, as John Dickinson expressed it, "the worthy against the licentious."[66]

One of the effects of the Revolution was to open up avenues of advancement to groups previously excluded from commercial and political influence. But as James Otis had warned in 1776, "When the pot boils, the scum will rise";[67] by the 1780s, it appeared to many that the social turbulence of the period had produced just that result in the political realm. State legislatures, the focal point of power under the Articles of Confederation, were seen as dominated by men who did not possess the proper education, family, and class attributes. "Specious, interested designing men," it was said, "men, respectable neither for their property, their virtue, nor their abilities" were taking the lead in public affairs, courting "the suffrage of the people by tantalizing them with improper indulgences." The Revolution, it was widely feared, had allowed government to fall "into the Hands of those whose ability or situation in Life does not entitle them to it." Many complained both publicly in the press and privately in correspondence, as one rather restrained observer put it, that "a set of unprincipled men, who sacrifice everything to their popularity and private views, seem to have acquired too much influence in all our Assemblies."[68]

A principal aim of the Federalists was to create a virtuous republic which did not depend upon a virtuous people. That such a republic could also be expected to exclude unprincipled, vicious, self-serving men from positions of dominance was by no means just an incidental advantage. It appeared that both ends could be accomplished simultaneously by creating a national government of such jurisdictional expanse and distance from the people that not only would the power of the licentious be undermined at the state level, but only the most worthy would be able to command the support necessary to gain national office. As John Jay wrote in the *Federalist,* ". . . although town or country or other contracted influence, may place men in State assemblies . . . more general and extensive reputation for talents and other qualifications will be necessary to recommend men to offices under the national government."[69] The Constitution was to serve as the functional equivalent of a stable class system.

Despite the adoption of the Constitution, however, the goal of establishing a firmly entrenched ruling elite proved to be elusive. In the highly inflamed political atmosphere of the 1790s, Washington continued to warn against faction and party and the men who would use these as instruments of their own ambition. Although Washington saw the most immediate danger in the emerging Jeffersonian opposition, he cast his admonitions in terms reminiscent of the Federalist critique of the 1780s. Noting that parties were invariably the bane of the public good, Washington argued that though such associations may occasionally serve "popular ends," they are likely "to become potent engines, by which cunning, ambitious, and unprincipled men will be enabled to subvert the power of the people; and to usurp to themselves the reins of government." The end result, he thought, would be to "gradually incline the minds of men to seek security and repose in the absolute power of an individual" whose elevation would be "on the ruins of public liberty."[70]

From Washington's perspective, Madison's assumption that the public good in the national government would be served by "the substitution of representatives whose enlightened views and virtuous sentiments render them superior to local prejudices"[71] had not been borne out by experience. "Men of factious tempers, of local prejudices, or of sinister designs," whom Madison had sought to confine within the bounds of state politics, had not been confined, and continued to threaten public morality. In order to augment the mechanical contrivances of the Constitution as a means of fostering virtue, Washington turned to a source rejected by Madison as just another cause of factious strife: "Of all the dispositions and habits which lead to political prosperity, religion and morality are indispensable supports," said Washington. "In vain would that man claim the tribute of patriotism, who should labour to subvert these great pillars of human happiness, these firmest props of the duties of men and citizens."[72] In looking to religion as a substitute for political virtue, Washington was embracing the ideas of John Adams, a man removed from the mainstream of Federalist thinking,[73] but one highly sensitive to the importance of religion in American political culture.

Among his contemporaries, it was Adams alone who fully understood the practical uses of religion in establishing and maintaining political authority. From his biting critique of church rule in *A Dissertation on the Canon and Feudal Law* to his much-maligned discussion of the republic of virtue in *Discourses on Davila,* he never lost sight of the importance of destroying the political power of the church without undermining its moral authority. Adams recognized that in a country where the church had been reduced to a voluntary association, and the battle for religious liberty substantially won, what remained was a highly functional Christian piety which could be employed as a civic religion. The Declaration of Rights in his own Massachusetts constitution of 1780, for example, contained the rather unusual provision that it was the "duty of all men in society, publicly, and at stated seasons, to worship the *supreme being,* the great Creator and Preserver of the universe."[74] The purpose of such a call to religious duty amid a declaration of revolutionary rights is not hard to surmise, although Adams did not always spell it out. If the laws of God and nature alone were insufficient restraints on the passions of men, thus necessitating a mixed constitution and a balanced government, as Adams argued, they were nevertheless a valuable prop to the durability of a mixed constitution.

While carrying on a dialogue with Bolingbroke in the margin

of his copy of that author's works, Adams scribbled the following note:

> But, My Lord, you have omitted the most essential foundation of the duty of patriotism, a belief in a future state of rewards and punishments. Without this faith patriotism can never be anything more than hypocrisy, i.e., ambition, avarice, envy, resentment, lust, or at least the love of fame hidden under a masque. Your other works, in which you have endeavored to destroy or to invalidate and render dubious all the arrangements of a future life, have destroyed your whole system of patriotism. . . .[75]

So profound was Adams's distrust of human nature that he did not regard even a well-ordered constitution as adequate to control the passion for distinction. He had to rely upon a future state of rewards and punishments as a sanction against political immorality —or what Hannah Arendt has called the attempt by Plato to discover a legitimate principle of coercion for the many which was later incorporated into church ideology.[76] Individuals as well as states live under the sentence of death; and the fear of hell or love of paradise by the individual could be the source of immortality for the state: pious men were law-abiding citizens.

The laws of God and of men were mutually reinforcing not only in a general sense of supporting the state's longevity, but in the particular sense of providing protection for rights of persons and property as well. As Adams put it, "If *'Thou shalt not covet'* and *'Thou shalt not steal'* were not commandments of Heaven, they must be made inviolable precepts in every society before it can be civilized or made free."[77] If rights of property were not held to be as sacred as the laws of God, then anarchy and tyranny would be the inevitable result. Denial of the fatherhood of God would be an invitation to nihilism and political terror. If the government of nations should fall into the hands of those who teach that "men are but fireflies and that this *all* is without a father," would it not make "murder itself as indifferent as shooting a plover, and the extermination of the Rohilla nation as innocent as the swallowing of mites on a morsel of cheese?" And should this happen, even sophisticated intellectuals would have reason to pray to their "almighty chance": "give us again the gods of the Greeks; give us again the

more intelligible as well as more comfortable systems of
Athanasius and Calvin; nay, give us again our popes and hierar-
chies, Benedictines and Jesuits, with all the superstition and fanaticism, impostures and tyranny."[78]

For Madison, who discounted entirely the efficacy of religious
morality as a means of restraining a factious majority, such a passionate concern for the political uses of religion made no sense at
all. But Adams recognized what Madison's new science of politics
sometimes overlooked, that America was different from Europe in
important respects, and that among those differences were their
widely disparate religious histories. Madison viewed the religious
impulse as just another source of popular strife and potential
oppression in a place where it was one of the few links binding
together a community of believers. Where he could see only opinion, and therefore, in his own terms, error, Adams recognized a
kind of natural piety that involved no great sectarian conflict, and
therefore a transcendental sanction for political authority that was
both potent and harmless.

Following Adams's ideas Washington suggested that the strictures of religion can be used as a bulwark against public disorder:
"Let it be simply asked, where is the security for property, for
reputation, for life, if the sense of religious obligations *desert* the
oaths, which are the instruments of investigation in courts of justice?" Likewise, following Adams, he suggested that religion can
be employed by the few as a substitute for political virtue among
the many: "It is substantially true, that virtue or morality is a
necessary spring of popular government." The implication is that
the two are interchangeable, and that in the absence of virtue,
morality will suffice. However, morality, among the masses at least,
is dependent upon the maintenance of religion: "And let us with
caution indulge the supposition, that morality can be maintained
without religion. Whatever may be conceded to the influence of
refined education on minds of peculiar structure, reason and experience both forbid us to expect that national morality can prevail
in exclusion of religious principle."[79] Adams himself could not
have made the point more clearly or delicately.

The authority of a constitutional order designed to protect its
citizens from their own worst tendencies, by restraining their ex-

cesses and compensating for their weaknesses, could thus be augmented, it was assumed, by inculcating religious piety. Constitutional fathers could join church fathers in calling upon the fatherhood of God as a source of authority for earthly control. The paternalism of the Constitution, however, depended not only on its providing a system of safety for its citizens, but also on the concealment of its own filial origins. This concealment was effected by placing the fraternal union of 1776 within a system of paternal constraint so that the Revolution could lend its legitimacy to the reaction.

There can be a convoluted complexity to a reactionary call for order and stability which recognizes the right of revolution. The Farewell Address accurately captured the convolutions of this position, if not all the complexities. Arguing that the Constitution was the "uninfluenced and unawed" choice of the people and that it therefore could justly claim their confidence and support, Washington said: "Respect for its authority, compliance with its laws, acquiescence in its measures, are duties enjoined by the fundamental maxims of true liberty." Acknowledging that the "basis of our political systems is the right of the people to make and alter their constitutions of government," he concluded that the constitution which exists at any time is "sacredly obligatory" upon all, until it is changed by an "explicit and authentic act of the whole people." The right of a people to establish government, he said, "presupposes the duty of every individual to obey the established government."[80]

Among the complexities ignored by this formulation was not only the fact that the Federalists sought to prevent fundamental constitutional change by minimizing the power of majorities, but also the degree to which they attempted to enlist the prejudices of the people in behalf of a constitution which, strictly speaking, was itself unconstitutional. For the convention of 1787 had originally been authorized only to recommend revisions in the Articles of Confederation, and it had plainly disregarded this limited mandate by proposing instead a wholly new constitutional system. Moreover, the ratification procedure it established, calling for adoption when nine of the thirteen states approved in specially convened assemblies, likewise circumvented the political machinery of the

Articles. Yet without such legal irregularities, it is doubtful that a new national government could have been created.

The Federalist attitude toward the people's right to make and alter their constitutions is reflected in Madison's response to the proposal by Jefferson that a convention be called for the purpose of altering a constitution whenever two of the three governmental branches concurred. Madison argued that frequent appeals to the people would "deprive the government of that veneration which time bestows on everything," without which it would not possess the "requisite stability." Among a nation of philosophers, this consideration could be disregarded, he said, but "in every other nation, the most rational government will not find it a superfluous advantage to have the prejudices of the community on its side."[81]

An even more serious objection to frequent constitutional conventions, however, was the danger, as Madison put it, of "interesting too strongly the public passions." Despite previous American success with such conventions, he thought they were "of too ticklish a nature to be unnecessarily multiplied." Previous constitutions, he argued, were formed "in the midst of a danger which repressed the passions most unfriendly to order and concord." They were created in an atmosphere tempered by public confidence in Revolutionary leadership and a universal commitment to republican forms, unmarred by the spirit of party. "The future situations in which we must expect to be usually placed do not present any equivalent security against the danger which is apprehended."[82] Thus the American practice of constitution-making must come to an end with the Constitution. Madison was saying to Jefferson that this tree of liberty needed no periodic refreshment with the blood of patriots and tyrants, nor even renewals less sanguinary. It required only the irrigating waters of veneration.

Among the sources of veneration which the Federalists sought to tap was the fraternal bond of 1776. The practical advantages of the Constitution could be added together endlessly, and the catalogue of horrors against the Confederation extended indefinitely, but this would all be of little import unless the utility of the proposed order could be linked to the Revolution. An opportunity to establish such a linkage was afforded by the ambiguity of the term "union." In attempting to create a new constitutional union, the

Federalists repeatedly invoked the union of 1776 as though the two were identical. They did not distinguish between the unity established during the Revolution and the institutions of governance they recommended for adoption, which meant that opponents of the Constitution were invariably characterized as opposing "the Union." As Hamilton defined the issue in 1787, the nation's only alternatives were either the "adoption of the new Constitution or a dismemberment of the Union." Such definitional ambiguity, however, did not prevent a clear distinction from being made between the Confederation and the Union: one of the major topics selected for discussion in the *Federalist* was the "insufficiency of the present Confederation to the preservation of the Union."[83]

This ambiguity about the meaning of "the Union," which permitted the Federalists to claim the Revolution as exclusively their own, served to conceal more than just a temporary strategic advantage in constitutional debate. It also helped to conceal the reality that the union of 1776 was to be used to legitimize a reactionary order designed to prevent not only revolution but significant institutional change of any kind, and even anticipated the installation of a new ruling elite. A fraternal union of republican equals, whose hallmark was a pledge of mutual renunciation of paternal power, was used, paradoxically, to help create a paternal union. The irony lay in the fact that these constitutional fathers sought to justify the illegality of their work by invoking the Declaration of Independence. The drafting of a new constitution, it appears, was to have been the final act of the last American revolution.[84]

Madison's intellectual agility, which served him well throughout his explication of the Constitution, did not fail him when it came to justifying the actions of the Philadelphia Convention. But his tortuous demonstration of the legality and propriety with which the convention carried out its commission is less noteworthy than his consideration of its revolutionary nature, or as Madison delicately put it, of "how far the duty they [the convention delegates] owed to their country could supply any defect of regular authority."[85] By his interpretation, the convention was to be viewed as a republican forum exercising the people's right to make revolution. Writing as "Publius," he pictured the delegates as necessarily reflecting that in all great changes of established governments forms ought to give way to substance; that a rigid adherence in such cases to the former would render nominal and nugatory the transcendent and precious right of the people to "abolish or alter their governments as to them shall seem most likely to effect their safety and happiness," since it is impossible for the people spontaneously and universally to move in concert towards their object; and it is therefore essential that such changes be instituted by some *informal and unauthorized propositions,* made by some patriotic and respectable citizen or number of citizens.[86]

They must have recalled too, Madison went on to say, that it was by this unauthorized means that the states were first united against the British, by this means liberty was defended and constitutions established, and that those who opposed the formal illegality of it all were actually only attempting to conceal their opposition to the substance.

There is no need to belabor the obvious contradiction between Madison's defense of the convention as a revolutionary forum and the reactionary purposes of the institutions it created. The implications of that contradiction, however, should not be overlooked. If the task of the convention was "to decide forever the fate of republican government,"[87] as Madison and Hamilton told the delegates, then it would require that posterity be forever excluded from attempting to improve upon their work. No other "patriotic and respectable citizen" could be permitted to reenact the Revolution and reshape institutions on the basis of "some informal and unauthorized propositions." Nor could subsequent generations of citizens be allowed access to the legitimizing experience of the founders; they would have to passively accept the role assigned them by the Constitution as obedient subjects and active engines of economic self-interest.

For the most part, posterity has obligingly met these requirements, but the exceptions are notable. One such exception was Abraham Lincoln, who not only demanded and received access to Madison's revolutionary forum, but reenacted the Revolution and refounded the Constitution according to his own requirements.

The Federalist goal of saving the Revolution by ending it, and preserving it forever in nominal form in the Constitution, was well served by Washington's Farewell Address. Just as his voluntary retirement from office lent legitimacy to the electoral machinery of the Constitution, so his advice sought to enhance acceptance of the political theory on which it was based. It offered Hamilton's demonstration of the commercial and military advantages of union; it provided a plea to let experience decide the practicability of an extended republic, accompanied by the admonition to "discountenance irregular oppositions" to the government's "acknowledged authority" and to resist the "spirit of innovation upon its principles"; it warned against faction and party and the "ambitious, unprincipled" men who would use these as instruments of their ambitions; it defended balanced government as the surest guardian of liberty; it emphasized the need for religious morality. Finally, it was a call for union which recognized no discrepancy between 1776 and 1789, and thus implied that citizens would be united on the basis of fraternity, benevolence, honesty ("honesty is always the best policy").

Most of Washington's advice was not heeded by his contemporaries, who were distracted by the tumult of partisan and sectional recriminations. Republican party opposition, which eventually gave Jefferson the presidency in the "revolution of 1800," was met by Federalist repression. Only ten years after the adoption of the Constitution, one of those repressive measures, the Alien and Sedition Acts, was declared null and void by the Virginia and Kentucky legislatures. Under the guidance of Madison and Jefferson, these states claimed the right to judge the constitutionality of federal acts and to interpose themselves between their citizens and the central government. A few years later, Massachusetts adjudged the Embargo of 1807 to be unconstitutional and not legally binding on its citizens, and Connecticut followed suit by invalidating a federal order calling out the state militia. It would not be long, either, before John C. Calhoun would begin his elaboration of Madison's theory of minority rights and propose improvements on the mechanism of 1789. It was one thing to create instruments of national power and quite another to infuse those instruments with sufficient legitimacy to overcome the centrifugal loyalties and interests of state and section. There was a difference between exhorting the people to cherish the Union as their palladium and compelling their acceptance of it as such.

The failure to establish the Constitution's intrinsic authority, however, was at least partially hidden for a time. Madison seems to have accepted Machiavelli's teaching on the need of republics for expansion, and in so doing, also endorsed the need for periodic renewal as a means of avoiding disintegration. Expansion itself would provide a ritual of renewal which did not require the return to first principles except in a symbolic way. It was by extension of the sphere of government, said Madison, that factions would be prevented from destroying the fabric of society. Through "enlarging the basis of our system and increasing the number of states," said President Monroe in announcing his famous doctrine, "the system itself has been greatly strengthened. . . . Consolidation and disunion have thereby been rendered equally impracticable."[88] Just as external expansion could replace internal renewal as a reaffirmation of authority, so the experiment of an extended republic could be transformed into a quest for empire. If the Federalists did not fully succeed in establishing the authority of the Constitution, they at least instructed posterity on how that failure might be overlooked—until the process of expansion and microcosmic renewal would itself force a crisis of authority, and the West could no longer function as a safety valve for constitutional discontent.[89]

WEEMS AS ROUSSEAU

[Civil religion] is good in that it unites the divine cult with love of the laws, and, making country the object of the citizens' adoration, teaches them that service done to the State is service done to its tutelary god.
—Jean Jacques Rousseau, 1762

When Lincoln recalled Parson Weems to the New Jersey senate, he prefaced his remarks by asking for the indulgence of his audience: "May I be pardoned if, upon this occasion, I mention that away back in my childhood, the earliest days of my being able to read, I got hold of a small book, such a one as few of the younger members have ever seen, 'Weems's Life of Washington.' " He went on to say that he remembered all the accounts there given of the battlefields and the struggles for the liberties of the country, but that none fixed themselves upon his imagination so deeply as the struggle at Trenton. "I am exceedingly anxious," he said, "that this Union, the Constitution, and the liberties of the people shall be perpetuated in accordance with the original idea for which that struggle was made. . . ."[90]

It is understandable that Lincoln would feel somewhat uncomfortable referring to Weems's book in such close proximity to what, in retrospect, turned out to be one of his most serious statements of presidential purpose. It is also understandable that he would mention the oddity of the book ("such a one as few of the younger members have ever seen") because Lincoln's statement of purpose echoed the central message of Washington's Farewell Address, but it was a message which he had first encountered enshrined by Weems's inimitable editorial embellishments. The oddity of the book, in other words, was the enthusiasm with which Weems sought to offset Washington's rather abstruse style by providing for a young reader the necessary clarification and emphasis. And Weems's adornments were almost as memorable as the thing adorned.

Having introduced the Farewell Address with the hope that its publication would check "that fatal flame of discord" which had destroyed all the ancient republics and now threatened the United States, Weems concluded his book with an expostulation of its relevance to contemporary life: "In this admirable bequest, like a true teacher sent from God, he dwells chiefly on our union and brotherly love. That, the *first birth of true religion* appears, to him as the *one thing needful,* the spring of political life, and *bond* of perfection." On this topic, said Weems, Washington employs all the energies of his mind, and "in words worthy to be written in gold, emphatically beseeches his countrymen to guard with holiest care *'the unity of the government,'* as the *'main pillar and palladium of their liberty, their independence, and everything most dear to them on earth.'* "[91]

In reading Weems, Lincoln was able to confront Washington; in reading Washington, he was able to confront the political thought of the men of 1789. But, as telescoped through the eyes of Weems, the ideas and personalities of the founders were inevitably aggrandized and distorted. Weems's Washington was a demigod whose superhuman qualities marked him for greatness at a very early age. But again and again Weems emphasized that the source of his greatness was his religion. He returned repeatedly to the theme set forth on the first page of the book that "greatness of public character" is often deceiving, that although in public any man can appear great, the true test of greatness was the virtue displayed in private. The examples were legion: Charles Lee, Hamilton, Burr, Benedict Arnold. These, as well as others selected from classical and biblical history, were proof that valor and genius alone were insufficient to guarantee greatness; for in each case, the potential for greatness was flawed by lack of religion.

Human laws alone were not sufficient as restraints on the actions of men who would seek greatness: "Great God! what bloody tragedies have been acted on the poor ones of the earth, by kings and great men, who were *above* the laws, and had no sense of religion to keep them in awe!" And even men who did not set themselves above the law, what horrid crimes, ". . . what cruel murders may they not commit in *secret,* if they be not withheld by the sacred arm of religion!" Weems repeatedly quoted the Farewell Address on the need of religion as a support for the political order.[92] What distinguished Washington above all else, according to Weems, was both his religious devotion and his recognition that religion was the basis of all sound morality.

Always quick to draw the biblical parallel, Weems also took note of the spirit of disunity abroad in the land, and projected the consequences in terms of Old Testament retribution. The disorganizing schemes of what Washington called "cunning, ambitious, and unprincipled men," said Weems, were leading us to the brink of civil war. Like other instances of fraternal strife, it would be horrible beyond contemplation—though Weems did not hesitate to suggest some possible images: sisters mute with grief, aged parents wringing withered hands and hoping for an early death, the country strewn with mangled carcasses, wives and children being dragged, screaming, from their houses. "Nor does this tragedy (of a free government madly divided and destroying itself) terminate here." If nations abused their liberty, God would take it away. "And since they would not let God reign over them with a golden sceptre of reason and *equal laws,* he will set a Master over them with a scourge of scorpions and an iron rod; some proud tyrant, who . . . shall . . . destroy our sons in his ambitious wars, and beggar us with exactions. . . ."[93]

But all was not yet lost, Weems assured his readers, if people would hear the voice of the Divine Founder who spoke through his servant Washington: above all things, Americans should hold dear their national union, accustom themselves to estimate its infinite value to their individual and national happiness, look upon it as their palladium. They should be filled with the spirit of '76 and rally around the sacred standard of their country: respect her authority, comply with her laws, acquiesce in her measures. Then other nations, following their example, would aspire to the same honor and felicity, until at last a new earth would be born, and there, freed from their imperfections, men would dwell together in love and joy eternal.[94]

Whatever one may think of Weems's characterization of Washington, there can be no doubt about the success of his book. With the full cooperation of the American public, he transformed a hated villain of the Jeffersonians at the time of Jay's Treaty into an irreproachable national hero within just a few years. In fact, one historian has concluded that Weems's book was one of the most influential works about American history ever written.[95] Even that may be too modest an estimate of its importance. Through this book Lincoln apparently first engaged the founding fathers in conversation, and out of that encounter came Lincoln's reply to the Farewell Address—the Lyceum speech in which he projected himself into the role of tyrant and proposed the establishment of a political religion to complete the work of the founders. Could it be that in the major drama of nineteenth-century American history Weems was to play Rousseau to Lincoln's Robespierre?

2

Dreams of Elysium:
Visions of Death and Immortality

HERNDON AND LINCOLN'S RELIGION

. . . I have never denied the truth of the Scriptures. . . .
—A. Lincoln, 1846

No aspect of Lincoln has perplexed his observers more than the matter of his religion or lack thereof. Much ink has been spilled —most of it needlessly—to prove either his infidelity or his orthodoxy. The issue first arose in connection with a series of lectures delivered by Lincoln's former law partner, William Herndon, during the winter of 1865–66, in which he asserted, among other things, that Lincoln had not been "a technical Christian man." The ensuing reaction by those who sought to protect Lincoln's Christian reputation, and the counter-response by Herndon, who wished to protect Lincoln's integrity as well as his own, precipitated a crisis of national proportions which rapidly degenerated into farce.[1]

Shortly after Lincoln's death, Herndon began to accumulate information for a biography he hoped to write by conducting a series of interviews with Lincoln's former friends and associates. On the basis of this material, Herndon developed his first series of lectures, which were generally well received by audiences and press alike. The one dissonant note which portended future trouble was the omission by the press of those remarks relating to Lincoln's religion. This greatly angered Herndon, but for him the worst was yet to come.

While the lawyer was working on his material and negotiating for its publication, Josiah Holland's *Life of Abraham Lincoln*[2] appeared and became an immediate popular success. Although Herndon acknowledged that the book had merit, he was deeply disturbed by Holland's portrayal of Lincoln as a Christian saint, based largely upon the testimony of a casual Springfield acquaintance, Newton Bateman. Herndon knew from personal experience, as well as his own investigations, of Lincoln's skepticism and even atheism; he was aware that Lincoln had read Paine and Volney and had written an essay denying the divinity of the Bible—a manuscript which Herndon later claimed was snatched from Lincoln's hands by his friend and employer Samuel Hill, and thrust into the stove, thus safeguarding his political future.[3] Herndon believed that by picturing Lincoln as a Christian, Holland was only making him appear a hypocrite; for if Lincoln had truly been converted, there would have been no reason for concealment. Indeed, the public announcement of such a conversion would have worked to Lincoln's political and social advantage. But in denying Lincoln's infidelity, his apologists were inadvertently setting the stage for future revelations that would do permanent damage to his reputation.

It was in anticipation of such future revelations that Herndon devised his lecture on Ann Rutledge. Should concrete evidence of Lincoln's atheism turn up, Herndon would provide the context in which it could be best interpreted and even explained away: Lincoln had written the "infidel book" in a fit of deep depression after the death of his true love, Ann Rutledge. At the same time, such a story would provide an explanation of the Lincolns' marital troubles which did neither party serious injury, and was therefore a relatively harmless way for Herndon to vent his animus against Mary Todd Lincoln.

Herndon's romantic tale of love and death—of a young woman driven to her demise by the conflict between previous commitments and immediate yearnings, of a young man disconsolate in his grief at her loss—placed in the pastoral setting of the Sangamon Valley, was an immediate sensation, though its author was thoroughly excoriated by the press as an iconoclast and traducer of the dead. One of the bitterest attacks came from the Reverend James Smith, who had been appointed by Lincoln as an American consul in Scotland and had previously been minister of the Springfield church attended by Mrs. Lincoln. Shortly after reading of the Rutledge lecture, Smith received an insolent letter from Herndon demanding that he produce evidence of Lincoln's conversion to Christianity, implying that Smith's testimony could not be believed in any case. The minister was outraged. In a widely published reply, Smith compared Herndon's villainy to that of Booth, and asserted that Lincoln had indeed affirmed his belief in the divinity of the Scriptures (as a result of reading Smith's book, *The Christian's Defense*), but that he would not discuss the issue with a man so despicable as to cause the president's family needless suffering.

After 1867, Herndon seemed to lose interest in his projected biography, and everything else. Plagued by a dying law practice and an unsuccessful venture in farming, he seized the opportunity to sell a copy of his Lincoln records to Ward Hill Lamon. The Lamon biography (actually written by Chauncey Black), as it finally appeared in 1872, was a devastating portrait of Lincoln, containing not only the stories of the Rutledge affair and the "infidel book," but Herndon's account of the illegitimacy of Lincoln's mother and elaborate testimony by former Lincoln associates on the nature and specifics of his irreligion.[4] The Lamon-Black view, largely based upon Herndon's records, was that Lincoln did not change his mind on religious matters, though he did come to recognize the political consequences of infidelity in a highly religious age. As they put it: "He perceived no reason for changing his convictions, but he did perceive many good and cogent reasons for not making them public."[5]

With the Christian reputation of a Republican national hero at stake, Josiah Holland was quick to respond. Not content with his own rebuke of the Lamon book in a review in *Scribner's Monthly* (of which he was editor), Holland also published the lecture of a Springfield minister, James A. Reed, which was designed to show that in his presidential years, Lincoln thought much about religion, and acted as a Christian. In support of his position, Reed cited the testimony of various Washington and Springfield preachers, including that of James Smith and Newton Bateman. Thus Republicans could rejoice that the slanderers of their Lincoln had been repudiated, and the Christian reputation of the national martyr restored.

Prodded by Black, who thought the popularity of the Reed lecture was creating a market for a new book on Lincoln, and by Mrs. Herndon, who believed the Reed lecture impugned her husband's veracity, Herndon responded with another lecture, designed to refute Reed's interpretation of Lincoln's religion and indirectly to advertise the book proposed by Black. Dismissing the testimony used by Reed as either fraudulent or otherwise unbelievable (as in the case of Smith's), Herndon held that since no one questioned that Lincoln had been a freethinker as a young man, it was incumbent upon the "defenders of the faith" to establish that he had been converted to Christianity at some later point. Herndon was certain that no such conversion had occurred. He cited a letter from the president's secretary, John G. Nicolay, which said, "Mr. Lincoln did not, to my knowledge, in any way change his religious views, opinions, or beliefs, from the time he left Springfield to the day of his death," and included the statement of Mrs. Lincoln that her husband "was not a technical Christian."

The controversy might have ended there except that Mrs. Lincoln, about to be committed to a mental sanitarium, was prevailed upon to repudiate the statement attributed to her by Herndon. This gave Herndon the opportunity to have the last word, which he eagerly accepted. Publishing his notes of the interview with Mrs. Lincoln, he gained a final victory over a woman whom he had never liked and who never liked him. It was not a pretty story, but an appropriately trivial conclusion to a debate that always generated more heat than light, never rising much above the level of gossip, fraud, and hucksterism. Even when the argument did reach a higher plane, it was virtually impossible to separate the personal and political purposes of the contending parties from the issue at stake. The irony is that, at least according to some historians, there was really never a genuine issue in the first place.

In his 1846 campaign for Congress, Lincoln felt obliged to issue a statement answering charges of infidelity made by his opponent—a statement not discovered until nearly a century after it had been made—which Herndon's biographer believes is "the final word on the religion controversy":[6]

That I am not a member of any Christian Church, is true; but I
have never denied the truth of the Scriptures; and I have never
spoken with intentional disrespect of religion in general, or of any
denomination of Christians in particular. It is true that in early life
I was inclined to believe in what I understand is called the "Doctrine of Necessity"—that is, that the human mind is impelled to
action, or held in rest by some power, over which the mind itself
has no control; and I have sometimes . . . tried to maintain this
opinion in argument. The habit of arguing thus however, I have
entirely left off for more than five years.

I do not think I could myself, be brought to support a man for
office, whom I knew to be an enemy of, and scoffer at, religion.
Leaving the higher matter of eternal consequences, between him
and his Maker, I still do not think any man has the right thus to
insult the feelings, and injure the morals, of the community in
which he may live.[7]

If that is the final word on Lincoln's religion, Herndon was
essentially correct in his assessment after all—no matter how overstated and self-serving that assessment may have been. For if there
was ever an opportunity for Lincoln to announce his belief in
Christianity, this would have been it. Pressed by his opponent, the
Reverend Peter Cartwright, a well-known Methodist circuit rider,
who circulated rumors of Lincoln's infidelity during this campaign
for the House, he had every reason to acknowledge his conversion
or at least affirm his acceptance of Christian principles—even if it
meant bending the truth a little. But Lincoln resolutely resisted
that temptation. His carefully worded statement did nothing more
than deny that he was an "open scoffer at Christianity": he did not
say he had never denied the divinity of the Scriptures, but only
their "truth"; he did not say he had abandoned his belief in the
doctrine of necessity, but only that he had "left off" arguing it.
Surely no man running for public office could afford to ignore or
insult the beliefs of his fellow citizens if he expected to be elected;
nor would so foolish a man be worthy of support.

But if Lincoln was not a Christian believer, how then does one
account for the abundant evidence of his Christianity? How to
account for the testimony of so many of Lincoln's clerical "confessors"? Can it simply be dismissed as the prating of men duped

through their own gullibility and what Lamon called Lincoln's "shrewd game" of deception? How then to explain Lincoln's own invocation of God as a source of strength and guidance for himself as well as the nation? More deception? How to account for the religious imagery and metaphors which so distinguished his speeches? Did Lincoln read the Bible only for its poetry? How to explain his apocalyptic view of the Civil War, in which he professed to see the hand of God working out His purpose? How are we to understand, in short, the motivation of a man whose words and deeds aimed at Christianizing the nation, but who himself did not believe?

For most observers, this is a superficial paradox to be explained away by what one of them calls the "several crises of the spirit" through which Lincoln passed, whose cumulative effect was a kind of conversion: the broken engagement to Mary Todd in 1841, the death of his son Eddie in 1850, the press of events after the 1860 election, the burdens of the war, the death of his beloved son William.[8] Of these, the preinaugural crisis is often singled out for special attention, not only because it was during this crucial period that Lincoln was formulating the policies which would initially guide his administration but also because of Lincoln's statement as reported by Noah Brooks in 1864: ". . . referring to what he called a change of heart, he said he did not remember any precise time when he passed through any special change of purpose, or of heart; but he would say, that his own election to office, and the crisis immediately following, influentially determined him in what he called 'a process of crystallization,' then going on in his mind."[9]

A process of crystallization may not be the same as a conversion. Indeed, Lincoln seems to have distinguished between them, unlike those observers who would cite this as evidence of his religious transformation.[10] What did Lincoln have in mind when he made this reference, if not his personal conversion? There can be no certain answer, but the evidence strongly indicates that during the time before his inauguration, Lincoln began to realize that the crisis precipitated by the secessionist movement could be resolved only by founding the Union anew, and that he personally could become the instrument of this national rebirth by establishing a political religion for the nation. The process of crystallization of

which Lincoln spoke may have referred to his deepening conviction that in order to save the Constitution it would be necessary
to reach back to the Declaration of Independence as a source of
authority. This refoundation would be stabilized by supplying
what, according to Weems, Washington believed to be the one
thing needed in his Union: "the first birth of true religion."

THE LYCEUM ADDRESS:
FANTASIES OF GREATNESS

Towering genius disdains a beaten path.
—A. Lincoln, 1838

Madison's Constitution placed great faith in mechanisms and very
little faith in men. The founders seemed to believe that only they
had both the capacity and the opportunity for political greatness.
They assumed it was the duty of the sons to honor the achievements of the fathers. Should the progeny falter in this duty, they
would be the inheritors of a self-regulating mechanism which
could compensate for their weaknesses. Relieved of the terrible
burdens of political creativity, subsequent generations of Americans would be free to go forth, take possession of a continent, and
prosper. The founders, like most fathers, thought of their sons as
mere children—a source of pride, but not necessarily an object of
respect. As always, it would be the sons who were to have the last
word.[11]

Speaking before the Young Men's Lyceum of Springfield,
Abraham Lincoln, the twenty-eight-year-old state legislator from
Sangamon County, selected as his topic "the perpetuation of our
political institutions."[12] He began the discussion as the loyal son,
faithful and true to the work of the fathers, by invoking a familiar
theme from Washington: "We find ourselves in the peaceful possession, of the fairest portion of the earth, as regards extent of
territory, fertility of soil, and salubrity of climate. We find ourselves under the government of a system of political institutions,
conducing more essentially to the ends of civil and religious lib-

erty, than any of which the history of former times tells us." Contemporary Americans had neither established the institutions nor acquired the land but were, he said, obliged only to transmit the land, "unprofaned by the foot of an invader," and the political edifice, "undecayed by the lapse of time, and untorn by usurpation, [to the] latest generation that fate shall permit the world to know."

How should this duty be performed? At what point would the dangers arise? Certainly not from a foreign invader, said Lincoln. All the armies of Europe, Asia, and Africa combined could not win a military victory against the United States. If danger arose, it would not come from abroad, but from among ourselves. "If destruction be our lot, we must ourselves be its author and finisher. As a nation of freemen, we must live through all time or die by suicide."

At this point Lincoln, taking note of the increasing incidence of mob violence in the country, broached a subject of some sensitivity to his Springfield audience. A few weeks before the Lyceum speech the abolitionist editor Elijah Parish Lovejoy had been killed by a mob in nearby Alton, Illinois. Lovejoy, who previously had published his newspaper in St. Louis, had been forced to flee across the river into Illinois following his castigation of a St. Louis mob for lynching a mulatto, and his denunciation of the judge, who in effect ordered that no indictments be returned against the guilty parties. As Lovejoy's Alton reception suggested, however, anti-abolitionist sentiment ran high on both sides of the river. A year before, the Illinois state legislature had passed a series of resolutions denouncing abolitionism, to which Lincoln had later registered a mild dissent. By taking up the theme of mob violence, Lincoln had to steer a course between denunciation of the mob at Alton, which might have aroused the anti-abolitionist passions of his audience, and defense of Lovejoy, which might have furthered a cause equally intent on unlawful violence. If he hoped to receive a fair hearing for his defense of law and order, he had to avoid those passions which at that moment threatened to overwhelm both the law and whatever order it supplied.[13]

The examples Lincoln selected to illustrate the "mobocratic spirit" abroad in the land were only obliquely related to the death of Lovejoy. In Mississippi: the hanging of gamblers, Negroes suspected of insurrectionary conspiracy, whites accused of being in league with them, and finally strangers passing through from neighboring states. "Thus went on this process of hanging . . . till, dead men were seen literally dangling from the boughs of trees upon every roadside; and in numbers almost sufficient, to rival the native Spanish moss of the country, as a drapery of the forest." And in St. Louis: "A mulatto man, by the name of McIntosh, was seized in the street, dragged to the suburbs of the city, chained to a tree, and actually burned to death; and all within a single hour from the time he had been a freeman. . . ."

The direct evils of such action could be minimized: the mulatto had forfeited his life by committing an outrageous murder; the gamblers were "worse than useless," so their deaths could not be a matter of regret. It was the indirect consequences of such acts, said Lincoln, which produced the real evil. Acting upon such examples, the mobs of tomorrow would punish the innocent as well as the guilty; and seeing that such acts go unpunished, ". . . the lawless in spirit, are encouraged to become lawless in practice; and having been used to no restraint, but dread of punishment, they thus become, absolutely unrestrained." Meanwhile law-abiding men, seeing their property destroyed and their lives endangered, would become disgusted with a government that offered them no protection, undermining their attachment to it as a result. Under these circumstances, "men of sufficient talent and ambition will not be wanting to seize the opportunity, strike the blow, and overturn that fair fabric, which for the last half century, has been the fondest hope, of the lovers of freedom, throughout the world."

There was more at stake for Lincoln in the killing of Lovejoy than the right of free speech. His defense of Lovejoy—if that is what it was—took the peculiar form of downgrading the intrinsic evil of similar acts of violence so that he could call attention to their ultimately more disastrous implications. Any friends of the Alton mob in the audience could listen comfortably to his real message because he seemed to be virtually exonerating them of any direct evil. It was a shrewd tactic. As he put it a few years later, "When the conduct of men is designed to be influenced, *persuasion*, kind, unassuming persuasion, should ever be adopted. It is an old and a true maxim, that a 'drop of honey catches more flies than a gallon of gall.' So with men. If you would win a man to your cause, *first* convince him that you are his sincere friend. Therein . . . is the great high road to his reason. . . ."[14]

Lincoln was speaking to a wider audience than just the Springfield assembly. Though addressing matters of current interest, he also wanted to have a word with the founders. His argument up to this point had been that dangers arise to the nation's political institutions from the "mobocratic" spirit abroad in the land. Now he returned to the question of how to fortify against it. The answer, he said, was simple:

> Let every American, every lover of liberty, every well wisher to his posterity, swear by the blood of the Revolution, never to violate in the least particular, the laws of the country; and never to tolerate their violation by others. As the patriots of seventy-six did to the support of the Declaration of Independence, so to the support of the Constitution and Laws, let every American pledge his life, his property, and his sacred honor;—let every man remember that to violate the law, is to trample on the blood of his father, and to tear the charter of his own, and his children's liberty. Let reverence for the laws, be breathed by every American mother, to the lisping babe, that prattles on her lap—let it be taught in schools, in seminaries, and in colleges;—let it be written in Primers, spelling books, and in Almanacs;—let it be preached from the pulpit, proclaimed in legislative halls, and enforced in courts of justice. And, in short, let it become the *political religion* of the nation; and let the old and the young, the rich and the poor, the grave and the gay, of all sexes and tongues, and colors and conditions, sacrifice unceasingly upon its altars.

The fathers would have been proud of this son. Here was a call for law and order which was a distinct improvement over their own formulations, but one entirely supportive of their work. For Washington the entreaty to cherish constitutional order was entirely separate from his acknowledgment of the usefulness of religion as an "indispensable" support for that order. Washington could call the Union "sacred," but that did not make it so; he and the other founders knew, as Adams admitted, that the government was "contrived merely by the use of reason and the senses," that it had no more divinity in it than a ship or a house, or at best, no more than a poem, a painting, or a scientific invention.[15] They were left with the hope that the individual quest for religious salvation could lend a redemptive quality to their political order, or at least conceal its nonredemptive nature, so that obedience to the law could be secured, and become the means of achieving immortality for the state. It was a slender hope at best, because the political order they recommended was itself unregenerative, and its authority rather tenuous.

Such a separation between the sacred and the profane did not occur in Lincoln's formulation, nor in Parson Weems's. It was no coincidence that the danger for which Lincoln prescribed "political religion" as the remedy was the same cited by Weems to be overcome by "political salvation": the spirit of lawlessness abroad in the land which was leading the nation to the brink of civil war. It was no coincidence that the remedy proposed by Lincoln was essentially the same as that advanced by Weems: both "political religion" and "political salvation" were invitations to embrace the work of the fathers—and the terms acknowledged no discrepancy between the realms of the sacred and the profane.[16] Lincoln clearly was relying upon the assistance of Weems to improve upon the ideas of the founders, just as the latter had occasionally attempted to improve upon the words of Washington.

But it was one thing for Weems to hold that the Constitution and Washington's injunctions regarding its maintenance were sacred, and quite another for Lincoln to do so. Weems, after all, saw American history as but a variation on a biblical theme in which the hand of God was everywhere writ large. On what basis could Lincoln make a similar assumption? Though he had no sound basis for it, he certainly intimated one. Lincoln understood that the Declaration of Independence was sacred because lives, fortunes, and honor had been pledged in its defense, and, at times, had been sacrificed in its behalf. To swear by the blood of the Revolution was to reaffirm ritualistically the sacrifice and thus the sacredness of the Declaration. Lincoln was later to view the yearly fourth of July celebration as just such a reenactment: the ritual by which not only the descendants of the men of the Revolution, but later immigrants as well, were collectively regenerated by renewed contact with the moral principles of the Declaration.[17] He also knew that no lives or fortunes had been sacrificed for the sake of the Constitution, and that whatever honor had been committed to the cause, it was largely self-serving, being inseparably linked to the ambitions of the founders. In calling upon his fellow-citizens to take up the pledge of 1776 in behalf of the Constitution and its laws, he was tacitly admitting that the Constitution was not yet sacred; at the same time, he was also suggesting how it could become so: "Let reverence for the laws . . . become the *political religion* of the nation; and let [everyone] . . . sacrifice unceasingly upon its altars."

If Lincoln could play the loyal son, willing to suggest improvements on the bequest of the fathers, yet always faithful to their memory, he did not accept such constraints without considerable tension, and even resentment. A hint of resentment is to be found in the introduction of the speech, where he says that it was our task "only" to transmit the legacy of the fathers to the last generation. The meaning of that "only" became clear when he took up the question of why it was necessary to suppose that political institutions in existence for more than fifty years were now endangered. In view of the unqualified admiration he had already expressed for the work of the founders, his answer to that question was entirely unexpected: he not only suggested that the great reputation of the founders was undeserved, but identified himself with the forces which might destroy their achievements.

"That our government should have been maintained in its original form from its establishment until now, is not much to be wondered at. It had many props to support it through that period, which now are decayed, and crumbled away." Then, all who sought fame and distinction staked everything upon the success of an experiment designed to test the capability of a people for self-government. The experiment was successful, and thousands had won their immortality by making it so. "But the game is caught; and I believe it is true, that with the catching, end the pleasures of the chase. This field of glory is harvested, and the crop is already appropriated. But new reapers will arise, and *they*, too, will seek a field." And when new men of ambition spring up among us, they too will "seek the gratification of their ruling passion." The question then was, could that gratification be found in supporting an edifice erected by others?

> Most certainly it cannot. Many great and good men sufficiently qualified for any task they should undertake, may ever be found, whose ambition would aspire to nothing beyond a seat in Congress, a gubernatorial or a presidential chair; *but such belong not to the family of the lion, or the tribe of the eagle.* What! think you these places would satisfy an Alexander, a Caesar, or a Napoleon? Never! Towering genius disdains a beaten path. It seeks regions hitherto unexplored. It sees *no distinction* in adding story to story, upon the monuments of fame, erected to the memory of others. It *denies* that it is glory enough to serve under any chief. It *scorns* to tread in the footsteps of *any* predecessor, however illustrious. It thirsts and burns for distinction; and, if possible, it will have it, whether at the expense of emancipating slaves, or enslaving freemen.

When Herndon called this speech "sophomoric," he may have been right in a way he barely understood.[18] Here was Lincoln as rebel, unsatisfied with simply being about his fathers' business, downgrading their accomplishments, and even projecting himself ("and I believe it is true") into the very role against which he warned his audience—a Caesarean role in which the player would have his distinction no matter what the cost, whether by freeing slaves or enslaving free men. And it was this "startlingly prophetic" speech, as Edmund Wilson called it, which makes Lincoln observers tremble a little in the presence of a young man who seemed to anticipate not only his own historical role, with all the terrible ambiguity surrounding it, but all possible future criticisms of it as well. "It was as if," wrote Wilson, "he had not only foreseen the drama but even seen all around it with a kind of poetic objectivity, aware of the various points of view that the world must take toward its protagonist."[19]

Lincoln's poetic foresight, however, was heavily indebted to that of Weems. It was Weems who first projected civil war as the consequence of falling away from the advice of Washington, and, as a biblical gloss on Washington's warning against cunning, ambitious, and unprincipled men, prophesied that God would punish an ungrateful Israel by setting over them a master, "some proud tyrant" who would "destroy our sons in his ambitious wars, and beggar us with exactions."[20] And it was Weems's view that what distinguished Washington above all other great leaders was the self-restraint imposed by his religion. Washington had refused a crown though it was his for the taking, and as a result, had won everlasting fame and distinction. Towering genius disdains a beaten path. What would an irreligious Washington have done had he found the field of virtuous conduct already harvested? As Lincoln said of his tyrant, "Distinction will be his paramount object; and although he would as willingly, perhaps more so, acquire it by doing good as harm; yet, that opportunity being past, and nothing left to be done in the way of building up, he would set boldly to the task of pulling down."

What fantasy of greatness remained for a young man acutely aware of his own impiety and his own ambition but to fix upon the field left untouched by Washington? The general characteristics of Lincoln's Caesarean figure can be easily inferred by standing Weems's Washington on his head, or more precisely, by standing him in Lincoln's place. The general context, as well, in which such a figure might rise to the forefront of American politics can be derived from Weems's own prophecy. Both Lincoln and Weems agreed that the one way to frustrate the designs of any such despot would be to have the people united with one another in their attachment to the government and its laws.

Acknowledging Lincoln's indebtedness to Weems, however, should not obscure that it was Washington whom he was addressing. And if out of frustration and resentment Lincoln wished to shake the vine and fig tree under which Washington rested, in the end he did not want to disturb the grave, except by transcending it. What he suggested was why the appeal of the Farewell Address and the testimony of the founders were no longer effective as deterrents against disunity or adequate as props for maintaining the political institutions; and to propose how those goals could be accomplished in the future, thus preserving the legacy of the fathers.

According to Washington, the passions of the people were one of the many obstacles the founders had to overcome. Lincoln disagreed. During the Revolution, he argued, petty jealousies were temporarily rendered inactive, while the deep-rooted passions of hate and revenge, by being directed exclusively against the British, were transformed into active agents for the advancement of the noblest of causes. In this respect Lincoln was agreeing with Madison in *Federalist* No. 49, who argued that governments established during the Revolution "were formed in the midst of a danger which repressed the passions most unfriendly to order and concord," and in an atmosphere of universal commitment to revolutionary values. "But," according to Lincoln, "this state of feeling *must fade, is fading, has faded,* with the circumstances that produced it." Not that scenes from the Revolution would ever be entirely forgotten; but ". . . they *can not be* so universally known, nor so vividly felt, as they were by the generation just gone to rest." What were once living histories to be found in every family as evidenced by the mangled limbs and other scars of war—mute but undeniable testimony of the sacrifice—were now gone. "They *were* a fortress of strength; but what the invading foemen could never do, the silent artillery of time *has done;* the leveling of its walls. They are gone."

Lincoln agreed with Madison that the Revolutionary experience channeled passions toward constructive ends. But he did not share the assumption that time necessarily bestowed veneration upon governmental institutions, nor reverence for the laws. Time may bestow only forgetfulness, a loss of memory, and as a result, a loss of the Revolutionary experience. For the previous generation of Americans, the Revolution was real because they had been participants in that struggle; their sacrifices were visible to all. These living histories were a source of strength because they were a source of community: a universal recognition of the common purpose which bound the people together in a cause, as Lincoln later put it, that held out "a great promise to all the people of the world to all time to come." Political meaning, as he indicated previously in his plea for political religion, is created by sacrifice, and common meaning or community by common sacrifice or its immediate recognition. Time may bestow indifference as well as veneration, but in any case, time does not bestow reverence; it is only by sacrifice that the profane becomes sacred. In parting with Madison, Lincoln was also suggesting his agreement with Jefferson: the tree of liberty needs periodic refurbishment with the blood of patriots (at least) lest it become "a lonely trunk, despoiled of its verdure, shorn of its foliage; unshading and unshaded, to murmur in a few more gentle breezes, and to combat with its mutilated limbs, a few more ruder storms, then to sink, and be no more."

For Lincoln those living histories lost to his generation had to be replaced if the political institutions were to be perpetuated. The stories of the Revolution and, by implication, the exemplary testimony of Washington which had come to him through Weems were no longer adequate: "They *were* the pillars of the temple of liberty; and now, that they have crumbled away, that temple must fall, unless we, their descendants, supply their places with other pillars, hewn from the quarry of sober reason. Passion has helped us; but can do so no more. It will in future be our enemy." The language echoed Washington's, but the message suggested that new meanings must be created for Washington's words if the experiences which they represented were to survive. "Reason, cold, calculating, unimpassioned reason, must furnish all the materials for our future support and defence. Let those materials be moulded into *general intelligence, sound morality* and, in particular, *a reverence for the Constitution and laws. . . .*" Reason might furnish the materials of future support and defense, but how could these materials be molded into new meanings, and particularly, into reverence for the Constitution and its laws? Lincoln did not say, but again he hinted at an answer. His own calculating reason would mold the passions of the people into support of Washington's advice to posterity so that the preparation for the day of judgment could be made and the immortality of Washington and the nation simultaneously attained: "that we improved to the last; that we remained free to the last; that we revered his name to the last; that, during his long sleep, we permitted no hostile foot to pass over or desecrate his resting place; shall be that which to learn the last trump shall awaken our WASHINGTON."[21]

Lincoln ended his Lyceum Address as he began it, by invoking Washington. But this son clearly was no passive receptacle for the faith of the fathers. There were some terrible ambiguities involved in his acceptance of their legacy. He said that reason, rather than passion, could provide the means of achieving Washington's goals for the nation; but he also implied that reverence came only from sacrifice, and that perhaps something more apocalyptic than a call for respect of Washington's name and advice would be necessary. His final words were: "Upon these let the proud fabric of freedom rest, as the rock of its basis; and as truly as has been said of the only greater institution, *'the gates of hell shall not prevail against it.'* " The implication of this comparison between church and state was given added meaning by Lincoln's plea for establishment of a political religion. For, whatever his own religious views, Lincoln understood that the seed of the church was sown in the blood of martyrs. And whatever he owed to Weems, there could be no comparison between a hustling itinerant preacher whose prophetic calling was matched by a keener sense of the profitable, and an ambitious young man, playing for much higher stakes, who had the talent to maneuver himself into a position where his prophecies could be armed with the power of the state.

ELYSIAN ROOTS: DEATH AND MADNESS

> . . . *I must die or be better, it appears to me.*
> —A. Lincoln, 1841

"That man who thinks Lincoln calmly sat down and gathered his robes about him, waiting for the people to call him, has a very erroneous knowledge of Lincoln. He was always calculating, and always planning ahead. His ambition was a little engine that knew no rest."[22] This comment of Herndon's is not as profound an insight as might be suggested by the frequency with which it is cited. Lincoln never concealed his ambition for political office; and if his "commonness" was a studied effect in concealment, its purpose, as it had been for other Whig politicians, was only to enhance his chances for political success—though no doubt Lincoln had more uncommonness to conceal than most. Lincoln's ambition was not a "little engine" in any real sense; for if, as that term would suggest, he welcomed the small gratifications that public office could provide and worked diligently in their attainment, he sought much more from the political arena than Herndon—or anyone else—fully acknowledges. Ultimately, what Lincoln sought through political action was to transcend the finitude of the human condition, to triumph over death, by identifying his personal transcendence with the immortality of the Union. Ambition provided the means of this identification, and that suggests no small engine at work.

Lincoln's ambition was rooted in what can only be described as an obsession about death. Recent interpretations of Freud have emphasized that the Oedipal complex involves not simply lust and sexual competitiveness, stressed in his early writings, but the flight from passivity, helplessness, and obliteration, cited in his later work. "The essence of the Oedipal complex," writes Norman O. Brown, "is the project of becoming God. . . ." It exhibits "infantile narcissism perverted by the flight from death."[23] In other words, as Ernest Becker has put it, "the child wants to conquer death by becoming the *father of himself,* the creator and sustainer of his own life."[24] This flight from death and obliteration, the desire to conquer death by becoming father of himself, had a particular urgency with Lincoln. His project of becoming "God" worked itself out in both a private and a public context, against both his natural father and his political father, with the result that a personal death anxiety became transformed into a symbolic immortality both for himself and for the nation.

No general theory of human psychology is adequate to explain the special obsessive quality of Lincoln's anxiety about death. He not only feared death but wished for it; he saw death not only as an enemy but as an ally. Both as a concept and as a metaphor death appeared in his premonitions and his dreams, his public speeches and his private correspondence, his poetry and his humor. He expressed anxiety about it on a personal as well as a political level, consciously as well as unconsciously, with great seriousness as well as casual levity.

Some assistance in understanding Lincoln's preoccupation with death is offered by Erik Erikson's comments on the "young great man" in the years before he becomes the "great young man." Erikson had Martin Luther in mind, but his words de-

scribe Lincoln just as well: ". . . inwardly he harbors a quite inarticulate stubbornness, a secret furious inviolacy, a gathering of
impressions for use within some as yet dormant new configuration of thought . . . [,] waiting it out for a day of vengeance
when the semideliberate straggler will suddenly be found at the
helm. . . ." Accompanying this period of waiting, said Erikson, is
often a fear of an early death which would "keep the vengeance
from ripening into leadership." Yet, at the same time, such a
young man often shows signs "of precocious aging, of a melancholy wish for an early end, as if the anticipation of prospective
deeds tired him."[25]

As many of his early speeches attest, there was nothing particularly inarticulate about Lincoln's inward stubbornness, nor secret
about his furious inviolacy; but his associates often commented on
his brooding aloofness and inaccessibility, despite all his apparent
efforts at conviviality. There was, however, a definite sense of
preparation for a "day of vengeance" in Lincoln's early speeches,
a sense that he was readying himself for some great work, the
nature of which only he understood. The young man Lincoln often
seems to have been a case of a consciousness in search of an
appropriate forum in which to express itself, of words in search of
events with sufficient gravity to be worthy of the signification with
which he endowed them. In reporting that Lincoln did not believe
in freedom of the will, Herndon said: "We often argued the question, I taking the opposite view; he changed the expression, calling
it freedom of the mind, and insisted that man always acted from
a motive. I once contended that man was free and could act without a motive. He smiled at my philosophy, and answered that it was
impossible because the motive was born before the man."[26]

Lincoln's motive, his flight from death, revealed as the "necessity" out of which he spoke and acted, also had a counterpart, as
Erikson suggests, in his wish to end the project before it was
completed. Lincoln's many periods of melancholy and despondency did not simply reflect a wish to die. In one crucial instance,
the period from 1850 to 1854—which will be discussed in the next
section—a significant change occurred in how Lincoln sought to
act upon his motive and realize his ambition: rather than emulating
Weems's Washington, the father of his country, he would emulate

Lincoln's Washington, the revolutionary son. The constant factor in both modes of identity, however, was the fear of death.

As previously indicated, Lincoln expressed his obsession with death in a variety of ways. In the Lyceum Address the personal and the political were combined in the expressed fear that the founding fathers, in winning their "deathless names," had so foreclosed the field of glory as to impose upon subsequent generations of Americans a kind of inevitable death sentence. It was for this reason, perhaps, that Lincoln projected himself into the role of tyrant as a way of circumventing the more ignominious fate of political obscurity. Understanding that the temple of immortality erected by the founders was crumbling as the memory of the Revolution faded, he saw the opportunity for new acts of greatness in the task of revitalizing the Constitution and in renewing the Revolutionary community.

Lincoln's anxiety about death was not always expressed with such high seriousness. There was the almost casual disclosure of an 1836 letter to the *Sangamo Journal,* "If alive the first Monday in November, I shall vote for Hugh L. White for President"; and a typical rhetorical exaggeration which suggested a rather vivid image of death, ". . . I am willing to pledge myself in black and white to cut my own throat from car to ear, if . . . you believe me capable of betraying my friends for any price."[27] Lincoln warned his friend Joshua Speed, who was about to be married, that the absence of business and the conversation of friends to divert the mind can turn even the "sweetest idea" into the "bitterness of death." Again to Speed on the subject of his marriage, Lincoln wrote, "I now have no doubt that it is the peculiar misfortune of both you and me, to dream dreams of Elysium far exceeding all that any thing earthly can realize."[28] He was trying to quiet Speed's jittery bachelor nerves in this case, but for Lincoln the reference to Elysium took on larger implications.

It is wholly appropriate that the very first entry in Lincoln's *Collected Works* contains a verse highly suggestive of the famous line from *Macbeth* ("Tomorrow and tomorrow and tomorrow . . ."), which Lincoln in the last years of his life regarded as Shakespeare's greatest play.[29] As a youth, Lincoln wrote in his copybook: "Time What an emty vapor/ tis and days how swift they are swift

as in indian arrow/ fly on like a shooting star the presant moment.
Just is here/ then slides away in haste that we can never say they're
ours/ but only say they're past."[30] Shakespeare's greater felicity
cannot entirely conceal Lincoln's early recognition that life is but
a walking shadow, a tale told by an idiot, full of sound and fury,
signifying nothing.

Two poems provide an insight into Lincoln's unhappy consciousness. The first, a generally undistinguished work by William
Knox entitled "Oh, Why Should the Spirit of Mortal Be Proud?,"
was a favorite of Lincoln's, one which he quoted repeatedly, and
about which he said, "I would give all I am worth, and go in debt,
to be able to write so fine a piece as I think that is."[31] The theme
of the poem is the flux of time without progression, the pointless-
ness of life, the inevitability of death which wipes away all permanence and meaning. Four of the stanzas quoted by Lincoln on the
occasion of Zachary Taylor's death will give an indication of its
possible appeal:

> So the multitude goes, like the flower or the weed,
> That withers away to let others succeed;
> So the multitude comes, even those we behold,
> To repeat every tale that has ever been told.
>
> For we are the same, our fathers have been,
> We see the same sights our fathers have seen;
> We drink the same streams and see the same sun
> And run the same course our fathers have run.
>
> They died! Aye, they died; we things that are now;
> That work on the turf that lies on their brow,
> And make in their dwellings a transient abode,
> Meet the things that they met on their pilgrimage road.
>
> Yea! hope and despondency, pleasure and pain,
> Are mingled together in sun-shine and rain;
> And the smile and the tear, and the song and the dirge,
> Still follow each other, like surge upon surge.[32]

This is not a poem that cries out for exposition; but in view of
Lincoln's fondness for it, some consideration must be given to its
possible meaning for him. There may have been an element of wry
humor involved in Lincoln's use of the poem on this occasion. To

associate Taylor with the "multitude . . . the flower or the weed,/ That withers away to let others succeed" would seem to be a sly disparagement of Taylor's importance, as well as a suggestion of his own ambition. Of more significance to Lincoln was the poem's denial of the reality of an heroic era. By the poet's legerdemain, the differences between the sons and the fathers are eliminated: the game is not once and for all time caught, nor the pleasures of the chase permanently ended—the field of glory may again be cultivated and new crops appropriated, even on the "turf" which covers the fathers' graves. Death is an enemy, but it is also an ally, as the hint of celebration in Lincoln's announcement about General Taylor would suggest: "The conqueror at last is conquered."[33] The cycle of life and death was not simply a cause for despair; it was also a source of hope because it permitted the challenges of the fathers to be met anew by the sons.

"And this, too, shall pass away" was one of Lincoln's favorite themes. "How chastening in the hour of pride!" he exclaimed, "—how consoling in the depths of affliction!" But Lincoln did not accept this bit of timeless wisdom, as he characterized it, without qualification. "And yet," he said, "let us hope it is not *quite* true."[34] The hedge was that memory could preserve what nature obliterated. He made this point indirectly in his eulogy of Taylor. The president's death, he argued, may be useful in "reminding us, that *we,* too, must die." Abstractly considered, he said, death is the same with the high and the low, ". . . but practically, we are not so much aroused to the contemplation of our own mortal natures, by the fall of *many* undistinguished, as that of *one* great, and well known name."[35] In death all men are created equal; but even though the high must fall with the low, a name can be remembered. Lincoln made the same point more directly in his eulogy of Henry Clay two years later. Clay is dead, he said, but his "name has been, and will continue to be, hallowed in two hemispheres, for it is—'One of the few the immortal names/that were not born to die.' "[36]

Lincoln was always anxious to establish a "name" for himself, and was very uneasy about the one he had inherited. It was widely believed in Indiana, where he had lived as a boy, that his mother, Nancy Hanks, had been an illegitimate child. Lincoln's anxiety on the matter was reflected by the fact that he once, perhaps wishfully, told Herndon that his maternal grandfather had been a "well bred Virginia planter."[37] He was even less comfortable with his father's origins. According to Herndon's sources, the family was virtually unknown in the Hardin County region of Kentucky prior to Lincoln's national prominence. Lincoln himself often made inquiries of others bearing the name, hoping to discover a family connection and history—in one case explaining that he had failed to mention that Thomas, his father's name, was widely used in the family for the reason that it was so "common." He blamed his ignorance of family history on the fact that his father was an orphan and had become a "wholly uneducated man."[38] The disregard in which Lincoln held his father was made clear by an 1851 letter to his stepbrother, John D. Johnston, in which Lincoln said he could not come to visit his dying father. Tell him to place his trust in his Maker, Lincoln told Johnston. "He notes the fall of a sparrow, and numbers the hairs of our heads; and He will not forget the dying man. . . ."[39] The marked contrast between this cold rejection and his warm praise of Taylor and Clay is inescapable. It was clear that Lincoln preferred to identify himself, as the Lyceum Address suggests, with the family of the lion or the tribe of the eagle, rather than the flock of sparrows from which he came.

The appeal of Knox's poem for Lincoln must have been closely related to his own feelings of illegitimacy. The promise of "And this, too, shall pass away" gave hope to the disinherited, and, in this respect, closely resembled the appeal of the Declaration of Independence, a declaration which made bastardy itself the basis for legitimacy—or, as Lincoln put it, "clears the *path* for all—gives *hope* to all."[40] If Lincoln saw death as a threatening father who foreclosed the field of autonomous action, and as a friend who helped clear the path for his own achievements, he also saw it as the embrace of a loving mother. The second significant poem, which also addressed the theme of human mortality but is more interesting because it is Lincoln's own work, reveals some of the sources for his dreams of Elysium.

On a campaign trip in 1844, Lincoln visited his boyhood home in Indiana, where his "mother and only sister were buried." "That part of the country," he said, "is, within itself, as unpoetical as any spot of the earth; but still, seeing it and its objects and inhabitants

aroused feelings in me which were certainly poetry. . . ."[41] He
expressed those feelings as follows:

> My childhood's home I see again,
>   And sadden with the view;
> And still, as memory crowds my brain,
>   There's pleasure in it too.
>
> O Memory! thou midway world
>   'Twixt earth and paradise,
> Where things decayed and loved ones lost
>   In dreamy shadows rise.
>
> And, freed from all that's earthly vile,
>   Seem hallowed, pure, and bright,
> Like scenes in some enchanted isle
>   All bathed in liquid light.

The next five stanzas set the scenes of his childhood, which he
experienced again with a sense of loss at the recognition of how
time had brought change and death to the familiar, which now
could live on only in his memory. He ended the first section of the
poem on this note:

> I hear the loved survivors tell
>   How nought from death could save,
> Till every sound appears a knell,
>   And every spot a grave.
>
> I range the fields with pensive tread,
>   And pace the hollow rooms,
> And feel (companion of the dead)
>   I'm living in the tombs.

The paradise envisioned in the first part of the poem required an
extraordinary act of imagination; for the reality he subsequently
dwelt upon was grim, depressingly wretched, and everywhere
tainted with death. But then dreams of Elysium are not born out
of the satisfactions of a comfortable life; instead, they are rooted,
it would seem, in the desolation of death and deprivation as an
immediate experience.

Deprivation, squalor, and death were daily realities during Lincoln's childhood. The sordidness of these conditions can be made

apparent by a brief look at his early years. Having sold his holdings in Kentucky in 1816 for whiskey so as to avoid litigation, Thomas Lincoln literally drifted into Indiana by raft on the Ohio River in search of a new homesite for himself, his wife, and his two children. They eventually settled in the sparsely populated area of Pigeon Creek, a malarial swamp region where the vegetation was so dense that sunlight could barely penetrate it. The Lincolns lived the first year in an open-sided lean-to made of poles and brush, and provisioned themselves with wild game. The following year a small cabin was built and some land was cleared, but living conditions remained crude. The Lincolns were then joined by Betsy and Thomas Sparrow, Nancy's aunt and uncle, and a cousin, Dennis Hanks, who occupied the lean-to. There was no sanitation, and disease was widespread. The Sparrows fell ill and died within eighteen months of their arrival. A neighbor woman, attended to by Nancy, also became sick and died. Shortly thereafter Nancy herself was stricken with the disease and died. Following her death, Beveridge reports, living conditions deteriorated even further: ". . . for the Lincolns 1819 was a year of squalor—mostly flesh for food, unfit water, wretched cooking, no knives or forks, bare feet, bodies partly clad, filthy beds of leaves and skins."[42]

These bestial circumstances were unrelieved by social life. The people were illiterate, unkempt, unruly, and superstitious. Beveridge, the Progressive, says "incredible" quantities of whiskey were regularly consumed by men, women, and clergy alike. He describes social relations as "loose and undisciplined," by which he apparently meant that rape, divorce, bigamy, slander, assault, and adultery were common.[43] Lincoln went to school briefly at age ten, but did not return until four or five years later, when he learned to read. Home life and physical comfort improved markedly under the influence of his stepmother, Sarah Bush; but Lincoln did not get along well with his father, who treated him roughly and appeared to favor his stepson to Abraham. One explanation for this abrasive father-son relationship is suggested by the fact that Lincoln's contemporaries described him as "lazy," that is, disdainful of farm work and bookish. Dennis Hanks doubted whether "Abe Loved his farther [sic] Very well or Not . . . I Don't think he Did."[44] In any case, Lincoln left his family at the earliest opportunity, upon reaching his majority, and seldom saw them again.

This "abode of solitude and gloom," as Beveridge termed Lincoln's boyhood home, is recalled even more vividly in the second section of Lincoln's 1844 poem. Here the subject was an insane man, Matthew Gentry, with whom Lincoln had gone to school, and about whom he said, "He was a rather bright lad, and the son of *the* rich man of our very poor neighbourhood. At the age of nineteen he unaccountably became furiously mad, from which condition he gradually settled down into harmless insanity."[45] Lincoln could not have avoided seeing something of himself in such a man, who as a boy was somewhat better off than himself, and who presumably owed his insanity to the same circumstances which shaped Lincoln's own childhood. What is made apparent by the poem is Lincoln's identification with Matthew as well as his recognition that more horrible than death itself is the living death of insanity:

> But here's an object more of dread
>   Than aught the grave contains—
> A human form with reason fled,
>   While wretched life remains.
>
> Poor Matthew! Once of genius bright,
>   A fortune-favored child—
> Now locked for aye, in mental night,
>   A haggard mad-man wild.

Lincoln then recounted in four stanzas how Matthew, after maiming himself, fighting his father, and attempting to kill his mother, had his arms and legs bound by frightened neighbors, to which he responded with cries of rage, coupled with "maniac laughter."

> And when at length, tho' drear and long,
>   Time soothed thy fiercer woes,
> How plaintively thy mournful song
>   Upon the still night rose.
>
> I've heard it oft, as if I dreamed,
>   Far distant, sweet, and lone—
> The funeral dirge, it ever seemed
>   Of reason dead and gone.

To drink it's strains, I've stole away,
  All stealthily and still,
Ere yet the rising God of day
  Had streaked the Eastern hill.

Air held his breath; trees, with the spell,
  Seemed sorrowing angels round,
Whose swelling tears in dew-drops fell
  Upon the listening ground.

To examine possible sources of insanity in the America of Lincoln's youth, it might be useful to recall that this was also Tocqueville's America, an America wherein men were "born equal," to be sure, but also ridden with anxieties in their longing for community and connections:

> The woof of time is every instant broken and the track of genera-
> tions effaced. . . . Thus not only does democracy make every man
> forget his ancestors, but it hides his descendants and separates his
> contemporaries from him; it throws him forever upon himself
> alone and threatens in the end to confine him entirely within the
> solitude of his own heart.[46]

Confined within the solitude of his own heart, Lincoln, in the first section of the poem, conjures up perfect scenes of childhood to replace actual ones. Memory does not recall or recollect, it "hallows"; it frees "things decayed and loved ones lost" from "all that's gross or vile" and transforms them into "scenes in some enchanted isle." Memory, in other words, sublimates actual death into symbols of immortality, and regenerates actual social life into an Elysian community.

But what was it about that mournful song of Matthew, breaking the stillness of an Indiana night, which Lincoln as a youth found soothing, and which led him to steal away and drink its strains amid a glistening forest in the early morning? Perhaps in the faint echo of Matthew's rage he heard something of his own protest against conditions which could be experienced only in their squalor, misery, and death, yet which, as prescribed by an emerging American mythology, were to be viewed as earthly paradise. Perhaps in that desperate cry could be heard his own longing for an enduring meaning and a human connectedness commensurate with his own capacity to imagine them. In any case, for the young Lincoln there was something seductive and compelling about Matthew's madness, as well as something "more of dread/ Than aught the grave contains." The grave, it should be noted, contained his mother.

What was it that prompted Lincoln as a thirty-five-year-old politician to render this episode in poetic form? Some possible clues are provided by the text, as well as by the facts of Lincoln's personal life. In the poem, Lincoln employed the present perfect tense with reference to Matthew's cry: "I've heard it oft, as if I dreamed,/ Far distant, sweet, and lone—/ The funeral dirge, it ever seemed/ Of reason dead and gone." Whether or not it was his intent to say that he continued to be compelled by Matthew's song after leaving Indiana, Lincoln's behavior in the years preceding the return to his boyhood home indicated that he had indeed heard the funeral dirge of reason dead and gone on more than one occasion.

The most significant of these appeared to have occurred three years earlier, in 1841, on the "fatal first of Jany," as Lincoln characterized it, when he broke his engagement to Mary Todd.[47] At the time, Lincoln was Whig floor leader in the Illinois house, and had proved himself an energetic and effective legislative manager, rarely missing a roll-call vote. For three weeks, however, beginning with the new year, he was absent except for brief periods, and thereafter for an additional three weeks attended irregularly, failing to exercise leadership on key party issues.[48] During this period, his friend Speed became so concerned about Lincoln's depression that he removed all razors and knives from their room, fearing that Lincoln might commit suicide. At the same time, his associates reported that Lincoln "went crazy as a Loon."[49] Another observer saw different symptoms but concurred in the general diagnosis: Lincoln, it was said, "had two Cat fits and a Duck fit."[50] Lincoln himself characterized his malaise as follows:

I am now the most miserable man living. If what I feel were equally distributed to the whole human family, there would not be one cheerful face on the earth. Whether I shall ever be better I can not tell; I awfully forebode I shall not. To remain as I am is impossible; I must die or be better, it appears to me.[51]

It is impossible to know the precise causes for this episode of psychological deterioration. It is known that Lincoln found the incident painfully embarrassing, especially because of Mary Todd's humiliation. He even sought medical assistance, admitting that he "had been making a most discreditable exhibition of myself in the way of hypochondriaism."[52] It is also known that Lincoln had been despondent at the time of Ann Rutledge's death, and New Salem associates had thought that he was going insane then too.[53] Assuming that there had been a romantic relationship between Ann and Abraham, there also would have been a close connection in Lincoln's mind between love and death—a connection formed perhaps by the death of his mother when Lincoln was nine years old. It is clear from Lincoln's 1842 letters to Speed on the subject of Speed's marriage that he did associate love with death, perhaps even unconsciously expressing a love *of* death. His use of "Elysium" as a standard of marital happiness points to this conclusion. More importantly, Lincoln not only told Speed that one of the reasons for Speed's anxiety about marriage was that even the "sweetest idea" (marriage) can be turned into the "bitterness of death"; he also advised him that the proof of his love for Fanny Henning, Speed's bride-to-be, was his fear she would meet an early end.[54] Such a test of marital love, since it was Lincoln's own, might in fairness be applied to Lincoln's relationship with Mary Todd.

In his February 3, 1842, letter Lincoln said, referring to Fanny, "Why Speed, if you did not love her, although you might not wish her death, you would most calmly be resigned to it. Perhaps this point is no longer a question with you. . . . You know the Hell I have suffered on that point, and how tender I am upon it."[55] One might ask, what hell had Lincoln suffered on this point? Presumably, the test he was proposing to Speed as a way of resolving Speed's doubts in favor of marriage would not produce the same results in Lincoln's case. That is, Lincoln could not say he loved Mary because he *would* be calmly resigned to her death. If, however, the additional factor was included in the equation—the wish for her death—then perhaps the results would be different. Was Lincoln saying in effect, following the pattern of his mother and Ann Rutledge, that he could love Mary only if she were dead and thus transformed into an object which could be hallowed in memory? It's a chilling possibility, but one that might help explain the great emotional turmoil which Lincoln experienced during this period.

Whatever the causes of this episode, Lincoln was finally able to control the effects. He and Mary Todd were joined in what proved to be an unhappy union in November 1842. He reestablished his tarnished reputation with the Whigs and became their nominee for the United States House of Representatives in August 1846, winning the election by an unprecedented margin. He looked forward to beginning a new political career at the national level. This transformation was reflected, seemingly, in the poem about Matthew, which Lincoln was still revising in February and September of 1846, admitting that he was having "a deal of trouble to finish it."[56] As both he and his Springfield associates acknowledged, Lincoln had indeed continued to hear the "sweet" song of Matthew's madness, the dirge of reason dead and gone, in the years after leaving Indiana. It was time for Lincoln the poet, in rendering Matthew's appeal to Lincoln the youth, to bid farewell to all of that:

> But this is past, and nought remains
>   That raised you o'er the brute.
> Your mad'ning shrieks and soothing strains
>   Are like forever mute.
>
> Now fare thee well: more thou the cause
>   Than subject now of woe.
> All mental pangs, but time's kind laws,
>   Hast lost the power to know.
>
> And now away to seek some scene
>   Less painful than the last—
> With less of horror mingled in
>   The present and the past.[57]

This poetic resolution of the appeal which insanity had for Lincoln did not altogether allay his anxiety about death. His other attempts at poetry also dealt with the theme of death. His only other serious poem, "The Bear Hunt," treated the violence of the hunt in vivid images of death ("And, spouting blood from every part,/ He reels and sinks, and dies," etc.); it also offered a comment upon the false pride humans take in their meager accomplishments.[58] A couple of light verses given as souvenirs dealt with time, the loss of youth, and, by implication, death.[59]

Public speech, not verse, was Lincoln's poetic medium, and his speeches also revealed a man hounded by a death anxiety that could not be denied expression even in public. In his early speeches, Lincoln sometimes made use of death as a metaphor or illustration even though it was not necessary to his argument or even particularly appropriate to do so. In an 1839 speech on the Sub-Treasury, Lincoln concluded by saying that he felt his soul expand to godlike dimensions when he saw himself as the sole defender of his country's cause. He had previously argued that men knew nothing of the future except by analogies drawn from past experience. What had happened before would happen again when the same circumstances were present. To illustrate, Lincoln asked, how do we know a blast of wind will extinguish the flame of a burning candle? We know from having seen it happen before. Having made his point, Lincoln went on to cite the similar example of how we know we are going to die, as if somehow a candle in the wind ineluctably brought to his mind the precarious impermanence of life itself: "Again, we all feel to *know* that we have to die. How? We have never died yet. We know it, because we know, or at least we think we know, that of all the beings, just like ourselves, who have been coming into the world for six thousand years, not one is now living who was here two hundred years ago."[60] The point is superfluous to his argument, but not to an understanding of the psychology of a young man who needed so desperately to feel his soul expand to metaphysical dimensions that he professed to see an opportunity for that kind of transcendence in opposing the election of Democrats to public office.

Likewise in the 1858 debates, when Lincoln's "house divided" speech was attacked by Douglas as calling in effect for sectional war, Lincoln responded by saying, "In that passage I indicated no wish or purpose of my own; I simply expressed my *expectation.* Cannot the Judge perceive the distinction between a *purpose* and an *expectation.* I have often expressed an expectation to die, but I have never expressed a *wish* to die."[61] But in quoting the relevant passages from the speech, Lincoln omitted, apparently by accident, the sentence which expressed his expectations most vividly, i.e., that "I do not expect the Union to be dissolved—I do not expect the House to fall—but I *do* expect it will cease to be divided." Curiously, in the entire course of the Lincoln–Douglas debates, and even thereafter, Lincoln never again omitted that reference to the Union, and never again made that comparison between his expectations regarding the ultimate character of the government and his expectation of death, even though he answered Douglas's charges on this point repeatedly in otherwise almost exactly the same terms. It was as if the identification he felt between himself and the Union was so close on an unconscious level that mention of the expectation of his own death foreclosed mention of his expectation that the Union would survive. It is worth noting, though, that the Union with which Lincoln apparently so closely identified himself was not that established in 1789. For as he also said in his "house divided" speech, the government could not "endure permanently half slave and half free"—it would become all one thing or all the other. The only Union with which Lincoln could identify would be one that was all free.

Another possible explanation for this omission, one that is less speculative though not necessarily inconsistent, would be that it was simply accidental, and that subsequently Lincoln, realizing the inappropriateness of the analogy between his expectation of death and his expectations regarding the Union, simply abandoned it. So certain an expectation on the part of a policy-maker can hardly be distinguished from a purpose. In any case, this reference by Lincoln to his death was not only inappropriate, except on an unconscious level, but damaging to the argument he consciously wanted to make.

Another "coincidental" identification between himself and the Union, involving death and destruction respectively, is to be found in the Cooper Union Address. Here the identification occurs because of the language Lincoln used in an analogy drawn between the threats of a highwayman who says, "Stand and deliver, or I shall kill you, and then you will be a murderer!" and the South which says that the election of a Republican president will destroy the Union, and his supporters will then be responsible. About this Lincoln said, ". . . the threat of death to me, to extort my money, and the threat of destruction to the Union, to extort my vote, can scarcely be distinguished in principle."[62] The only coincidence here was in Lincoln's choice of pronouns. There is some evidence to indicate that Lincoln may have taken secret delight in smuggling himself into the discussion when the subject of the Union arose.

In his eulogy of Henry Clay, for example, Lincoln quoted extensively from another eulogy which had been previously published in a Democratic journal. In the latter encomium, Clay was hailed as an unequaled champion of the Union, a man who belonged not merely to his party and country, but to the world. "His career has been national—his fame has filled the earth—his memory will endure to 'the last syllable of recorded time!' " That tribute also included the following statement, of which Lincoln must have heartily approved in view of some of his earlier speeches: "Perchance, in the whole circle of the great and gifted of our land, there remains but one on whose shoulders the mighty mantle of the departed statesman may fall—one, while we now write, is doubtless pouring his tears over the bier of his brother and his friend—brother, friend ever, yet in political sentiment, as far apart as party could make them."[63]

The author of this eulogy was obviously hoping for a Democratic savior; but Lincoln probably still had some hopes for a particular Whig from Illinois when he returned to this theme in the conclusion of his own eulogy and said: "Such a man [as Clay] the times have demanded, and such, in the providence of God was given us. But he is gone. Let us strive to deserve, as far as mortals may, the continued care of Divine Providence, trusting that, in future national emergencies, He will not fail to provide us the instruments of safety and security."[64] Lincoln's failure to muster much enthusiasm for his subject on this occasion probably reflects his personal feeling that in 1852 his political fortunes were at their nadir. Within a few years, however, with the passage of the Kansas-Nebraska Act and the announcement of the Dred Scott decision, they were to improve spectacularly. And when Lincoln first began his long debate with Douglas in 1854, he very self-consciously took on the mantle of Henry Clay as defender of the Union and opponent of slavery's advance.

Not all the evidence of Lincoln's concern for his own mortality, and of his personal identification with the cause of his country, rests upon speculation and indirect inference. In a remarkable statement apparently prepared for his private use during the Douglas debates, parts of which later found their way into his public speeches, Lincoln brought together several elements of this theme and developed them in the most explicit terms possible. He began by defending his ambition: "I have never professed an indifference to the honors of official station; and were I to do so now, I should only make myself ridiculous. Yet I have never failed—do not now fail—to remember that in the republican cause there is a higher aim than that of mere office." Referring to the British abolition of the slave trade, he said he had never allowed himself to forget that it was a struggle which lasted a hundred years before its final success, and that during this time, it was the opponents of abolition who won office while the advocates were defeated. "But I have also remembered that though they [i.e., the opponents] blazed, like tallow-candles for a century, at last they flickered in the socket, died out, stank in the dark for a brief season, and were remembered no more, even by the smell." Even schoolboys, Lincoln wrote, knew the names of those who helped forward that cause (Wilberforce and Sharp), but who could name a single man who labored to retard it? "Remembering these things I can not but regard it as possible that the higher object of this contest may not be completely attained within the term of my natural life. But I can not doubt either that it will come in due time. Even in this view, I am proud, in my passing speck of time, to contribute an humble mite to that glorious consummation, which my own poor eyes may not last to see."[65]

Ambition provided the means by which immortality could be attained, but immortality did not come to those who merely won and held office. As Lincoln had put it in his Lyceum Address, many men can be found whose ambition aspires to nothing more than a seat in Congress, the statehouse, or even the White House, but these places would never satisfy a man who seeks true distinction. To win immortality is to live on in the memory of subsequent generations, and thus to be out of the ordinary, to disdain the beaten path, to seek regions hitherto unexplored. The opponents of abolition of the slave trade had won all the offices, but in their opposition and immediate political success, had also been consigned to historical obscurity. Wilberforce and Sharp, on the other hand, in backing an unpopular cause, had won the most elusive of historical prizes, the remembrance of posterity. According to Lincoln, ". . . he who moulds public sentiment, goes deeper than he who enacts statutes or pronounces decisions. He makes statutes and decisions possible or impossible to be executed."[66] But the molder of public sentiment, in playing for greater historical stakes, must also be willing to forfeit immediate success.

It is in this light that Lincoln's 1858 statements on his ambition can be best interpreted. Perhaps the most flamboyant of these was made just prior to the first formal debate with Douglas, in a speech at Lewistown. His conclusion to that speech deserves to be quoted at length:

> Think nothing of me—take no thought for the political fate of any man whomsoever—but come back to the truths that are in the Declaration of Independence. You may do anything with me you choose, if you will but heed these sacred principles. You may not only defeat me for the Senate, but you may take me and put me to death. While pretending no indifference to earthly honors, I *do claim* to be activated in this contest by something higher than anxiety for office. I charge you to drop every paltry and insignificant thought for any man's success. It is nothing; I am nothing; Judge Douglas is nothing. *But do not destroy that immortal emblem of Humanity—the Declaration of American Independence.*[67]

Lincoln did not seriously expect to be put to death, but there could have been no quicker way to win his own immortality than to be martyred in defense of the Declaration of Independence. In that sacrifice he would not only partake of the meaning of that immortal emblem of humanity, but contribute to it as well.

The crucial point to note here is that Lincoln's defense of "principle" was no restraint upon his ambition; quite the contrary, since his ambition preceded his principles in both time and importance, and in large measure determined what his principles would be. Here, at last, was an opportunity appropriate to the ambitions of a man who would emulate the founders. Douglas's idea of popular sovereignty and the Dred Scott decision, which, according

to Lincoln, threatened to open up both the Western territories and
the free states to the spread of slavery, provided an occasion worthy of the rhetorical grandeur displayed in the Lyceum and other
early speeches. It was an opportunity to cut a path of glory across
the infinite cycle of life and death without end and without meaning, to transcend the flux of human impermanence and gain a
distinction that could be preserved by remembrance. Lincoln did
not rise to the occasion so much as the occasion rose to him.

According to Lincoln, what distinguished the British abolitionists from their opponents was not their principles—though he
clearly implied that the principles of Wilberforce and Sharp were
superior to those of their opponents—but the fact that they were
remembered while their opponents were not. Likewise, what distinguished Lincoln from Douglas was not simply his principles—
though preventing the spread of slavery was morally better than
permitting its expansion under the guise of democracy—but that
where Lincoln sought historical greatness, Douglas merely sought
office. This can be seen in Lincoln's closing speech of the campaign, which he ended as he had begun it, with a disavowal of
ambition that only barely conceals how monumental his ambition
really was:

> Ambition has been ascribed to me. God knows how sincerely I
> prayed from the first that this field of ambition might not be
> opened. I claim no insensibility to political honors; but today
> could the Missouri restriction be restored, and the whole slavery
> question replaced on the old ground of "toleration" by *necessity*
> where it exists, with unyielding hostility to the spread of it, on
> principle, I would, in consideration, gladly agree, that Judge
> Douglas should never be *out,* and I never *in,* an office so long as
> we both or either, live.[68]

In order to restore the Missouri Compromise, Lincoln would
have had to win his battle not only against Douglas in Illinois, but
throughout a considerable portion of the rest of the nation as well.
Indeed, as both Lincoln apologists and revisionist historians have
acknowledged, had Lincoln not challenged Douglas on this issue,
there probably would have been no crisis after 1858. Douglas, at
this time, was emerging as the leader of a free-soil coalition which

had the support of many Republicans nationally, including such notables as Greeley, and even Seward. By opposing Douglas on the grounds that he did, Lincoln not only denied him access to the leadership of that coalition, and possibly the Republican party as well, but in the course of the debates forced him to adopt a position that ultimately resulted in a Democratic schism which was a valuable adjunct to, if not a necessary precondition for, a Republican presidential victory in 1860. In the process of driving a wedge between Douglas and both the Republicans and the South, Lincoln also laid claim to the support of radical Republicans through his "house divided" speech, which automatically branded him as an abolitionist in the South. Finally, the contest with Douglas catapulted Lincoln from relative obscurity into national prominence almost overnight, and made him a contender for his party's presidential nomination in 1860.[69]

These are no mean accomplishments for a man without ambition. Nevertheless, it is probably true that had the Missouri Compromise been restored, Lincoln could have easily agreed to let Douglas gain all the offices while he gained none, because Lincoln would have earned his immortality, and unlike the British abolitionists, perhaps even in his own lifetime. The restoration of the Missouri Compromise would have been Lincoln's accomplishment alone. As it was, he believed he had to content himself, like the British, with an immortality derived from a principle which would live on after him.

After the 1858 election, Lincoln confronted the proposal that Republicans should have supported Douglas in that contest. He argued that had they made Douglas their nominee for the Senate, it would have destroyed the Republican party nationally by impairing its principles. "I believed that the principles around which we have rallied and organized that party would live; they will live under all circumstances, while we die." Had Douglas intervened, however, it might have been twenty years before those principles could have been reassembled in a worthy organization.[70] Again a few months later, Lincoln said "that our principle, however baffled, or delayed, will finally triumph, I do not permit myself to doubt. Men will pass away—die—die, politically, and naturally; but the principle will live, and live forever."[71] The principles of which

Lincoln spoke were his principles. Before 1858, especially in Illinois, but in the nation as well, there were few Republican principles except as Lincoln defined them in the debates. Thus implicit within Lincoln's own analysis was the recognition that the contest with Douglas was undertaken not so much to establish a principle *per se* as to stake a claim on immortality.[72]

Lincoln's quest for immortality did not proceed along a single, uninterrupted course, as the foregoing analysis of his constant preoccupation with death might suggest. The ambiguity in his attitude toward the legacy of the founding fathers, as revealed in the Lyceum Address, found a corresponding expression in the different ways he sought to realize his ambition. Denied the opportunity of distinguishing himself in his early years by upholding the advice of Washington, Lincoln sought to distinguish himself in his later years by repudiating that advice. Eventually, he would win his immortality, even taking Washington's place as the father of his country, by becoming the very tyrant against whom Washington had warned in his Farewell Address, a tyrant who gained power under conditions of sectional strife, and presided over the disintegration of the settlement of 1789.

ANGELS AND FOOLS:
THE LIBERATION FROM OPPRESSION

. . . when you have extinguished [a man's] soul, and placed him where the ray of hope is blown out in darkness like that which broods over the spirits of the damned; are you quite sure that the demon which you have roused will not turn and rend you?

—A. Lincoln, 1858

The career of Lincoln's ambition seems to have had two distinct phases. The first, in which by his own efforts he managed to escape the squalor, misery, and illiteracy of his childhood to become a highly successful Whig politician, is marked by the development and display of Weemsian virtue. It is a phase in which Lincoln not only thought of Washington and hoped, as Weems advised his

young reader, but apparently modeled himself with considerable
deliberateness on Weems's portrayal of the father of his country.
The first phase came to an end with Lincoln's speech in the House
of Representatives on the Mexican War, which he apparently had
expected would attract national attention to himself by its display
of virtue, but which was ignored in Washington and both attacked
and ridiculed in Illinois. This failure, together with his frustration
at not receiving an appointment in the Taylor administration, sent
Lincoln into a period of extended despondency from which he did
not emerge until the fall of 1854, the date which marks the beginning of the second phase of his ambition. When Lincoln emerged
from this brooding moratorium, he did so with a vengeance—by
announcing that the "republican robe" had been soiled and must
be repurified in the spirit, if not the blood, of the Revolution. The
difference in these two phases is the difference between Lincoln's
emulation of Washington the father of his country, and his emulation of Washington the revolutionary son.

In his first public act as a new member of the House from
Illinois's seventh district, on December 22, 1847, he introduced a
series of resolutions which requested that the president inform the
House of the precise "spot" where, as he alleged, the Mexican
government had invaded U.S. territory and caused the blood of
American citizens to be shed on their own soil.[73] The resolutions
were tabled. Shortly thereafter, another Whig resolution, the Ashmun amendment, which declared that the Mexican war was "unnecessarily and unconstitutionally begun by the President," was
presented to the House and passed on a strict party vote.[74] A few
days later Lincoln, who had authored the "spot" resolutions and
supported Ashmun's rebuke of Polk's policy, rose to give his first
important speech in the House. He spoke for forty-five minutes,
elaborating the theme of his tabled resolutions and refuting point
by point the president's justifications for the war. He concluded by
accusing Polk of deception, incompetence, and immorality.[75]

It was an excellent speech—logical, factual, and precise, yet
also gracefully humorous, morally rigorous, and rhetorically compelling. It was also rather surprising. Lincoln knew how popular
the war was in Illinois; during the campaign of 1846, it had been
the principal focus of public attention. Thousands of young men

had volunteered to help defend against the "invasion," including several locally prominent politicians: former Congressman Hardin was killed at Buena Vista, future Senator Shields had been wounded at Cerro Gordo, and Congressman Baker had resigned his House seat—the one which Lincoln held—in order to seek glory on the battlefield. For the most part, Lincoln had been silent on the war, admitting privately that he "never was much interested in the Texas question";[76] but both he and his opponent, Cartwright, apparently supported the war during the campaign, and Lincoln actually spoke at a war rally in Springfield.[77] Moreover, Lincoln wanted to be returned to the House, even though, in order to keep peace in the local party, he had promised not to seek reelection. Regardless of this pledge, as he told Herndon just four days before his war speech, ". . . I could not refuse the people the right of sending me again."[78] Why, then, would a man who was not insensitive to the prudential requirements of democratic politics deliver such a speech?

The only possible answer seems to be that he hoped to so distinguish himself on a national level as a virtuous leader that all other considerations would pale by comparison. It was obviously not a desire to propitiate constituency interests which prompted him to speak out in this way; nor could it have been a wish to demonstrate his party loyalty. He had already done the latter by supporting the Ashmun resolution, and it was not necessary to further risk local censure on that account alone. Both the address itself and his correspondence with Herndon give some clues which point to another kind of motivation.

In December 1847 Lincoln wrote to Herndon, who served as his constituency contact, that he was going to be regularly sending him a copy of the *Congressional Globe,* the record of proceedings. The next day, in another letter, he again mentioned the *Globe* and concluded by telling Herndon, "As you are all so anxious for me to distinguish myself, I have concluded to do so, before long."[79] Nine days later he introduced the "spot" resolutions, which were printed in the *Globe.* Again, a few days prior to his war speech, he told Herndon that he expected to make a speech "within a week or two, in which I hope to succeed well enough to wish you to see it."[80] This was the same letter in which Lincoln said he could not

refuse the people the right of returning him to Congress if they so
chose, even suggesting that perhaps local party opposition to his
seeking reelection was being exaggerated. In short, the evidence
indicates that Lincoln wanted his views on the war to be widely
known, local opinion notwithstanding, that he was proud of those
views, and even hoped that their wide dissemination would result
in such universal acclaim that he might be swept back into office
by popular demand.

Lincoln opened his remarks by saying that he had remained
silent on the war until he took his seat in the House, and would
have continued to do so had the president allowed it. But by
insisting that "every silent vote given for supplies" was an endorsement of the justice and wisdom of his policy, Polk was compelling him to end his silence. By attempting "to prove, by telling
the *truth,* what he could not prove by telling the *whole truth,* " said
Lincoln, the president forced him into an examination of the official justifications for the war. What he discovered was that Polk's
account of American entitlement to the land where the violence
first occurred was "from beginning to end, the sheerest deception." Thus, said Lincoln, let the president answer the queries
which had been put to him by the "spot" resolutions. "Let him
answer, fully, fairly, and candidly. Let him answer with *facts,* and
not with arguments. Let him remember he sits where Washington
sat, and so remembering, let him answer, as Washington would
answer." If he should fail to do so, said Lincoln, ". . . I shall be
fully convinced . . . that he feels the blood of this war, like the blood
of Abel, is crying to Heaven against him."[81]

It is hard to believe that so shrewd a politician as Lincoln could
seriously have expected that such a speech would permit him to
"distinguish" himself in the ways he apparently hoped. Since most
of it was a detailed examination of the boundary question and a
critique of Polk's stated war aims, it was not the sort of speech
likely to capture the popular imagination. In that respect, perhaps,
Lincoln was more concerned with attracting the attention of his
congressional colleagues than his Illinois constituents. But whatever audience he had in mind, he failed to reach it, except in
unexpected ways; and, however naive, there was no question about
Lincoln's seriousness. He defended his vote on the Ashmun reso-

lution in a letter to Herndon by asking, "Would you have voted what you felt you knew to be a lie?" If your only alternative "is to tell the *truth* or tell a *lie,*" said Lincoln, "I can not doubt which you would do."[82] Such a passionate commitment to truth-telling suggests the degree to which Lincoln had committed himself to the emulation of Weems's Washington. Washington could not tell a lie; thus Polk, who sits where Washington sat, should not be permitted to tell a lie. Lincoln could not tell a lie either; but in this case, he apparently forgot Weems's implicit corollary: Washington did not have any friends.[83]

One indication of the extent to which Lincoln had modeled himself on Weems's Washington is the similarity between Lincoln's first campaign statement and Weems's stated purpose in writing his book. Weems said that in presenting Washington he was concentrating on the private virtues "because in these every youth may become a Washington—a Washington in piety and patriotism,—in industry and honour—and consequently a Washington, in what alone deserves the name, SELF ESTEEM and UNIVERSAL RESPECT."[84] Likewise, in launching his first campaign for the Illinois state legislature in 1832, the twenty-three-year-old Lincoln employed a solemnity of language which his listeners must have found startling, but which closely resembled Weems's. He concluded his campaign statement as follows: "Every man is said to have his peculiar ambition. Whether it be true or not, I can say for one that I have no other so great as that of being truly esteemed of my fellow men, by rendering myself worthy of their esteem. How far I shall succeed in gratifying this ambition, is yet to be developed."[85] This statement, which included an awkward reference to his "most humble" origins, was incongruous, given the situation, but quite appropriate to one who would emulate Weems's Washington.

"Imaginary fathers," Michael Rogin has written, "may exert a more powerful influence over sons than real ones."[86] This was especially true in Lincoln's case. In Washington Weems provided Lincoln with an ego ideal which could replace that represented by his own natural father, and thus with a means of triumph over the brutish conditions of his early life. Lincoln was not just speaking metaphorically when he said in his Temperance Address:

When all such of us, as have now reached the years of maturity,
first opened our eyes upon the stage of existence, we found intox-
icating liquor, recognized by every body, used by every body, and
repudiated by nobody. It commonly entered into the first draught
of the infant, and the last draught of the dying man. From the
sideboard of the parson, down to the ragged pocket of the house-
less loafer, it was constantly found. Physicians prescribed it in this,
that, and the other disease. Government provided it for its soldiers
and sailors; and to have a rolling or raising, a husking or hoe-
down, any where without it, was *positively insufferable.* [87]

By concentrating on Washington's private virtues, Weems was
offering Lincoln a model of self-discipline by which he could escape the death, both symbolic and actual, of not only alcoholism,
but illiteracy, deprivation, and madness as well. It was a model
which he followed closely.

Like Washington, Lincoln was self-educated, eagerly engaging,
as Weems put it, in the "noble pursuit of knowledge" by reading
and often memorizing whatever printed material he could obtain.
Like Washington, he was industrious (in all but farm work, at least),
and, like Weems, always associated idleness with death. Like Washington, whose word, according to Weems, was accepted as law
among his fellows, and whose athletic prowess was unequaled,
Lincoln developed the reputation among his young friends for
great physical strength and courage, and became their (the "Clary
Grove Boys") acknowledged leader, adjudicating their disputes,
restraining their mischievousness, but also standing with them
against outsiders. Like Washington, Lincoln could not tell a lie—his
name became a "synonym for fair dealing," said Beveridge—and
thus he became a respected judge in athletic contests, one whose
word was never questioned. Like Washington, Lincoln controlled
what Weems called the "malignant passions" of hatred and revenge
by his use of reason; he had "no ears to hear horrid oaths nor
obscene language" (Beveridge: Lincoln did not swear); he had "no
leisure for impure passions nor criminal amours" (Beveridge: Lincoln was not fond of girls); and he "enjoyed that purity of soul
which is rightly called its *sunshine*" (Beveridge: Lincoln displayed
"sweetness" of temperament). Like Washington, Lincoln became a
surveyor, and volunteered to help put down an Indian uprising,

achieving a position of command which he hoped to parlay into a political position, and like Washington, he was unsuccessful in doing so.

Unlike Washington, however, Lincoln had a sense of humor; and one of the ways in which he used reason to control his demonic impulse, his "bad" or "malignant" passions,[88] was through his irreverent wit. On Washington's birthday in 1842, Lincoln gave an address before the Washington Temperance Society of Springfield, which ostensibly was a straightforward discussion of the contemporary American temperance movement, but which actually used the consumption of alcohol as a metaphorical device for consideration of a more general concept of intemperance, the thirst for power and domination. The occasion proved to be an irresistible opportunity for Lincoln to have some fun, mostly at the expense of his audience, by commenting on the intemperance of temperance reformers, mimicking the style of a temperance reformer himself, and seeming to talk about "dram-sellers," "dram-drinkers," and their self-styled saviors, while actually discussing slave traders, slave owners, and abolitionists. But if the occasion called for irony and wit, it did not prevent Lincoln from making some serious points at the same time.

The thesis of the speech, in brief, was that exemplary self-reform is the best way to achieve social reform. The Washingtonians, a society of reformed drunks, have redeemed the cause of temperance reform, Lincoln argued, because rather than engaging in the tactics of denunciation used by previous reformers, they proceed with a benevolence born of personal experience with the problem. In Lincoln's view, those who have suffered from intemperance personally, and have reformed, are the "most powerful and efficient instruments to push the reformation to ultimate success." Those who have not fallen victim to intemperance, said Lincoln, have been spared more by the "absence of appetite" than by any "mental or moral superiority." In fact, habitual drunkards as a group compare favorably with any other group. "There seems ever to have been a proneness in the brilliant, and the warm-blooded, to fall into this vice. The demon of intemperance ever seems to have delighted in sucking the blood of genius and of generosity. . . . He ever seems to have gone forth, like the Egyptian angel of death, commissioned to slay if not the first, the fairest born of every family."[89]

How shall this demon be arrested? Everyone, suggested Lincoln, drunkards and nondrinkers alike, must take the Washingtonian pledge of abstinence. In that event, a greater revolution will have occurred than occurred in 1776. For by the temperance revolution "we shall find a stronger bondage broken; a viler slavery, manumitted; a greater tyrant deposed"—and at no cost in human suffering or bloodshed. And yet temperance will also be an ally to the cause of political freedom, which, so aided, will march on until every "son of earth" shall drink the "sorrow quenching draughts of perfect liberty. . . . Happy day, when, all appetites controlled, all passions subdued, all matters subjected, *mind,* all conquering mind, shall live and move the monarch of the world. Glorious consummation! Hail fall of fury! Reign of Reason, all hail!"[90]

It is little wonder that not all of Lincoln's listeners were amused by this performance. For not only were many in the audience clergymen and reformers of the type whose tactics he disdained, they were also being made the butt of a joke. To illustrate his point that the universal sense of mankind on any subject is an influence not easily overcome, Lincoln said that belief in the existence of an "over-ruling Providence" depends mainly on that sense; ". . . and men ought not, in justice, to be denounced for yielding to it, in any case, or for giving it up slowly, *especially,* where they are backed by interest, fixed habits, or burning appetites."[91] It was perhaps this kind of remark, in addition to Lincoln's contention that drunkenness was the best training for a temperance reformer, which led Herndon to conclude that the charges of infidelity made during the 1846 Congressional campaign were traceable to this speech.[92]

Lincoln's iconoclasm was also revealed in the similarities between this speech and his Lyceum Address. The passion for distinction in the earlier speech was here portrayed as the demon of intemperance; in both cases it was a menacing presence, associated with both genius and destruction: in one instance, an ambitious tyrant who would destroy the government in order to achieve fame, and, in the other, an avenging angel who locks the "fairest born" in the "chains of moral death." Likewise, as in the Lyceum speech, Lincoln argued that the protection against this menace was for the people to be united by a pledge of mutual forbearance, the pledge of 1776 in the former case and the Washingtonian pledge in the latter, suggesting in both that passions and appetites will be controlled by reason. Finally, Lincoln concluded in both speeches with a paean to Washington, "the mightiest name of earth," as he put it here, *"long since* mightiest in the cause of civil liberty,"* and, presumably because he had not given in to the demon of intemperance when he had the opportunity to become tyrant, *"still* the mightiest in moral reformation." On that name, said Lincoln, no eulogy can be given. "To add brightness to the sun, or glory to the name of Washington, is alike impossible. Let none attempt it. In solemn awe pronounce the name, and in its naked deathless splendor, leave it shining on."[93]

Despite Lincoln's ironic detachment and irreverent tone, he ended this speech, as he had the Lyceum Address, still formally committed to Washington as moral exemplar and ultimate authority. There was nothing in the content of the speech inconsistent with this conclusion either, suggesting that his demonic impulse, though not suppressed, was firmly under the control of his reason. Lincoln was not always so self-restrained, however. In an 1839 Whig campaign speech on the Sub-Treasury, he seems to have let his malignant passions gain the upper hand in a moment of rhetorical extravagance, unconsciously revealing that he sometimes fantasized the realization of his ambition not as upholding Washington's example and precepts, but as witnessing their destruction.

Referring to an opponent's assertion that every state would vote for Van Buren in the next election, Lincoln declared: "It *may* be true, and if it *must,* let it. Many free countries have lost their liberty; and *ours may* lose hers; but if she shall, be it my proudest plume, not that I was the *last* to desert, but that I *never* deserted her." Conjuring up an amusing image of the city of Washington as a great volcano, belching forth the lava of political corruption under the direction of the evil spirit Van Buren, Lincoln said that all who dared resist might be swept away. But then, suddenly, the humor was gone:

Broken by it, I, too, may be; bow to it I never will. The *probability* that we may fall in the struggle *ought not* to deter us from the support of a cause we believe to be just; it *shall not* deter me. If ever I feel the soul within me elevate and expand to those dimensions not wholly unworthy of its Almighty Architect, it is when I contemplate the cause of my country, deserted by all the world beside, and I standing up boldly and alone and hurling defiance at her victorious oppressors. Here, without contemplating consequences, before High Heaven, and in the face of the world, I swear eternal fidelity to the just cause, as I deem it, of the land of my life, my liberty and my love.[94]

Ostensibly Lincoln was talking about the possibility of a Democratic victory in upcoming elections; but, aside from the absurdity of an obscure Whig politician casting himself in such a heroic role under these circumstances, this passage is noteworthy for both its superficial similarity to and its fundamental difference from a statement incorrectly attributed by Weems to Washington's first Inaugural Address. In his inaugural, according to Weems, Washington said, "Integrity and firmness are all I can promise. These, I know will never forsake me, although I may be deserted, by all men: and of the consolations to be derived from these, under no circumstances can the world ever deprive me."[95] Both statements aver the authors' integrity and fidelity in the face of extreme political isolation and even death. The difference is that Lincoln imagined himself playing out his heroic role under conditions of the country's destruction by "hurling defiance at her victorious oppressors." In other words, the country to which Washington pledged his integrity and firmness would have to be destroyed before Lincoln's oath of "eternal fidelity" could have any reality. He even suggested, by his choice of language, that only under such circumstances could his project of becoming "God," his flight from oblivion and death, be realized: he felt his soul expand to godlike dimensions when, standing alone, he resisted the country's oppressors.

Nevertheless, such lapses of self-control by Lincoln were rare. For the most part, Lincoln's demonic impulse was carefully restrained by his reason. Throughout his early years, he remained, outwardly at least, committed to the emulation of Weems's Washington. This commitment was expressed in his attack on Polk's war policy, and apparently was the basis for his expectation that such a display of virtue would win for himself the distinction he sought. In this he was badly disappointed.

A measure of the speech's insignificance in Washington was provided by the fact that President Polk, who usually recorded the most minute details of daily life in his diary, took no notice of it; also, the city's newspapers gave it not a single line of attention.[96] Lincoln was not so fortunate in Illinois. The Democratic press in Springfield immediately launched an attack on the speech under the caption "OUT DAMNED SPOT." Public meetings were held, sometimes nonpartisan gatherings, which adopted parodies of Lincoln's "spot" resolutions, accusing him of slandering the war dead and defending the "butchery" at the Alamo. "Henceforth," said one such resolution, "will this Benedict Arnold of our district be known here only as the Ranchero Spotty of one term." Another meeting declared of Lincoln and his measures, ". . . may they be long remembered by his constituents, but may they cease to remember him, except to rebuke him. . . ."[97] The sobriquet "spotty Lincoln" caught on, and was still being used against him in the 1858 contest with Douglas. Lincoln was eventually to get his revenge for these attacks by employing a variation of Polk's Mexican War strategy at Fort Sumter; but in the meantime he suffered in silence.

Another humiliation also awaited Lincoln at the end of his House term. Early in the first session he had helped organize a congressional club of young Whigs for the advancement of General Taylor's candidacy for president. As the time for the nominating convention approached, he urged his Illinois friends to support delegates favorable to Taylor on the grounds that only he among the Whigs could be elected.[98] At the convention itself he took an active role in securing Taylor's nomination, working against the forces of his old party idol, Henry Clay. After the convention he traveled to Massachusetts entirely on his own initiative, attempting to keep the Whigs there from bolting the party in favor of the Free-Soilers.[99] Lincoln apparently avoided campaigning in Illinois until after the congressional election; but he did return to work for Taylor in the presidential contest, and after Taylor's victory, returned to Washington to finish out his House term, hoping to receive an appointment in the new administration.

Not only, however, was he not offered a significant appointment, but the job he wanted, commissioner of the General Land Office, was given, over his objections, to a Clay man from Chicago. The final insult came when he did receive the offer of an appointment —an embarrassingly insignificant one, secretary of Oregon, which he promptly rejected.

Thus Lincoln returned to Springfield in 1849, apparently feeling that his political career was at an end. He spent much of the next five years in mourning its passing. Invited to join a partnership with a successful Chicago lawyer, Lincoln refused on the grounds that "he would have to sit down and study hard . . . [which] would kill him. . . ." Instead, he told David Davis, "he would rather go round the circuit . . . than to sit down and die in Chicago."[100] Actually, Lincoln found a third alternative: to ride around the circuit and die symbolically in Springfield. According to the testimony of his closest associates during this time, he did no serious studying, as had always been his habit; he became childishly dependent upon the indulgence and generosity of others; he regularly fell into periods of depression, marked by occasional manic outbursts, in which he was oblivious to everyone around him; and he was filled with self-pity and helpless rage.

During his two years in Washington, Lincoln's law practice had completely lapsed; Herndon now insisted that he rejoin the firm as the senior partner, and that they carry on as before. Always more interested in politics than law, Lincoln became more desultory than ever in his approach to legal work. After his return from Congress, he never made an entry in the firm's account book, always leaving finances to Herndon. He kept no records of his legal activities, preferring to simply divide his fees with Herndon on an informal basis.[101] Lincoln's reading during this period was haphazard, superficial, and unrelated to his legal profession. On a typical day, he would arrive at the office about nine o'clock, immediately stretch out on the couch, and, to Herndon's great annoyance, begin reading the newspapers out loud. Often, when he was not on the circuit, entire mornings were spent swapping stories with local clients and cronies. When he was traveling the circuit, the times which his friend and companion Judge Davis thought were his happiest, the same mood of carefree merriment and camaraderie characterized his legal practice.[102]

Lincoln's apparent gaiety and unconcern did not reflect an inner contentment. A few months after delivering his Mexican War speech, he asked his wife to discontinue affixing the title "Honorable" to his name when addressing letters to him.[103] He gave no explanation, but this is a rather surprising request from a man who attached great importance to the prestige of a public name. Immediately upon his return to Springfield, he became completely indifferent to his personal appearance, much to his wife's embarrassment, even though in Washington he had been rather fastidious about his dress. Similarly, after the House term Lincoln neglected his personal business obligations, allowing two separate judgments against him in favor of New Salem creditors to go unsatisfied. This was in marked contrast to the usual care he took to preserve his well-known reputation for honesty and integrity, and a clear violation of his stern warnings to his father on the need to honor financial obligations.[104] These were some of the outward signs of Lincoln's lowered self-esteem, of the "melancholy" which Herndon said "dripped from him as he walked."[105]

All of Lincoln's closest associates commented upon his despondency, sadness, and gloom—his "abstraction," as they often characterized it. Visitors to his house noted that he would sometimes sit for long periods staring straight ahead, completely oblivious to his surroundings. Traveling companions on the court circuit testified that he would frequently stay awake all night staring into the fire, mumbling incoherently to himself. Acquaintances said that he would be in self-absorbed dejection for hours at a time, defying the interruption of friends. This constant gloom, however, was also interwoven, as Beveridge puts it, "with hours of abnormal gayety—black despondency and boisterous humor following one another like cloud and sunshine in a day of doubtful storm." Thus a house visitor said that after sitting abstractedly for half an hour he would suddenly "burst out in a joke, though his thoughts were not on a joke." Herndon told of many times when Lincoln would be staring vacantly at the office wall, unaware of Herndon's presence, and then suddenly "spring to his feet, burst into wild laughter, and rush from the room." On other occasions, Lincoln would interrupt these reveries by reciting Knox's poem "Oh, Why Should the Spirit of Mortal Be Proud?"[106]

Whether it was intentional or not, one effect of such behavior was that Lincoln succeeded in getting his friends and associates to join him in mourning his own symbolic death. All made allowances for his strange behavior; none questioned it or even spoke with him about it. His despondency was so conspicuous and intense that it always elicited the commiseration of others. As one associate put it, "His sad countenance aroused universal sympathy." Lincoln frequently put this sympathy to an extreme test. Herndon said that when he brought his children to the office he would turn them loose, "and they soon gutted the room, gutted the shelves of books, rifled the drawers and riddled boxes, battered the points of my gold pen . . . turned over the inkstands on the papers, scattered letters over the office and danced over them and the like."[107] Such permissiveness by Lincoln is often cited as evidence of his kindness as a father; but since there is no kindness in such paternal laxity, it was more likely an indication of his own self-hatred and rage. It did reflect, at least, the same pattern of dependence on the indulgence of others which characterized many of Lincoln's relationships.

Lincoln's associates had various explanations for this behavior. One attributed his depression to a "sluggish liver," for which he was advised to take "blue-mass pills." Judge Davis thought it was due to marital unhappiness. Herndon ascribed the causes in part to "derangement of secretions," in part to Mary Lincoln's bad temper, and (getting closer to the truth) in part to Lincoln's political disappointments.[108] But it was not merely political failure which sent Lincoln into this prolonged period of depression. The public reaction to his Mexican War speech was not simply a temporary reversal, but a repudiation of the very model of political action by which Lincoln sought to establish his own legitimacy; it was a rejection of the *modus operandi* by which political greatness was promised to those who emulated Washington's private virtues in suppressing the demonic impulse through the use of reason.

A clue to the extent of Lincoln's disillusionment with this model, an indication of the depth of his loss, is provided by the comments of his associates on his reading habits. Observing that he preferred poetry, mathematics, and science to history, two of his lawyer friends (Gillespie and Stuart) said that Lincoln thought "history as generally written was altogether too unreliable." And biography he refused to read at all. "Biographies as written are false and misleading," he told Herndon.

> The author of the life of his hero paints him as a perfect man— magnifies his perfections and suppresses his imperfections—describes the success of his hero in glowing terms, never once hinting at his failures and blunders. Why do not book merchants and sellers have blank biographies on their shelves always ready for sale, so that when a man dies, if his heirs—children and friends— wish to perpetuate the memory of the dead, they can purchase one already written, *but with blanks* which they can fill up eloquently and grandly at pleasure thus commemorating a lie; an injury to the living and to the name of the dead.[109]

The most significant biography in Lincoln's reading experience had been Weems's *Washington*. After his disillusioning and frustrating congressional term, he had ample reason to think Weems had commemorated a lie. The harm in such work, however, was not merely that it did injury to the name of the dead; it also injured the heirs of the dead—it injured "children and friends" who were misled by such distortions. In expressing his interest in science, Lincoln told Herndon: "Men are greedy to publish the successes of [their] efforts, but meanly shy as to publishing the failures of men. Men are ruined by this one sided practice of concealment of blunders and failures."[110] Lincoln had reason to believe that he had been ruined by this practice of concealment. In the future, however, he would engage in concealment of his own and make certain that the blank pages of his biography were filled not merely with lies, but with his own truths—truths which were a significant departure from the paternal counsels of Weems's *Washington*.

In the period between the summer of 1850 and the fall of 1854, except for the obligatory eulogy of Henry Clay and some desultory remarks to the Scott Club of Springfield, Lincoln made no important public speeches. It was a period of dejection, despondency, and disillusionment. Beginning in late August of 1854, however,

Lincoln returned to public life by speaking out on the Kansas–Nebraska Act. His Peoria speech of October 1854 set forth the essentials of the position that would transform Lincoln from an obscure Whig politician into president of the United States within six years. It marked the emergence of a new Lincoln, one who identified himself not with Washington, the father of his country, but with "Mr. Jefferson, the author of the Declaration of Independence . . . who was, is, and *perhaps* will continue to be, the most distinguished politician of our history. . . ."[111] It was an identity in which, as the qualification "perhaps" would suggest, Lincoln found new possibilities for himself by speaking and acting not from filial piety, but with a revolutionary vengeance; an identity in which Lincoln used reason to liberate rather than suppress his malignant passions. It was an identity which represented a course of action Lincoln had hoped would not be necessary; but, denied the opportunity of achieving distinction by following his political father's advice, Lincoln would become father of himself by repudiating that advice.

The differences between these two modes of identity are thrown into sharp relief by contrasting Lincoln's speeches after 1854 with an earlier talk delivered in the House on internal improvements. In the latter, Lincoln digressed to comment on the "general proposition of amending the constitution." His comments were virtually a direct quotation from the Farewell Address. As a general rule, he said, it is better to leave the Constitution alone; better not to take the first step, as that may lead to a habit of altering it. "Better, rather, habituate ourselves to think of it, as unalterable. It can scarcely be made better than it is." New provisions would create new appetites for still further change. "No sir, let it stand as it is. New hands have never touched it. The men who made it, have done their work, and have passed away. Who shall improve, on what *they* did?"[112]

This was Lincoln, in 1848, as the dutiful son. After renewing his public career in 1854, he made virtually no further references to the Constitution, except to note that its authors did not believe it forbade the prohibition of slavery in the territories. Beginning in 1854 and continuing throughout his six-year contest with Douglas, Lincoln looked instead, as he said at Peoria, "away back of the constitution," to the "pure fresh, free breath of the revolution"; he reasserted what he called "our ancient faith" that all men are created equal, as opposed to the "new faith" that some men have the right to enslave others.[113] He identified his personal vengefulness against Washington and the founders of the Constitution, for denying that he was their equal, with the "monstrous injustice" of Negro slavery, thereby disavowing the institutions which had enslaved them both, even threatening violence as a means of mutual liberation. After 1854, in short, Lincoln turned against the inheritance of 1789 as embodied in the Farewell Address.

Lincoln's position, which he maintained throughout the Douglas debates, was that government rests on public opinion, and whoever can change public opinion can change government. "Public opinion, on any subject, always has a *'central idea'* from which all its minor thoughts radiate. That 'central idea' in our political public opinion, at the beginning was, and until recently has continued to be, 'the equality of men.' "[114] It was Lincoln's contention that the Declaration of Independence, which he always regarded as marking the beginning of the nation, included all men, black and white, under its aegis. Not that all men were equal in all respects, but that all men were equal in their inalienable rights to life, liberty, and the pursuit of happiness. Now since the assertion of equality was of no practical use in effecting the separation with Great Britain, Lincoln concluded that it was placed in the Declaration for future use. The assertion that all men were created equal was intended as a "standard maxim for a free society, which should be familiar to all, and revered by all; constantly looked up to, constantly labored for, and even though never perfectly attained, constantly approximated, and therefore constantly . . . augmenting the happiness and value of life to all people of all colors everywhere."[115] Thus when Douglas's "don't care" policy with respect to slavery became public law in the Kansas–Nebraska Act, Lincoln's objection was not simply that the Missouri Compromise had been repealed, but that the founding principles of the Declaration of Independence were being repudiated.

Douglas, on the other hand, who marked the beginning of the nation in 1787, argued that the founders had made a government divided into free and slave states, and guaranteed to each state the right to do as it pleased on the question of slavery. He did not challenge the relevance of the Declaration of Independence, but disagreed sharply with Lincoln's interpretation of the signers' intentions. Douglas thought the Declaration was adopted for the limited purpose of justifying before the eyes of the world the withdrawal of allegiance from the British crown, and referred only to the rights of white men as British subjects.[116] Douglas saw in Lincoln's denial that territories had the right to decide the question of slavery for themselves the same abridgment of self-government which led the colonies to sever their connection with the British empire.[117] For Douglas, slaves were property like any other, and to exclude them from the territories was a denial of property rights.

Douglas can be criticized, of course, for failing to acknowledge the extent to which the men of 1776 thought slavery was wrong, and for ignoring the revolutionary aspects of the Declaration. Nevertheless, he was much more closely in touch with the realities of 1776 than was Lincoln. Actually Lincoln's parody of Douglas's version of the Declaration of Independence—"We hold these truths to be self-evident that all British subjects who were on this continent eighty-one years ago, were created equal to all British subjects born and *then* residing in Great Britain"[118]—was closer to the truth than his own version of the signers' intentions. He was also wrong in claiming that the assertion of equality had no usefulness in effecting the separation with Great Britain; the assertion of equality provided proof that monarchy was itself illegitimate, and therefore was of considerable use in justifying independence. More important, by tracing the origins of the government to 1776, Lincoln consistently ignored the origins of 1789, the Constitution of the United States.

As previously indicated, Lincoln hardly mentioned the Constitution, except to show that the founders did not believe it forbade the prohibition of slavery in the territories. No doubt he did not mention it for the understandable reason that on this point Douglas was surely right: the Union was founded on a compromise over slavery, and the Constitution legitimized that institution as part of an established order. If the founders hoped for the ultimate extinction of slavery, they did not seem seriously to expect it, as

Lincoln maintained, for they recognized that the price of union was compromise on this issue, and could not conceive of a society in which blacks and whites might live together in civility, let alone brotherhood.[119]

Perhaps the extent to which Lincoln's position challenged the principles of the Constitution was never more clearly revealed than when he said of Douglas: "He contends that whatever community wants slaves has a right to have them. So they have if it is not a wrong. But if it is a wrong, he cannot say people have a right to do wrong."[120] The right to do wrong in a moral sense is precisely what the Constitution did guarantee its citizens by defining liberty only as the absence of restraint, and by introducing no test of right and wrong other than a consensual one: right and wrong would be measured by the political strength of contending forces. Or again, when Lincoln condemned indifference to the spread of slavery as tantamount to admitting there is no right principle of action except self-interest, he conveniently overlooked the judgment of the founders that altruism in politics was more to be feared than honest self-interest, and that the Constitution endorsed no other principle of action.[121] In arguing that his were the principles of the founders, Lincoln had virtually to ignore the Constitution, which both sanctioned slavery and fostered a utilitarianism that could permit any compromise of principle contending parties were willing to accept, in favor of the Declaration of Independence, whose legal status was nonexistent, and whose moral authority had been seriously impaired by the Constitution.

Lincoln had not said much about slavery prior to 1854, mentioning it in a public speech for the first time in his 1852 eulogy of Clay. His silence on the issue was consistent with the practice of political parties prior to the 1850s of consciously excluding sectional ideologies and issues from politics.[122] The Kansas–Nebraska bill, by repealing the Missouri Compromise, dramatically ended such restraint, however, and Lincoln entered the fray along with others, openly expressing his passions. As he said at Peoria, ". . . the opening of new countries to slavery, tends to the perpetuation of the institution. . . . This result we do not FEEL like favoring, and we are under no legal obligation to suppress our feelings in this respect."[123]

Lincoln did not hesitate to express his feelings in this or in other respects. During an 1857 speech at Springfield, discussing the Declaration of Independence, he seemed to have lost his train of thought momentarily, digressing into what was for him a rare non-sequitur. Noting that the framers of the Declaration would scarcely recognize their work in recent times, he suddenly changed the subject: "All the powers of earth seem rapidly combining against him," he said.

> They have him in his prison house; they have searched his person, and left no prying instrument with him. One after another they have closed the heavy iron doors upon him, and now they have him, as it were, bolted in with a lock of a hundred keys, which can never be unlocked without the concurrence of every key; the keys in the hands of a hundred different men, and they scattered to a hundred different and distant places; and they stand musing as to what inventions, in all the dominions of mind and matter, can be produced to make the impossibility of his escape more complete than it is.[124]

It is clear from the larger context of the speech that Lincoln's reference here was to the Negro slave; but it is also clear that he too felt himself to be equally imprisoned in a life of political obscurity. A year earlier at the Illinois state Republican convention in Bloomington, Lincoln had given an electrifying speech—the famous "lost speech"—which his supporters thought put him "on the track for the Presidency." Later that same month he received 110 votes on the first ballot for the vice-presidential nomination at the national Republican convention, thereby gaining recognition for himself among party leaders outside of Illinois. Even after Republican candidate Frémont's 1856 defeat, Lincoln was being touted in the Western press as a man the party should place in a station commensurate with his abilities.[125] Yet in 1857, at the very moment Lincoln digressed to mention "all the powers of earth . . . combining against him," eastern Republicans were preparing to support Douglas for reelection to the Senate, and, much to Lincoln's annoyance, were praising Douglas's accomplishments in the party press. A Democratic newspaper probably captured Lincoln's own feelings accurately when it said: "Hon. Abe Lincoln is undoubtedly the most unfortunate politician that has ever attempted to rise in Illinois. In everything he undertakes, politically, he seems doomed to failure. He has been prostrated often enough in his political schemes to have crushed the life out of any ordinary man."[126] Prostrated and imprisoned, Lincoln sought to fashion an escape for himself by linking his own ambition to the cause of the "oppressed of [his] species."[127]

This connection was given dramatic illustration the following year by a comment Lincoln made as he was discussing the possible consequences of the Dred Scott decision. When you have extinguished a man's soul, he said, "and placed him where the ray of hope is blown out in darkness like that which broods over the spirit of the damned; are you quite sure the demon which you have roused *will not turn and rend you?*"[128] Lincoln's reference here was also ostensibly to the slave; but he too had felt hope vanish, and, damned to obscurity, had brooded in a darkness which extinguished his filial soul. And when he finally roused himself from this darkness in 1854, he turned to rend the inheritance of 1789. By identifying his personal vengefulness against constitutional fathers with the cause of equality, Lincoln discovered a means of liberation both for himself and for the slave.

"Let no one be deceived," said Lincoln at Peoria. "The spirit of seventy-six and the spirit of Nebraska, are utter antagonisms. . . . " Let there be no deception either about the implications of that statement: the Declaration and the Constitution, Lincoln was saying, are in conflict, and he would clearly choose the former over the latter, the ancient faith that all men are created equal over the new faith that some men have a right to enslave others. After examining the Constitution and finding that there was no direct mention of slavery, Lincoln concluded, "Thus, the thing is hid away, in the constitution, just as an afflicted man hides away a wen or a cancer, which he dares not cut out at once, lest he bleed to death; with the promise, nevertheless, that the cutting may begin at the end of a given time."[129] Lincoln would eventually carve for himself a place in history by performing surgery on the "afflicted" Constitution. In the meantime, he used the knife only as a "prying instrument" of escape from political bondage, an instrument he employed with care and precision.

Lincoln was never an abolitionist. Joining the Republican party in 1856, he carefully maintained his position among Whig moderates, who held the balance of power within the party, by opposing only the extension of slavery. At the same time, he remained committed to the ultimate extinction of slavery and established for himself, through his "house divided" speech, a position somewhat in advance of the antislavery sentiment of the party.[130] This seems to have been a carefully calculated stratagem. At the Springfield convention in 1858, where Lincoln was nominated to oppose Douglas for the Senate, many of his supporters urged that he omit the "house divided" reference in his acceptance speech. Lincoln insisted on retaining it, because, he said, "I want to use some universally known figure . . . that may strike home to the minds of men in order to raise them up to the peril of the times."[131] The strategy worked; the speech had its desired effect. Always a man with solid Whig credentials, Lincoln now became acceptable to party radicals. He thus entered the 1860 nominating convention as "the second choice of everybody" for president.[132] Through shrewd calculation and patient maneuvering, he had succeeded in assembling the holders of the hundred different keys whose concurrence would release him from his bondage.

Lincoln concluded his 1858 senatorial campaign by saying, "God knows how sincerely I prayed from the first that this field of ambition might not be opened."[133] Although he did not say that he *did* pray sincerely, it is clear that he had fervently hoped, at least, that this field would not have to be opened. He had hoped to distinguish himself through a demonstration of Weemsian virtue, by controlling his demonic impulse—that is, by emulating Washington's character, and following Washington's advice. He had not succeeded in doing so; to the contrary, his virtuous efforts had been met with ridicule and rejection. Denied the opportunity of "building up," this ambitious genius "would set boldly to the task of pulling down." He made fun of his former identification with Weems's Washington in a way that hinted at his bitterness: "In my poor, lean, lank, face, nobody has ever seen that any cabbages were sprouting out."[134] He invoked Jefferson as an alternative model, but also implied a certain challenge to Jefferson's stature as the nation's "most distinguished politician." He looked beyond the Constitution and discovered a way of linking his own passions of hate and revenge, as he had said of the revolutionaries of 1776, with the "advancement of the noblest of causes."

Lincoln had indeed hoped that this field of ambition might not be opened—he even continued to warn people against his "wickedness" or his "foolishness," as he also characterized it, upon being elected to the presidency. When this field was opened, however, with the Kansas–Nebraska Act, Lincoln vented his passions by repeating themes from his Lyceum Address. In Peoria he began his attack on Douglas's idea of popular sovereignty by quoting the poet: "Fools rush in where angels fear to tread."[135] The virtuous, if not the angelic, Lincoln had been ignored and humiliated; now the foolish Lincoln, the "Ranchero Spotty of one term," would enter the forbidden fields with bitterness and wrath. He denounced Douglas's Nebraska bill as simply a utilitarian Union-saving measure, saying, "It hath no relish of salvation in it." He called for a sacrificial cleansing of the nation's political institutions: "Our republican robe is soiled, and trailed in the dust. Let us repurify it. Let us turn and wash it white, in the spirit, if not the blood, of the Revolution." He urged that the nation's political values be renewed and reestablished: "Let us re-adopt the Declaration of Independence. . . . Let north and south—let all Americans . . . join in the great and good work. If we do this, we shall not only have saved the Union; but we shall have so saved it, as to make and keep it, forever worthy of the saving."[136]

Obviously, Lincoln's Union-saving would provide the "relish of salvation in it." Faced with the dissolution of the Union as president-elect in 1861, he resolved not only to save the Union, but to save it in a way that would make it "forever worthy of the saving," by compelling the nation to readopt the Declaration of Independence so that it could be included within the Constitution. He would do this by attempting to establish a political religion which joined the sacrifices of 1776 to the promise of national redemption and constitutional immortality. It was against such "foolishness" that Lincoln warned his countrymen as he took the presidential chair, to sit where Washington sat.

CLAIMS OF DIVINE AUTHORITY:
A REHEARSAL FOR MARTYRDOM

May my right hand forget its cunning and my tongue cleave to the roof of my mouth, if I ever prove false to these teachings.
—A. Lincoln, 1861

As Lincoln's train carried him from Springfield to Washington, where he would assume the presidency of the United States, he grappled with the size of the task that lay before him. How could a relatively unknown politician who had held no major state or national office, whose one claim to prominence prior to 1860 was a losing campaign for the Senate, and who had polled but 40 percent of the popular vote in the presidential contest become the spokesman for the nation? How could a man "without a name, perhaps without a reason why . . . [he] should have a name" succeed in establishing national authority where Washington had failed, faced with even greater problems of disunity than Washington had faced? How could someone acutely aware of his own mortality—even haunted by forebodings of his death—be expected to preserve the perpetual union of the United States when those states had ceased to be united? Perhaps most difficult of all, how could a revolutionary become a defender of the very constitutional order from which he had declared his personal independence? These were the seemingly irreconcilable polarities that Lincoln was struggling to reconcile. And the closer he got to Independence Hall in Philadelphia, the more certain his answers became.

During the debates with Douglas, Lincoln had called the Declaration of Independence an "immortal emblem of humanity." He also believed that the Declaration was an emblem of human immortality both for the nation and for individual citizens. It was the principle of "liberty to all" which lay behind the Constitution and the Union that was primarily responsible for American prosperity, for this principle "clears the *path* for all—gives *hope* to all—and, by consequence, *enterprize,* and *industry* to all." With or without this principle, Lincoln said, we could have declared our independence; but without it, we could not have secured free government and prosperity. "No oppressed people will *fight*, and *endure*, as our fathers did, without the promise of something better, than a mere change of masters." Thus, as in a metaphor suggested, ironically, by Alexander Stephens, the future vice-president of the Confederacy, the Declaration should be viewed as an "apple of gold" framed in the "picture of silver" supplied by the Constitution and the Union. "The picture was made not to *conceal*, or *destroy* the apple; but to *adorn*, and *preserve* it. The *picture* was made *for* the apple—*not* the apple for the picture."[137]

That the Constitution could take its meaning only from the Revolution was an order of priority which the founders of 1787–89 sometimes lost sight of in their haste to justify the utility of the Union. Although Madison strove mightily to cloak the Constitution in Revolutionary colors, Lincoln had no difficulty in seeing through the disguise. It was as if in their concern to establish the conditions of political immortality for the nation, the founders had confused immortality with stability and had banished the true source of immortality: a means of political regeneration. Lincoln understood that while there could be no permanence in the affairs of men, "and this too shall pass away" was not merely an expression of despair; it was also a source of hope, a promise of change. He believed that the true greatness of America depended upon the Revolution, the essence of which was a principle that gave hope to all mankind.

By January 1861, the question was not how the Declaration and the Constitution both could be preserved, but how they might be renovated and restored. Lincoln had proposed a solution to this problem once before in his address to the Springfield Lyceum, and it was to that proposal that he now turned. In one of his first speeches after leaving Springfield, he raised the same question he had posed twenty-three years earlier: "Shall the Union and shall the liberties of this country be preserved to the latest generation?" And once again his answer was the same: "When the people rise in masses in behalf of the Union and the liberties of their country, truly may it be said, 'The gates of hell shall not prevail against them.' "[138] How would the people be mobilized in support of their liberties and the Union? In the Lyceum Address, Lincoln said, "Reason, cold, calculating, unimpassioned reason, must furnish all the materials for our future support and defense." Lincoln would be the instrument by which those materials would be molded into a general intelligence, sound morality, and, in particular, a reverence for the Constitution and laws. The question was, how would he fashion himself into such an instrument?

At a Republican rally in Springfield prior to the election, Lincoln had received a tumultuous welcome from the crowd, which stampeded his carriage and carried him aloft to the speaker's platform. He had not expected to make a speech on this occasion, but under the circumstances one could hardly have been avoided. He said he was "profoundly gratified" by the display of enthusiasm and affection shown him. "I am gratified, because it is a tribute such as can be paid to no man as a man. It is the evidence that four years from this time you will give a like manifestation to the next man who is the representative . . . though I be dead and gone."[139] The remark was not an appropriate response to this distinctly personal tribute. It was, however, an indication of the way Lincoln was to turn the transient insignificance of his life, of which he was so keenly aware, into something more than the strained pose of humility which he often affected. By downgrading his personal importance, he became the ideal instrument for the higher purpose he wished to serve.[140]

In his 1916 tribute to Lincoln, Woodrow Wilson offered an insight which he would himself appreciate within just a few years. Wilson said: "There is a very holy and very terrible isolation for the conscience of every man who seeks to read the destiny in affairs for others as well as for himself, for a nation as well as for individuals."[141] Wilson's reference was not necessarily to the period prior to Lincoln's inauguration, a period which Lincoln said was characterized by a "process of crystallization" in his thinking, but during this time he seemed to impose upon himself a terrible isolation that was ultimately even holy: he saw visions of duty where no men looked on. As he worked alone in a dingy backroom above a store across the street from the capitol in Springfield, it was as if he were preparing himself for a religious rite. According to one Lincoln scholar, in the week before he began his trip to Washington, a "noticeable change" came over him: "Outwardly he remained as jocular as ever, but new lines of worry began to show in his face, and at times a deathly pallor."[142]

That Lincoln had begun to define himself as a man apart, outside the mundane order of things, first revealed itself in his language. Rather than the term "our Washington" used in the Lyceum Address, Lincoln now spoke of "the Father of *his* country"; rather than "our liberties" or "our Declaration of Independence," as in the Douglas debates, it was now "the liberties of their country." Referring to the forts in South Carolina, Lincoln said, ". . . I will, if our Washington friends concur, announce publically at once that they are to be retaken. . . . This will give the Union men a rallying cry, and preparation will proceed somewhat on *their side,* as well as on the other."[143] Similarly, in a revision to the first draft of his Inaugural Address, he deleted the word "our" and substituted "your" so that a rather crucial sentence read as follows: "If the Almighty Ruler of nations, with his eternal truth and justice, be on *your* side, or on yours, that truth and that justice will surely prevail. . . . "[144] If this was just an error, as Lincoln's editor believes, it was the error of a man assembling himself in lonely isolation to become an impartial instrument of the nation's destiny which only he could read.

Lincoln was also experiencing another kind of isolation as he made the journey east, the isolation of a man who lived with the foreboding of death. Following his renomination in 1864, he reported that after his first election, while lying exhausted on a sofa, he had seen a double image of himself reflected in the wall mirror, with one image paler than the other. Lincoln attempted to re-create the double image several times, each time with the same result. He had interpreted this as a sign that he would be elected to a second term but that he would not live to complete it.[145] Whether or not it was this incident Lincoln had in his mind as he bade his Springfield friends goodbye with ominous finality ("I now leave, not knowing when, or whether ever, I may return. . . ."), he often expressed anxiety about his personal longevity. His pre-election statement at the Republican rally in Springfield ("though I be dead and gone") was repeated several times as he made the journey east, as if he knew from the beginning what the consequences of his hubris would be: that the price of his immortality was his own death.

These were the major themes of Lincoln's speeches as he talked his way across the country, sometimes extemporaneously, sometimes formally: first, that he personally was of no significance, but merely a temporary, even "accidental" instrument of a higher purpose, a man selected to fill an office for a brief period whose influence would soon pass away; and secondly, that his primary concern was the perpetuation of American political institutions. Since the latter theme was the subject of his Lyceum Address, and the former figured rather prominently in its conclusion, it will be useful to examine the articulation of these themes more carefully.

The manner in which Lincoln defined himself as an instrument varied somewhat from speech to speech, in part depending on whom he was addressing, and perhaps in part to avoid excessive repetition. But it seems likely that the variation was due partially to some indecisiveness. In the first speeches after leaving Springfield, he saw himself simply as the recipient of the nonpartisan respect and honor that would be given any incumbent president. At Pittsburgh, the emphasis changed somewhat, as he acknowledged the reception there to be one given not to him personally, but to the cause he represented. In Cleveland, he enlarged upon this interpretation to say, "You have assembled to testify your respect to the Union, the constitution and the laws," adding that had Douglas been elected, he would have received the same welcome. Likewise at Buffalo, he said of the various receptions accorded him: "They are tendered to the country, to the institutions of the country, and to the perpetuity of the liberties of the country for which these institutions were made and created."[146]

By thus minimizing his personal importance, Lincoln was in fact greatly enhancing it. By retreating into a kind of institutional anonymity, and posing as "the humblest of all individuals that have ever been elevated to the Presidency," he was actually defining himself as "the representative of the majesty of this great nation."[147] As symbol of the nation, representative of the majesty of the people and their Constitution (his phraseology varied), he spoke with the full authority of the American political tradition behind him.

But Lincoln was not content merely to cast himself as an instrument of tradition. The tradition, as he understood it, was under serious challenge in both the South and the North, both by Southern secessionists and by Northerners who wished to be rid of them, both by slaveholders and by abolitionists. He needed a source of authority which transcended a compromised and disputed tradition. As he left Springfield he said, "Without the assistance of that Divine Being, who ever attended him [Washington], I cannot succeed. With that assistance I cannot fail." There can be no doubt that the decision to seek divine sanction for his cause was made in advance of his departure; in addition to the statement cited above to the effect that the justice of the "Almighty Ruler of nations" would surely prevail, whether he be on the side of the North or of the South, his inaugural (drafted in January) also included the following statement: "Intelligence, patriotism, Christianity, and a firm reliance on Him, who has never yet forsaken this favored land, are still competent to adjust, in the best way, all our present difficulty."[148] Lincoln here was not proposing compromise with the South; quite the reverse, he was simply revising his earlier list of the components necessary for perpetuation of the nation's political institutions (from general intelligence, sound morality, and reverence for the Constitution and laws) to include a source of constitutional reverence untainted by disputed tradition—i.e., the God of Washington, the God who had never forsaken the American people.

Lincoln returned repeatedly to this theme in subsequent speeches. At Cincinnati, he assured his audience that with the good sense of the American people ". . . under the Providence of God, who has never deserted us . . . we shall be brethren again." In Columbus, he said that for support in the great task that lay ahead he looked to "the American people and to that God who has never forsaken them." He expanded the point somewhat at Buffalo and Albany to say that for ability and confidence ". . . I must trust in that Supreme Being who has never forsaken this favored land, through the instrumentality of this great and intelligent people.

Without that assistance I shall surely fail. With it I cannot fail."[149] Similar variations on this theme are to be found in speeches made at Steubenville, Ohio; Newark and Trenton, New Jersey; and Harrisburg, Pennsylvania.

What is so striking about these references to God is that prior to his Springfield farewell, Lincoln had never before made a personal appeal for divine assistance. Yet inside of eleven days of preinaugural speechmaking, he was to make nearly as many separate such appeals. Nor is that all. Only rarely in the past had Lincoln ever allowed for the possibility of divine intervention in the affairs of men and, with two notable exceptions, never viewed that intervention in particularistic terms—i.e., as God acting in history in behalf of a particular cause or country. Indeed, he had ridiculed proslavery theology on precisely these grounds: "Certainly there is no contending against the will of God; but still there is some difficulty in ascertaining, and applying it, to particular cases." When Douglas contended that there was a line "drawn by the Almighty" across the continent separating slave territory from free, Lincoln sardonically pointed out that an institution with divine sanction in one part of the country could hardly be excluded from the remainder on moral grounds.[150]

The references Lincoln characteristically made to divinity prior to assuming his presidential role were general and abstract. The God which found its way into his speeches was the God of the Declaration of Independence: Creator of the Universe, Almighty Architect, Ruler of the Universe, or, more simply, the Almighty. The manner in which he usually interpreted divine presence in secular affairs was equally abstract, as, for example, in the following: "Our reliance is in the *love of liberty* which God has planted in our bosoms." Or again: ". . . God reigns over you, and has inspired your mind, and given you a sense of propriety, and continues to give you hope. . . . " Occasionally Lincoln came close to identifying God with his cause without actually doing so. Of Republican party principles he once said: "But I do hope that as there is a just and righteous God in Heaven, our principles will and shall prevail sooner or later."[151] He sometimes referred to the eventual disappearance of slavery as happening in "God's own good time and way." There was, then, nothing in Lincoln's typical usage to suggest the kind of theology he began to articulate immediately upon adopting the persona of impartial instrument of the nation's destiny.

There were two important exceptions. The first is to be found in the passage previously quoted from his eulogy to Henry Clay in which he said, "Let us strive to deserve, as far as mortals may, the continual care of Divine Providence, trusting that, in future national emergencies, He will not fail to provide us the instruments of safety and security." The statement was carefully qualified, but the remarkable thing about it is that since Lincoln may have had himself in mind, however wistfully, as a candidate for providential selection, it suggests how readily the "necessity" by which he was driven might have lent itself to a nonsecular interpretation. This is confirmed by a comment made in a letter to Speed on Lincoln's role as a marital adviser: "I am not sure there was any merit, with me, in the part I took in your difficulty; I was drawn to it as by fate. . . . I always was superstitious; and as part of my superstition, I believe God made me one of the instruments of bringing your Fanny and you together. . . ."[152] It was perhaps out of a similar superstition that he defined his presidential identity, but in this case at least, there was more art involved than fate.

The second instance in which Lincoln alluded to the possibility of direct intervention by God into history occurred when he quoted Jefferson's statement, "I tremble for my country when I remember that God is just!" As Lincoln interpreted his meaning, there was danger to the country in Douglas's doctrine of popular sovereignty—the danger of the avenging justice of God. Referring to Jefferson, he said, "He supposed there was a question of God's eternal justice wrapped up in the enslaving of any race of men, or any man, and that those who did so braved the arm of Jehovah— that when a nation thus dared the Almighty every friend of that nation had cause to dread His wrath."[153] The unusual feature of this interpretation is that the nation risked divine wrath not only for enslaving a race of men, but for enslaving "any man." Recalling Jefferson's fear of divine justice, Lincoln did not include Jefferson's next phrase, "that His justice cannot sleep forever." Though omitted, the phrase was not forgotten. The Inaugural Address contained the rather startling assertion that God's "justice will surely prevail, by the judgment of this great tribunal, the American people," whether he be on "your side or on yours." In this impressive display of impartiality lay a cold anger that was surely a worthy instrument of God's avenging justice. It is little wonder that Lincoln's appearance sometimes betrayed a deathly pallor.

Lincoln's invocation of the God who had never forsaken the American people is unusual, given his previous reluctance to see signs of divinity revealed in the affairs of men. But the instances in which he did profess to see such signs were certainly consistent with the task he now set for himself. For if the "accident" of his presidency was an indication of providential selection, he could do no less than serve the purposes of divine justice. And since his task was greater than that of Washington, it was insufficient to claim authority simply on the basis of an appeal to the tradition which Washington represented. Lincoln's task was greater because that tradition, as he saw it, was on the verge of collapse, the meaning of the Revolution forgotten. Thus Lincoln would fail, as he admitted, unless he could find a higher source of authority, unless he could link the majesty of the nation to the divinity of God. This is exactly what he accomplished by invoking the God who had never forsaken the American people. For if the American people was the instrument of God, and Lincoln the instrument of the people, then, Q.E.D.: Lincoln was the instrument of God himself.

Lincoln's purpose in attempting to establish his credentials as a divine instrument was not to serve the glory of God—God would not remember. His purpose was rather to perpetuate the liberties and the political institutions of the American people in the hope they would remember; his goal as president had been set forth twenty-three years earlier at the Springfield Lyceum: to found a political religion. Appropriately, the speech in which he most succinctly brought together the divergent themes he had been addressing was the one given at Trenton, in which he recalled having read Weems's *Life of Washington*. Remembering his reading of Weems, Lincoln said:

> I recollect thinking then, boy even though I was, that there must have been something more than common that those men struggled for. I am exceedingly anxious that that thing which they

struggled for; that something even more than National Independence; that something that held out a great promise to all the
people of the world to all time to come; I am exceedingly anxious
that this Union, the Constitution, and the liberties of the people
shall be perpetuated in accordance with the original idea for which
that struggle was made, and I shall be most happy indeed if I shall
be an humble instrument in the hands of the Almighty, and of this,
his almost chosen people for perpetuating the object of that great
struggle.[154]

That Lincoln had long been anxious for the Constitution and
Union to be perpetuated in accordance with the Revolutionary
idea is confirmed by his conclusion in the Lyceum Address. But
there he said that new pillars in the temple of liberty must be
molded from the materials of cold, calculating reason, implying
that those new pillars were religious ones, that salvation was to be
found in adopting a political religion. Whether he now meant by
the phrase "his almost chosen people" that God's selection
awaited Lincoln's inauguration or that God's favor would not be
complete until the scales of heavenly justice had been righted is
not altogether clear. But given his self-definition, the phrase offered little basis for assuming that the ultimate consequences of
having braved the arm of Jehovah could be avoided. For Lincoln
would personally provide the avenging God of the Old Testament,
which had eluded the founders of 1789, as well as the forgiving
God of the New Testament; Lincoln would fulfill the founders'
prophecies on the consequences of constitutional backsliding by
removing the state of rewards and punishments from an uncertain,
ethereal future to an immediate, secular present; he would establish national authority anew by supplying, as Weems suggested,
the one thing needed in Washington's Union—the first birth of
true religion.

The burdens imposed by Lincoln's presidential purpose did
not rest lightly on his mind. In restating themes from his Lyceum
Address, Lincoln also repeated his earlier warnings against the
dangers of a malevolent political leadership, this time explicitly
identifying himself as the source of possible harm, and again suggesting that protection for the people lay in their attachment to
one another and to the Constitution. As he said in Lawrenceburg,

Indiana, ". . . should my administration prove to be a very wicked one, or what is more probable, a very foolish one, if you, the PEOPLE, are but true to yourselves and to the Constitution, there is but little harm I can do, *thank God!*"[155]

The same warning was incorporated into his Inaugural Address. Immediately following his statement that God's justice would surely prevail by the judgment of the American people, Lincoln noted that the framers of the government had given public servants "but little power for mischief." Then he said: "While the people remain patient, and true to themselves, no man, even in the presidential chair, by any extreme of wickedness or folly, can very seriously injure the government in the short space of four years."[156] If nothing else, the sequence of these two statements indicates that there was a close association in Lincoln's mind between the attempt to establish his divine authority and his capacity for wickedness and folly. Two elements of the Lyceum Address were now being combined into one: the evil genius would realize his ambition by establishing a political religion. If there were folly in such ambition, it was of the same sort Lincoln exhibited at Peoria when he said, fools rush in where angels fear to tread.

Lincoln's burdens also included the conflict he felt between his prior commitment to the Declaration of Independence and his newly acquired obligations to the Constitution. He was about to take an oath to "preserve, protect, and defend" a constitutional order which he considered morally indefensible and which he had been emotionally and ideologically committed to destroy. When Alexander Stephens expressed his apprehension in December 1860 that the Union was endangered by the failure of Republicans to condemn the fanaticism of John Brown, he told Lincoln, "A word fitly spoken by you now would be like 'apples of gold in pictures of silver.' " But Lincoln's uncommunicated response was that it was the principle of "liberty to all" that was the word fitly spoken, and that had proven to be an "apple of gold" framed by the "picture of silver" of the Constitution.[157] Although this was not necessarily an endorsement of John Brown, neither was it the "word" his old friend Stephens was hoping to hear. In any case, since seven states had seceded by the time Lincoln took office in March, it is clear that in terms of his own metaphor he was being required to become guardian of a broken picture that framed nothing but a faded canvas on which he might impose his own artistic conceptions. It was with little zeal, therefore, that Lincoln declared his intention to "take care . . . that the laws of the Union be faithfully executed in all the States." "Doing this," he said in his inaugural, "I deem to be only a simple duty on my part; and I shall perform it . . . unless my rightful masters, the American people, shall . . . direct the contrary."[158] Obviously for Lincoln such Union-saving had "no relish of salvation in it."

Painfully aware of the contradiction between his commitment to the Declaration and his duty to the Constitution, but still more compelled by the ancient faith than by the new, Lincoln struggled to avoid this contradiction in his public statements. Several times during his preinaugural speeches, he told his audiences, ". . . I hope to say nothing in opposition to the spirit of the Constitution . . . or . . . inimical to the liberties of the people. . . ." To do both simultaneously proved to be an almost impossible task. He accomplished the former at Cincinnati by repeating an earlier message to Kentuckians: "We mean to treat you . . . as Washington, Jefferson, and Madison treated you. We mean to leave you alone, and in no way interfere with your institution; to abide by all and every compromise of the constitution. . . ."[159] But a few days later in New York, Lincoln seemed to modify this promise considerably. Comparing the Union to a ship and liberty to its cargo, he said that a ship was made for the carrying and preservation of its cargo, ". . . and so long as the ship can be saved, with the cargo, it should never be abandoned. This Union should likewise never be abandoned unless it fails and the probability of its preservation shall cease to exist without throwing the passengers and cargo overboard."[160] This was a tortured way of admitting that should the cargo and passengers become endangered, it might be necessary to abandon ship.

Two days later, on February 22, in Philadelphia, Lincoln was forced to confront his contradictory obligations in a dramatic way. Asked to attend a ceremony in Independence Hall, Lincoln accepted the invitation by saying that he had always hoped to do nothing "inconsistent with the teachings of those holy and most sacred walls." Observing that this was the site where both the

Declaration and the Constitution had been framed, he said, "All my political warfare has been in favor of the teachings coming forth from that sacred hall. May my right hand forget its cunning and my tongue cleave to the roof of my mouth, if ever I prove false to those teachings."[161] As it happened, he did momentarily forget his cunning; but his tongue cleaved to the roof of his mouth so as to prevent his proving himself false to one half of the hall's sacred teachings, the Constitution of the United States.

Standing in Independence Hall on Washington's birthday, and "filled with deep emotion," Lincoln turned his attention entirely to the Declaration of Independence, making no mention of the Constitution. He said he had often pondered the danger incurred by the men who there adopted the Declaration, and the toils of the soldiers who achieved independence. He had often asked himself, he said, what principle or idea had kept the "Confederacy" together so long. It was not merely a matter of separation from Great Britain, but rather "something in that Declaration giving liberty, not alone to the people of this country, but hope to the world for all future time. It was that which gave promise that in due time the weights should be lifted from the shoulders of all men, and that *all* should have an equal chance." But could the country be saved on that basis? If not, declared Lincoln, ". . . if this country cannot be saved without giving up that principle—I was about to say I would rather be assassinated on this spot than to surrender it."[162]

There is an authentic, though not wholly spontaneous, ring of truth in that admission. Certainly there are no histrionics here, and not much art; Lincoln "meant it," as Erik Erikson has said of Martin Luther in a not altogether dissimilar context. At that moment he was at one with the men of the Revolution; he was there, like cosmological man in the sacred space, at the center of creation, in that place and in that time, reaffirming the pledge, ready to give up his life—ready to give the last full measure of devotion —if necessary, rather than abandon the principle of the Revolution. As an indication of how deeply involved he was in that reenactment, he seems to have come perilously close to giving up his commitment to the Union as well. What he was about to say was not that he would rather be assassinated than surrender the principle—that was his second thought, his recovery; what he was about to say was that if the country cannot be saved without giving up the principle of the Revolution, then the country could not or should not be saved.

Later, alluding to his possible mental lapse, he made his characteristic disclaimer that he had not come to the hall expecting to make a speech. "I may, therefore, have said something indiscreet, but I have said nothing but what I am willing to live by and, in the pleasure of Almighty God, die by."[163] He meant what he said, all right—he had said it before. But at that moment at least, he also meant what he did not say, that the Union without the principle which gave hope to all men was not worth saving. In his attempt to avoid saying the inadmissible, he was unaware of what he had done: symbolically, in atonement for having abandoned the Constitution, he had given up his own life.

3

The Founding of
a Political Religion

GOD'S AMERICAN ISRAEL

. . . God has a righteous controversy with us in this land. . . .
—Nicholas Street, 1777

Sometimes the behind-the-scenes trivia of history are more indicative of the essential nature of the times than the events occupying center stage. Shortly after Lee's surrender at Appomattox Court House, with Washington jubilant at the news of victory—bells pealing, flags waving, crowds celebrating in the streets—Secretary of War Stanton sent the following telegram to General Weitzel in Richmond: "It has just been reported to this Department that you have . . . consented that service should be performed in the Episcopal churches of Richmond to-day without the usual prayer said in loyal churches of that denomination for the President . . . and that you have agreed to waive that condition. If such has been your action it is strongly condemned by this Department."

Having secured a symbolic triumph of his own by establishing his headquarters in Jefferson Davis's former residence, Weitzel replied that the orders he gave in substance were "that no expression would be allowed in any part of the church service . . . which in any way implied a recognition of any other authority than that of the United States. . . ." Perhaps Weitzel meant to say that his orders permitted recognition of no other secular authority than that of the United States, but his unqualified statement did not satisfy Stanton. The following day the general received another wire from Washington: "The Secretary of War directs me to say that your explanation . . . is not satisfactory. . . . The Secretary also directs me to instruct you that officers commanding in Richmond are expected to require from all religious denominations . . . [in their prayers and rituals] no less respect for the President . . . than they practiced toward the rebel chief . . . before he was driven from the capitol."[1]

Amid the great pathos and exhilaration of the war's end, such an incident would seem to rate no more than a footnote. And yet the high drama of Lee's meeting with Grant to arrange surrender terms does not reveal the significance of the previous four years' struggle quite so vividly as Stanton's insistence that Southerners be required to pray for Lincoln, rather than simply desist in their prayers for Jefferson Davis. For Lincoln had defined the Civil War as a struggle against doctrinal hypocrisy and heresy in which the ultimate victor would be the sole claimant to the authority of Washington and the blessing of the national deity. It was a religious war, which, like most religious wars, had its economic and social dimensions, but which took its significance in the minds of the leading actors not from the processes of history but from a peculiarly American metaphysics, a tribal cosmology. It was palpable, undeniable evidence of God's justice—divine punishment for past sins, which offered the nation a means of atonement. Lincoln had been a leading spokesman for this theological view, though he was not its inventor; but a theologian as commander in chief proved that armed prophets succeed.

After the outbreak of armed hostilities, Lincoln lost little time in giving an interpretation of the war's meaning. Following the Northern defeat at Bull Run, and at the request of Congress, he proclaimed a national day of "humiliation, prayer, and fasting" which was accompanied by the following explanation:

And whereas, when our own beloved Country, once, by the blessing of God, united, prosperous and happy, is now afflicted with faction and civil war, it is peculiarly fit for us to recognize the hand of God in this terrible visitation, and in sorrowful remembrance of our own faults and crimes as a nation and as individuals, to humble ourselves before Him, and to pray for His mercy,—to pray that we may be spared further punishment, though most justly deserved; that our arms may be blessed and made effectual for the re-establishment of law, order and peace, throughout the wide extent of our country; and that the inestimable boon of civil and religious liberty, earned under His guidance and blessing, by the labors and sufferings of our fathers, may be restored in all its original excellence.[2]

This was a theology so old as to be rooted in the very base of American cosmology, a theology which reclaimed for the nation the covenant of the fathers, and reestablished the identity between civil and ecclesiastical orders. It was a Calvinism transformed and renewed by the evangelical spirit of the nineteenth-century American frontier, but which reached back to Puritan and Revolutionary origins, and thus drew upon the broadest possible spectrum of religious opinion. Indeed, it was a theology that was beyond the reach of any specific sectarian or denominational influence, and fundamentally was not even Christian: the God who had never forsaken the American people but who would now punish them for having broken the covenant was Jehovah just as the people were Israel. By reformulating this common fund of inherited meanings, Lincoln transformed American political history from an Old Testament story into a New Testament one, and thereby released the American Revolution from its Hebraic separatism so as to imbue it with a Christian universalism.

Lincoln's proclamation of a national fast day, which made the public confession of sins a prelude to seeking God's blessing and which viewed civil war as divine punishment for the nation's transgressions, closely followed the form of a ritual first observed on a national level in 1775.[3] At the recommendation of the Continental Congress, July 20 of that year was set aside as a "day of publick humiliation, fasting, and prayer" during which the people were to "confess and deplore" their sins, offering up "joint supplications, to the all-wise, omnipotent, and merciful Disposer of all events," humbly beseeching him to forgive their iniquities and to "avert those desolating judgments" which threatened the colonies. This was substantially the same ritual which had been used in New England for 150 years as a way of seeking the favor of Jehovah. Despite the ritual's Puritan origins, the Congressional recommendation found widespread acceptance not only in New England, but among Baptists, Presbyterians, and "low church" Anglicans throughout the colonies. As Perry Miller has remarked, this congressional call for public humiliation and a return to primitive piety had the effect of extending the New England covenant to the other nine colonies. The observance of such a ritual could be meaningful only as the solemn communal act of a covenanted people, standing in a direct relationship with God and responsible for their moral conduct.[4] As a result, in 1775, colonial peoples became united in a way which infused their informal and fragmentary political bonds with a spiritual energy imparted by an Old Testament God.

The significance of this renewal and extension of the Puritan covenant for the Revolution, whose stated purposes and acknowledged forms were largely secular, is easily overlooked. Covenant theology had served to legitimize fratricide and the judicial murder of a king in the English civil war,[5] and it could serve such purposes again. Seventeenth-century Puritans had found in God's promises to the Israelites a model of authority which replaced the inherited bonds of place, family, and hierarchy with a collectivist discipline which was voluntary, artificial, and abstract. This new covenant, by which "the saints volunteered to be God's instruments," had a special relevance in the new world.[6] When Abraham broke the bonds of land and kinship to seek a new home in the west, he did so with the understanding that God would make of him a great nation, provided he kept his part of the bargain. Similarly, New England saints found in the Old Testament covenant the means by which individual conversion into the body of Christ could be joined to ecclesiastical and political reform in the fulfillment of God's historical purpose.[7]

The Christian uses of the Old Testament covenant are illustrated well by John Winthrop's sermon "A Modell of Christian Charity," written and presumably delivered while on board the *Arrabella*. With the exodus to the wilderness underway, Winthrop exhorted his "Christian Tribes" to love one another "brotherly without dissimulation," as would befit a community of the regenerate; at the same time, however, he defined the company's purpose in terms of Old Testament sources, precedents, and analogues. We have entered into a covenant with God, Winthrop said, the terms of which God will have ratified by safely delivering our company to the new world. One of the authors of those terms himself, Winthrop warned that God would expect a "strickt performance" of the covenant: ". . . if wee shall neglect the observacion of the Articles . . . the Lord will surely breake out in wrathe against us [,] be revenged of such a perjured people and make us knowe the price of the breache of such a covenant." Thus Winthrop urged his tribe to "followe the Counsell of Micah" so that the "Lord will be our God and delight to dwell among us, as his owne people and will command a blessing upon us. . . ." We shall find that the "God of Israell" is among us, he said, when ". . . men shall say of suceeding plantacions: the lord make it like that of New England." Winthrop concluded the sermon by repeating the last farewell of Moses to Israel, that obedience to the covenant involved a choice between life and good, on one side, and death and evil on the other. "Therefore," said Winthrop, "lett us choose life."[8]

For the Puritans, to choose life meant to choose life after death, to choose the Brethren rather than brothers, to choose the Word over experience, God's authority over human bonds. To choose life meant to select a collective discipline in the covenant by which human beings became transformed into saints, the instruments of God's will. The covenant became the basis for a new purposive community in which individual salvation was inseparable from political reformation and, as Michael Walzer has said, both were "aspects of that divine politics which sought to establish order and discipline among men." That the colonists would readopt the New England covenant at the moment their illegitimacy within the British family was most keenly felt suggests the degree to which Puritan doctrine, the ideology of exiles and outsiders in early seventeenth-century England, could serve as the basis for a new legitimacy in America as well. Fellowship in the covenant not only gave solace to those uprooted from family ties, it required the sacrifice of such ties; serving as God's instrument not only authorized familial strife, it even justified fratricide. As Calvin put it, "you shall show yourselves rightly zealous of God's service in that you kill your own brethren without sparing, so as . . . to show that God is above all. . . ."[9] Hence the readoption of the covenant in 1775 also indicated how the authority of an earthly father (the king) could be replaced by the authority of a transcendent father (Jehovah), in a time of family dissolution.

The theology of Winthrop—a Calvinism modified and softened by covenant theology—did not survive long in seventeenth-century America. The contract with God was continually renegotiated to include more favorable terms for man until Puritan doctrine became what one scholar lauds and another decries as pragmatism.[10] Yet despite the failure of Winthrop's "Citty upon a Hill" to become a model for the world—despite "God's controversy with New England," as the Puritan poet Michael Wigglesworth depicted the declension of a subsequent generation of New Englanders—the Puritan sense of providential destiny was not lost to the eighteenth century. The typological interpretation of both Scripture and world history, which viewed Old Testament events as presaging New Testament events, and both as intimately bound up with the discovery and settlement of the new world, gave a cosmic dimension to everyday American life.[11] By this mode of analysis, American history was itself a biblical story, full of the urgency of divine purpose which added a revelatory and experimental character to ordinary experience, and fed hopes and fears of imminent apocalyptic upheaval.[12]

The eighteenth-century Great Awakening's sense of America's providential destiny is illustrated by the millennialist thought of the theologian Jonathan Edwards. Extrapolating from various Old Testament prophecies, Edwards calculated that God intended America to be the site of world renovation, the place where the "new heavens and new earth" would be created. He reasoned that since the old world had been given the honor of serving as both the place of birth and redemption of Christ, providential fairness would require that the glorious "application of redemption," the "great spiritual birth of Christ," would begin in the new world. Moreover, argued Edwards, when God "is about to turn the earth into a paradise, he does not begin his work where there is some good growth already, but in the wilderness, where nothing grows, and nothing is to be seen but dry sand and barren rocks. . . ." Such typological evidence was augmented by similar proofs derived from historical sources. Noting that America was discovered about the time of the Reformation, Edwards concluded that the conjunc-

tion of these two events reflected the providential intent to reno-
vate the world, an event which he strongly suspected would begin
in New England.[13]

Among the many and varied effects of the Great Awakening
were the rediscovery of Puritanism's emotional center in the conversion experience, and the creation of new bonds of fellowship
which crossed denominational and geographical boundaries. Edwards the Congregationalist, George Whitefield the Anglican, and
Gilbert Tennant the Presbyterian, all felt themselves to be of one
mind in a common undertaking. That all three achieved intercolonial fame, Whitefield being perhaps the first "American" public figure to be known from New England to Georgia, is a measure
of the Great Awakening's integrative and unifying cultural influence. Both the recovery of the bonds of conversion and the discovery of intercolonial unity added political force to millennial hopes,
stimulated by the Awakening, that the American peoples were
providentially fated for the realization of God's kingdom.[14] Nevertheless, faced with the prospect of civil war with England, the
colonists directed their immediate attention not to Revelations,
but to Old Testament sources—not to welcoming Christ's second
coming, but to propitiating Jehovah.

The spirit of the jeremiad, which had been lost during the
exuberance of the Awakening, was reestablished almost officially
by the Continental Congress's call for public humiliation, fasting,
and prayer. This fusion of politics and piety was effected by the
convergence of both religious and secular influences in the common conclusion that the Revolution was "an antidote to moral
decay."[15] Republican thinkers dreamed of recovering the glories
of the ancient Roman republic; but their analyses focused on the
themes of political declension and decadence, and the realization
of republican ideals required a morally regenerate people willing
to sacrifice private interests for the public good. Such analyses and
ideals were fully consistent with those articulated in the jeremiads
of Calvinist clergymen. Whereas the republicanism of an intellectual elite took its bearings from classical sources, the republicanism of the clergy looked to the Old Testament antecedent of a
covenanted community. The patriotic ministers translated the rev-

olutionary ideas of a secular rationalism into a religious language which could move the masses.[16]

In the years between the Stamp Act and the Treaty of Paris, the sermons of American clergymen exhaustively denounced the sins of the people and repeatedly called for acts of repentance as a way of seeking divine favor. American troubles were seen not as the result of British iniquity, but as "national punishment" inflicted by a just God on account of "national guilt." The shedding of American blood was viewed as having been provoked by American declension, sin, and abuse of divine trust. In effect, the clerical jeremiads of the Revolutionary period extended and updated God's seventeenth-century controversy with New England to include the rest of the colonies as well. The result of such a formidable scourging of the people for their sins was not merely public humiliation and self-abasement. Afflictions suffered because of a just God's wrath were a sure sign of chosenness; hence, as Perry Miller has written, the "jeremiad, which in origin had been an engine of Jehovah . . . became temporarily a service department of the Continental army."[17] Under the guidance of patriotic clergymen, resistance to British tyranny became a way of collectively purging the nation of sin and acquiring the favor of the Old Testament God.

The parallels between the new American states and ancient Israel were often explicitly drawn. The title of a 1777 sermon, typical of the period, by the Congregational minister Nicholas Street, accurately summarized his interpretation of the war's meaning: "The American States Acting Over the Part of the Children of Israel in the Wilderness and Thereby Impeding Their Entrance into Canaan's Rest." In Street's view, the British were acting out the role of Pharaoh in levying a "cruel and unnatural war" against God's chosen people. He warned his fellow citizens against assuming, however, as did Israel of old, that they were without sin themselves: ". . . God has a righteous controversy with us in this land; and our iniquities have arrived to that aggravated height, that they have called for these sore calamities that we feel!" In this sense, Street argued, the British are simply an instrument of God's anger "to chastise and correct his sinful, degenerate, backsliding people." Thus he urged that the people accept the

punishment for their sins and repent, so that God might restore
them to their original privileges and liberties.[18]

The vital role of the clergy in mobilizing support for the Revolution can be understood partly in terms of the psychological functions of such jeremiads. Sermons expounding upon the duties
enjoined by the covenant were not merely ritualistic incantations
or simply pieces of political propaganda. To a Bible-reading people, who saw everyday events alive with transcendent meaning, the
jeremiads provided an authoritative interpretation of how God
made his purposes known and of how the world was accessible for
a common participation. Interpretations of God's will that justified
fratricide on the basis of a higher authority also served to allay the
"guilt and danger and distress" which the Continental Congress
in 1776 said "always surrounded and frequently overwhelmed"
those who attempted to overturn a country's constitution.[19] The
need for such reassurance was amply illustrated by the fact that as
late as 1780 there were only a thousand fewer colonial Loyalists
serving in the British forces than the total number of men in
Washington's army.[20] The Revolutionaries not only fought British
brothers, but American brothers as well. By invoking the avenging
God of the Old Testament, the patriotic clergy simultaneously
provided compelling evidence of American chosenness and a
spiritual resolution of American guilt—both the reassurance of
God's justice and a cosmic explanation for what Nicholas Street
called "these sore calamities that we feel." With the war brought
to a victorious conclusion, the American triumph could be seen as
a sure sign of God's favor, which then became the basis for a new
political unity.

The political uses of God's ratification of the covenant were
illustrated by a 1783 election-day sermon of Ezra Stiles, president
of Yale College. Citing the history of the Hebrews as "allusively
prophetick of the future prosperity and splendour of the United
States," Stiles spoke at great length on the "political welfare of
God's American Israel." The Americans, he said, have reason
to expect a great future for their "experiment"; they have reason to believe that God will make "his American Israel 'high above
all nations which he hath made,' in members, 'and in praise, and
in name, and in honour.' " The source of Stiles's confident vision

of the future was the overwhelming evidence of providential blessing in the immediate past. "We have seen more wonders accomplished in eight years," he said, "than are usually unfolded in a
century." One of those wonders, also cited by Parson Weems, was
God's raising up Washington as an "American Joshua" for leading
the armies of "this American Joseph (now separated from his
brethren) and conducting this people through the severe, the ar-
duous conflict to Liberty and Independence." Of particular importance was God's intervention on Washington's behalf at Trenton,
which sealed American independence with military victory. These
and other "miracles" provided the proof, as far as Stiles was concerned, that in America's providential destiny could be read the
future of world history.[21]

The utilization of the covenant to define a new American unity
was not confined to pronouncements from the pulpit, or the single
fast day proclaimed by the Congress in 1775. Additional fast days
were established by Congress in March 1779 and April 1780, and
their appropriate sequel, days of thanksgiving, were annually observed throughout the colonies from 1777 to 1783.[22] The Continental Congress also recommended that the states encourage
"true religion and good morals" as "the only solid foundation of
public liberty and happiness" by suppressing such diversions as
theater and horse racing which lead to "idleness, dissipation, and
general depravity of principles and manners."[23]

A modified version of covenant language found its way into the
Declaration of Independence: the signers pledged to each other
their lives, fortunes, and sacred honor, but "with a firm reliance
on the protection of divine Providence." Both Jefferson and Franklin were persuaded of the aptness of the Hebraic analogy. They,
along with John Adams, were appointed as a committee by Congress to design an official seal for the new nation. Franklin proposed the image of Moses dividing the Red Sea while the Egyp-
tians were being overwhelmed by its waters, together with the
motto "Rebellion to tyrants is obedience to God"; Jefferson suggested the symbol of the children of Israel in the wilderness "led
by a cloud by day and a pillar of fire by night."[24] Although neither
of these proposals was finally adopted, their essential meaning has
been preserved in the Great Seal of the United States, which fea-

tures the "eye of God" over a pyramid, and the inscription *Annuit coeptis* ("He has favored our undertaking"), from Virgil's *Aeneid.*

Paradoxically, however, the ease with which Americans identified themselves collectively as a modern Israel was indirectly responsible for the profound disillusionment which swept the country after the war. Both secular and religious leadership had committed themselves, perhaps inadvertently, to the assumption that America would automatically become a society of the regenerate once the evils of British tyranny were removed.[25] The failure to realize this expectation, whether defined in terms of republican virtue or religious piety, is what made the "critical period" seem so critical to so many: the moral reformation promised by the Revolution had not in fact occurred. This recognition eventually led to the separation between evangelical schemes for achieving moral regeneration and the reliance upon institutional contrivances which made such reform unnecessary—the former culminating in the Second Great Awakening of 1800, the latter in the Constitution of 1789.[26] Yet, even in a time of separation between church and state, as imposed formally by the First Amendment, the covenant continued to be invoked as a source of authority and national unity.

Perhaps the clearest evidence that the secularization of politics in the United States did little to impair the vitality of the national faith was the establishment of a ritual of reaffirmation in the presidential inaugural address. In the inaugural ceremony, which symbolized the essence of republican government—the peaceful transfer of power by community participation—the individual who represented American government above all others would stand in Washington's place to repeat the oath of fidelity to the Constitution, and reaffirm his reliance upon the national deity. There was nothing in the Constitution to require that a president even make a speech on this occasion, let alone make reference to divine authority; but every inaugural address after Washington's second did so nevertheless.[27] It was not the Christian "God" which found its way into these early addresses—Christ was never mentioned—but "Providence," "Protector in all ages of the world of virtuous liberty" (Adams), "that Infinite Power which rules the destinies of the Universe" (Jefferson), "that Almighty Being whose power regulates the destiny of nations" (Madison). Americans did not celebrate the advent of Christ in their rites of priestly ordination, but their Old Testament calling to a future greatness.

The major tenets of this civic faith were set forth by Washington at his first inaugural. Accepting once more his country's call to service with characteristic humility, Washington said that it would be "peculiarly improper" for him to omit from this first official act his "fervent supplications to that Almighty Being who rules over the universe, who presides in the councils of nations, and whose providential aids can supply every human defect. . . . " "No people," he said, "can be bound to acknowledge and adore the Invisible Hand which conducts the affairs of men more than those of the United States." Every step by which they became an independent nation seems to have been "distinguished by some token of providential agency." Thus, he said, the distinctiveness of American unity cannot be recognized without acknowledging the providential blessings of the past and anticipating such blessings in the future. Divine favor, however, was not something that could be taken for granted: ". . . the propitious smiles of Heaven can never be expected on a nation that disregards the eternal rules of order and right which Heaven itself has ordained. . . ." Such disregard could involve nothing less than a betrayal of American destiny: ". . . the preservation of the sacred fire of liberty and the destiny of the republican model of government are justly considered, perhaps, as *deeply,* as *finally,* staked on the experiment entrusted to the hands of the American people."[28]

Washington's invocation of the nameless God of history as his first official presidential act, followed by the proclamation of a day of thanksgiving to inaugurate the new Constitution,[29] was an indication that the First Amendment did not necessarily deny the American people access to their ancient covenant. Although formal separation of church and state at the national level did discriminate against those Calvinist sects which insisted upon a close connection between the two, the First Amendment did not prohibit church establishments at the state level; nor did it inhibit the patriotic fervor of pietist sects which found in "denominationalism" the freedom to pursue various versions of the Puritan hope of realizing God's kingdom on earth.[30] Washington's appeal for the blessing of the national deity to inaugurate a new secular order indicated that the covenant did not require official constitutional sanction to be effective, for his call to faith was met with prompt acceptance among the churches as in Revolutionary times.[31] In terms of nineteenth-century uses of the civic religion, the one omission in Washington's ponderous formulation of the ceremonial creed was his failure to provide a Western focus for America's future. But his Proclamation of Neutrality and Farewell Address would turn the nation in a westerly direction, and, in any case, Jefferson soon corrected such deficiencies.

Upon taking office the first time, and with one eye on the "throes and convulsions of the ancient world" (i.e. Europe), Jefferson asked his fellow citizens to "unite with one heart and one mind." We are all Republicans, we are all Federalists, he said. Separated from the "exterminating havoc of Europe," and in possession of both a "chosen country with room enough for our descendents to the thousandth and thousandth generation" and a government that was the world's "best hope," what more could be necessary, he asked, for our prosperity and happiness? The one thing needed was an administration which would restrain men from injuring one another, but leave them free to pursue their private interests. Four years later he would be more explicit about the sources and extent of American unity:

> I shall need . . . the favor of that Being in whose hands we are, who led our fathers, as Israel of old, from their native land and planted them in a country flowing with all the necessaries and comforts of life; who has covered our infancy with His providence and our riper years with His wisdom and power, and to whose goodness I ask you to join in supplications with me that He will so enlighten the minds of your servants, guide their councils, and prosper their measures that whatsoever they do shall result in your good, and shall secure to you the peace, friendship, and approbation of all nations.[32]

Jefferson's endorsement of the God of Washington, which was also the God of the New England clergy and the revivalist frontier, the God of the intellectual gentry and the uneducated debtor farmer as well, secured the Hebraic consciousness as a fulcrum for national unity. It was not that Americans were all Republicans and all Federalists; it was rather that all Republicans and all Federalists had come to accept the same cosmology. Jefferson's peroration was not a call for rationalistic political consensus but a religious convocation which aimed at transcending differences of class and section by providing a collective identity, a sense of self-consciousness, which joined a favored past to the promise of an even greater future.

The same could be said of a hundred other public speeches during this period by less notable persons, for the early nineteenth century was the age of forensic eloquence, in which every occasion demanded a speech, and every speech was a celebration of American destiny.[33] This popular demand for public utterances which were creedal and prophetic was matched by a similar demand for edifying tales of American heroes. Weems's *Life of Washington,* by answering both demands, was spectacularly successful where others were only less so, perhaps because he mirrored so faithfully the assumptions Americans wanted to make about themselves: that they were called by God to a great purpose and that their leadership was divinely inspired. But if Old Testament myths provided a fulcrum for national unity and purpose, it was a flawed instrument which rested upon shifting sands.

The flaws in the covenant as a source of national unity after 1789 became apparent almost immediately. The Constitution released the churches from the burdens of responsibility for the political order. Although there was a broad Protestant consensus underpinning American denominationalism, which was Puritan in origin and spirit, the proliferation of newer denominations and sects after 1800 made it impossible for any one group of churchmen to speak for the nation.[34] Under the auspices of the revivalism of the Second Awakening, in the early nineteenth century, responsibility for enforcing the covenant devolved onto a multiplicity of religious communities. The signs of this disunity first became visible at a national level when President Adams proclaimed fast days in 1798 and 1799, ostensibly in response to epidemics of cholera and yellow fever. The Jeffersonians, however, saw this as a Federalist plot designed to trap the nation into praying for John Adams; and subsequently, Jefferson himself seized the opportunity provided by the objections of Connecticut Baptists to observing fast days of the established church there to declare that he would no longer proclaim such days, "as my predecessors did."[35] Such ceremonial observances, he explained later, were prohibited by the Constitution and were not even in the interest of the churches.

The fragility of covenant unity became especially clear when the ardent secularist James Madison attempted to impose an Old Testament perspective on the 1812 dispute with the British by asking the nation to view it as a manifestation of divine displeasure. New England responded not with public humiliation and prayer, but at the Hartford convention by registering its own displeasure with Madison's policies and the constitutional order as well. Similarly, in 1832 when Henry Clay introduced a Senate resolution requesting that President Jackson declare a day of humiliation because of a possible cholera epidemic, the Democrats would have no part of it. Denying both the reality of the threat and the constitutionality of the measure, the Democrats scotched it as a partisan maneuver.[36] Jackson, who had been hailed earlier in his career as the "due avenger" of New Orleans, and had even seen himself as "an instrument reserved by a magnificent Providence to save the political Israel of God,"[37] was prepared to veto the measure if necessary. The national faith, in other words, was not securely national; it was continually threatened by erosion from within so as to become a partisan parochialism and, paradoxically, by diffusion from without so as to become an uncertain universalism.

This paradox was illustrated clearly in John L. O'Sullivan's first editorial in the *Democratic Review*. Proudly announcing that democracy is the "cause of Humanity" and the "cause of Christianity," O'Sullivan said, "We feel safe under the banner of the democratic principle, which is borne onward by an unseen hand of Providence, to lead our race toward the high destinies of which every human soul contains the God-implanted germ; and of the advent of which—certain, however distant—a dim prophetic presentiment has existed, in one form or another, among nations in all ages." Having proclaimed the universality of the nation's mission, O'Sullivan then added the following stipulation: "One necessary inference from the views expressed above is that we consider the preservation of the present ascendancy of the Democratic party as of great, if not vital, importance to the future destinies of this holy cause."[38] The United States as a modern Israel was a concept which worked best as a negative definition, as a way of differentiating America from Europe. Beyond that, its meaning in the 1830s and 1840s was much less certain.

One factor which worked against the establishment of a political religion for the nation was that there was so little national consciousness upon which to draw. Weems's portrayal of Washington as a national hero was exceptional in this respect. Most of the leading actors of the early national period remained highly partisan figures until late in the nineteenth century, and most leading figures in a growing literature of hero worship were presented as sectional and local heroes. The first architect of the Daniel Boone legend, John Filson, entitled his book *The Discovery, Settlement, and Present State of Kentucke.* William Wirt, whose beatification of Patrick Henry rivaled that of Weems's Washington, presented Henry as the Great Virginian, and claimed for that state the leading role in the Revolution. Piqued at such an injustice, John Adams sought to defend the Revolutionary reputation of his own state and persuaded William Tudor to write a similar biography of James Otis. Tudor's Otis provided New England with a Revolutionary hero who was both earlier and greater than anyone Virginia had to offer.[39] In short, the early American pantheon tended to be filled with local heroes, and not even the Revolution was to be viewed as a truly national event.

In spite of all the early-nineteenth-century talk of declaring intellectual independence of Europe and developing a distinctively national culture, examples of such national independence are hard to discover. American literature, despite its distinctive flourishes, was heavily indebted to European concepts, forms, and myths. There was no history of the United States written from a national perspective prior to George Bancroft's, and his history, ironically enough in view of his personal influence as an apostle of American destiny, was written from an international perspective. There were few cultural events that could properly be called national. Virtually all national holidays were celebrated on a regular basis only after the Civil War, and three of them—Washington's Birthday, Memorial Day, and Thanksgiving—were regular-

ized under Lincoln's administration. Even Independence Day
prior to the semicentennial celebration was not a national holiday
so much as an occasion for partisan recrimination, with each party
claiming the day as its own. Perhaps the simultaneous deaths of
John Adams and Jefferson on July 4, 1826, by symbolically laying
to rest the old party antagonism, helped to establish the day as a
nonpartisan celebration thereafter. Their deaths were widely interpreted at the time as being a sign of divine favor (despite the
obvious plausibility of the opposite interpretation), indicating how
the hand of God could sometimes soothe partisan bitterness.

The same disunity characterized other symbols of American
nationalism. A uniform design for the national flag was not established until 1912. Thus an observer of the July 4, 1857, celebration
in New York amused himself by noting the zany variety of flags on
display: a majority of ships flew the Stars and Stripes with thirty
stars, though there were thirty-one states at the time, while other
flags featured a variety of designs, including a large star formed by
thirty-one smaller stars, thirty-one stars in the shape of an anchor,
and so forth. Similarly, "The Star-Spangled Banner" was not legally established as the national anthem until 1931, and was not
even played on ceremonial occasions by the military until the
1890s.[40]

If national consciousness was flawed by uncertainty, that uncertainty was simply universalized in Manifest Destiny. Just as God's
selection of Israel served a universal purpose, there had been a
universalism implicit within the Revolution, for the men of 1776
justified their actions to the whole world. While the eighteenth
century celebrated American uniqueness, the nineteenth century
grew restive of the exemplary mission, and by defining time as
space, sought to enlarge the future considerably. As Lincoln amus-
ingly phrased it in 1859, America "owns a large part of the world,
by right of possessing it; and all the rest by right of *wanting* it, and
intending to have it. As Plato had for the immortality of the soul,
so Young America has 'a pleasing hope—a fond desire—a longing
after' territory."[41] By midcentury, the nation's immortality seemed
to depend not so much upon an exemplary greatness as on continental expansion.

As many others have noted before, perhaps the great appeal of

Manifest Destiny lay in its vagueness. It was a definition of national purpose which could accommodate both the high-minded moralism of Emerson or Whitman and the single-minded imperialism of Thomas Hart Benton or Stephen A. Douglas; it justified the turning away from the European past, projected a seemingly limitless future, and could find divine sanction in the Old Testament or New. In short, Manifest Destiny was a perfect blend of democratic idealism and economic self-interest which found in westward expansion the fulfillment of the nation's providential destiny.

There was one unavoidable obstacle in the path of the universalization of America's mission: slavery. Since the characteristic justification for continental expansion was, as Jackson put it in 1843, to extend "the area of freedom," slavery was an inconsistency that could not be easily subsumed under the vague rubric of Manifest Destiny. The intellectual and political father of westward expansion in America, Thomas Jefferson, was also the leading spokesman for an agrarianism which saw the small freeholder as the mainstay of the republic, the chosen instrument of God. Not only did the extension of slavery come into conflict with the free-soil, capitalist ideology of American expansion, as indicated by the collapse of the South's attempts to establish close economic ties with the West,[42] its persistence threatened to undermine the American commitment to the redemption of the world. While not many Northerners would have agreed with William Lloyd Garrison's view "that the spirit of slavery was omnipresent, invading every sanctuary, infecting every pulpit, controlling every press, corrupting every household, and blinding every vision," a growing majority in the North would probably have accepted Seward's position that the slave system was "intolerable, unjust, and inhuman," and in fundamental conflict with the economic and political values of the nation.[43]

The stain of slavery on the purity of God's American Israel was painfully obvious from the beginning. In 1776, the Congregational theologian and Revolutionary pamphleteer Samuel Hopkins denounced the hypocrisy of the Sons of Liberty who were oppressors of Africans. For such a sin, he said, we are under divine judgment, and if we persist in this evil, the vengeance of God will be upon us. This warning echoed the 1774 jeremiad of his friend and colleague Levi Hart, who scourged his fellow citizens for their toleration of slavery and looked forward to the day when Americans would be *"consistently* engaged in the cause of liberty," a day which he saw as full of messianic promise. On that day, he said, "the hard bondage of sin and satan" will be thrown off and " the most perfect liberty" of Christ be established.[44]

This mood of impending doom and transformation, which combined fears of divine wrath with messianic and millennial hopes for redemption, produced what one historian calls "a strange sense of expectancy in ante-bellum America."[45] It was this pervasive, intuitive sense of expectancy which identified the transformation of religious consciousness in the United States between the Revolution and the Civil War—"this turning of the gaze," as Perry Miller has characterized it, "from what had been and could therefore be defined, to the illimitable horizon of the inconceivable."[46] Some insight into the inconceivable is provided by Francis Grierson's retrospective memoir of the 1850s, *The Valley of Shadows,* a book which Edmund Wilson has compared to *Uncle Tom's Cabin* because of its author's grasp of something felt but not yet fully articulated: "an ambiguous promise and menace, the fulfillment of some awful prophecy which had never quite been put into words."[47]

Writing about the Illinois of his youth on the eve of the Civil War, Grierson said that the people were being prepared for a new era by a series of scenes and incidents which only the term "mystical" could accurately describe. Grierson thought that all settlers, though preoccupied by material pursuits, "felt the unnameable influence of unfolding destiny." Things occurred, he said, not so much "by preconceived method as by impelling impulse." *Uncle Tom's Cabin* appeared as an "illumination"; the founding of the Republican party was an "inspiration"; "the great religious revivals and the appearance of two comets were not regarded as coincidences, but accepted as signs of divine preparation and warning." During the late 1850s, Grierson wrote, the nation's "collective consciousness . . . became aware of impending innovation and upheaval."[48]

Grierson's retrospective reading of the signs of impending upheaval was centered on the "imperative, spiritual impulse" provided by Abraham Lincoln, a man whom he would describe later as "the greatest practical mystic the world has known for nineteen hundred years"; but his interpretations find confirmation elsewhere as well. Harriet Beecher Stowe's *Uncle Tom's Cabin,* a book which she sometimes claimed had been written by God, did illuminate the teachings of Jesus ignored by Calvinist theology; it warned the churches not to forget that ". . . prophecy associates in dread fellowship the day of vengeance with the year of his redeemed."[49] The Republican party, likewise, was widely seen as having been "brought into being by Almighty God himself," an interpretation which owed its credibility to the presence of so many Protestant clergymen in its radical wing.[50] The presidential campaign of 1856 provided a forum for a greater degree of direct involvement by clergymen in national politics than at any time since the Revolution, and they took full advantage of it.[51] Combining the evangelicalism of the Second Awakening with the political ideology of moribund antislavery societies, northern churchmen gave a biblical, apocalyptic meaning to the sectional conflict, of which their own schisms in the 1840s were harbingers. Pronouncements from the pulpit bristled with prophecies of doom and redemption, and the comets mentioned by Grierson were a warning of things to come.[52] No astronomical event, however, had as much portent as the meteoric career of John Brown, whose raid on Harpers Ferry provided the nation with a symbolic rehearsal of civil war.

After the Pottawatomie massacre in Kansas, Brown planned to establish a revolutionary, abolitionist republic in the Appalachian Mountains from which he could wage war against slavery. Accordingly, he framed a provisional constitution which abolished slavery as "in utter disregard and violation of those eternal and self-evident truths set forth in our Declaration of Independence"; and created a provisional government to "direct the course and shape of the revolution," a government which would fly the same flag "our Fathers fought under in the Revolution."[53] Brown took his authority for this enterprise directly from God. As reported by his son Owen, he believed "God had created him to be the deliverer of the slaves the same as Moses had delivered the Children of Israel." In an attempt to gain financial support, Brown told friends that it was too late to settle the slavery question by political means, that their only recourse was to God, who willed that he (Brown) incite a slave insurrection. It was only by this means, Brown said, that this "slave cursed Republic" could be restored to the principles of 1776. "If God be for us, who can be against us?"[54]

On the night of October 16, 1859, Brown and his band of thirteen whites and five blacks seized the federal arsenal at Harpers Ferry, taking prisoner some leading townspeople, including the post's commanding officer, Colonel Lewis Washington, the grandnephew of George Washington. Apparently one of the reasons Brown had selected Harpers Ferry for his raid was precisely Colonel Washington's presence there. "I wanted you particularly for the moral effect it would give our cause . . . ," Brown told Washington later.[55] He also, apparently, wanted to take possession of Washington's sword, a ceremonial object that had once belonged to the father of the country, as a scepter for his calling.

Brown's attempt to wage fratricidal war in the name of divine authority and reestablish constitutional order on the basis of the Declaration of Independence was immediately quelled. Within two days he had been captured by a company of marines commanded by Robert E. Lee; within the month, he had been tried and convicted of murder, conspiracy, and treason against Virginia, and he was hanged a month later. Brown's last message, delivered on his way to the gallows, was that he had become "quite certain that the crimes of this guilty land will never be purged away but with Blood."[56]

Brown's actions were universally condemned by the Northern press, but such formal disdain for his fanaticism could not conceal the profound admiration accorded him by intellectuals who celebrated his martyrdom. Theodore Parker, one of Brown's financial supporters, who kept over his desk the musket used by his grandfather on Lexington Green as a reminder of his own Revolutionary heritage, saw Brown as the embodiment of the ideals of 1776. Both William Lloyd Garrison and Wendell Phillips, who usually deplored violence in favor of moral suasion as an antislavery tactic, viewed him as an instrument of divine justice, one who affirmed Revolutionary principles. Emerson and Thoreau found in Brown an example of transcendentalism in action, and they openly applauded his fanaticism as indicating that ". . . a man loves an idea better than all things in the world. . . ."⁵⁷ But it was Emerson's eulogy which best captured the legendary Brown who was to be celebrated in American poetry and song: "That new saint, than whom nothing purer or more brave was ever led by love of men into conflict and death . . . will make the gallows glorious like the cross."⁵⁸

"John Brown's body lies a-mould'ring in the grave" ran the verse of the Union army's favorite marching song, but "his soul goes marching on": "He's gone to be a soldier in the army of the Lord." Julia Ward Howe's "Battle Hymn of the Republic," which provided more exalted lyrics for this popular tune, also expressed more fully the sense of expectancy, both the menace and the promise, which Brown represented. In Mrs. Howe's rendering, with assistance from the book of Isaiah and a song of the English civil war, John Brown's "soul" became transformed into the vengeful God who "loosed the fateful lightning of his terrible swift sword" and whose truth marched on through the instrument of the Union armies.⁵⁹ This God, as shown by a subsequent stanza, promised to raise up a "Hero" who would receive divine grace in proportion to the amount of punishment he inflicted upon the enemies of Israel. Finally, there was in Mrs. Howe's lyric the suggestion that out of the cataclysm of civil war would come a political redemption for the nation: "As he [Christ] died to make men holy, let us die to make men free,/ While God is marching on."⁶⁰

The "Battle Hymn of the Republic," if not a definitive interpretation of the "impending innovation and upheaval" sensed by Grierson and others, was at least an accurate summary of the dynamics of religious consciousness in the antebellum period. Mrs. Howe's lyrics gave popular form to widely shared apocalyptic assumptions about political events which combined the inevitability of divine vengeance with the promise of human redemption. It also accurately captured the dominant intellectual and cultural mood of the period, a mood which found sober defenders of American institutions suddenly speaking the language of John Brown, rationalistic Unitarians invoking the harsh strictures of their seventeenth-century Puritan forebears, and nonviolent humanitarian reformers welcoming an armed crusade for the Union.

And it was this mood which defined the larger cultural context for attempts by political leadership during the 1860s to formally reestablish the covenant of 1776.

As previously indicated, Lincoln's first proclamation of a national day of "humiliation, prayer, and fasting," which viewed the war as divine punishment for the nation's sins, closely followed the form of a ritual first observed on a national level in 1775. Lincoln's proclamation, issued on August 12, 1861, was preceded by a similar proclamation from the provisional government of the Confederacy on May 28 of the same year, which, though Anglican in tone, also called upon people "to humble themselves under the dispensation of Divine Providence, to recognize his righteous government . . . and supplicate his merciful protection for the future."[61] Despite their differences in language, the effect of these rituals, invoked repeatedly by both sides throughout the war, was quite similar. Both were attempts to reestablish the covenant of the fathers; both represented a fusion of piety and politics which presumed an identity between the civil and religious orders; both provided a theodicy like that of the jeremiad which vindicated God's justice in the face of adversity. Both sets of rituals illustrated how in a time of family dissolution and disputed legitimacy, covenant theology could once again be used to justify fratricide and civil war, and perhaps serve as the basis for a new legitimacy as well.

The search for legitimacy by both North and South required that Lincoln and Jefferson Davis each wrestle with the problem of justifying the ways of God to man. Whereas Davis's interpretation of divine punishment focused upon the dimension of "hearth and home" and held out no promise of a collective spiritual regeneration for his countrymen, Lincoln's formulation supplied what had long been anticipated by Northern churchmen and subsequently accepted by intellectuals: a theory of atonement by which the suffering and sacrifices of his people could be linked to their salvation and redemption, a theology that joined death, the punishment for sinfulness, to rebirth and immortality. This would be Lincoln's distinctive contribution to the national faith, which, as set forth in his interpretation of the meaning of events at Gettysburg, would form the basis of a political religion in which he was both founder and leading exemplary figure, both Paul and Christ in one.

CONTROLLING EVENTS:
A THEODICY OF FAILURE

So true is it that man proposes, and God disposes.

—A. Lincoln, 1864

"Our Constitution," Henry Ward Beecher wrote to Lincoln near the end of the war, "has felt the hand of God laid upon it."[62] Indeed it had; but where clergyman Beecher could detect a divine presence only, closer observation reveals the firm grip of his correspondent.

Lincoln began his presidency by defining himself as God's instrument for saving the Union. In this role he interpreted the meaning of the war as divine punishment for collective sins, which offered the nation a means of atonement. By 1865, with the cost of saving the Union to be measured in terms of 600,000 Civil War dead, Lincoln had removed all evidence of his own intermediary presence, admitting that neither he nor anyone else could claim exclusive knowledge of divine intentions. Thus beyond the military defense of the Union and all the sacrifices which that policy entailed—beyond even the meaning which Lincoln authoritatively gave to that sacrifice—there was his own profound sense of personal guilt. It was the guilt of a man who had taken on the sins of his people, and had given them in return a means of salvation, but who himself could not be saved except by his own death. And ultimately, it was through the formal expiation of his own guilt that Lincoln caused the hand of God to be laid upon the Constitution.

Lincoln's founding of a new constitutional order, which transformed the utilitarian arrangement of 1789 into a mystical union, required that he fashion for himself a heroic identity which has few parallels in either history or literature. Nevertheless, two literary sources are useful in comprehending the magnitude and delicacy of his task as founder. The first is provided by Jean Jacques Rousseau's conception of the "legislator"; the second by Dostoevsky's "Grand Inquisitor."

"He who dares to undertake the making of a people's institutions," said Rousseau, "ought to feel himself capable . . . of transforming each individual, who is by himself a complete and solitary whole, into a part of a greater whole from which he . . . receives his life and being . . . and of substituting a partial and moral existence for the physical and independent existence nature has conferred on us all." To do this, the legislator must take away from man his own resources and give him new ones, alien resources, which are useless without the help of other men. In order to found such a community, the legislator needs access to divine authority so that the people will submit to the laws of the state as freely as they do the laws of nature, recognizing the same power in the formation of the state as in that of man. "But it is not anybody," according to Rousseau, "who can make the gods speak, or get himself believed when he proclaims himself their interpreter."[63] How, then, does a legislator gain access to divine authority?

For Rousseau the answer was deceptively simple: "The great soul of the legislator is the only miracle that can prove his mission." The legislator would have to be in possession of a superior intelligence which understood the passions of men without itself being subject to them. "This intelligence would have to be wholly unrelated to our nature, while knowing it through and through; its happiness would have to be independent of us, and yet ready to occupy itself with ours; and lastly, it would have, in the march of time, to look forward to a distant glory, and, working in one century, to be able to enjoy in the next."[64]

Dostoevsky's Grand Inquisitor defined the task of founding more brazenly, and more succinctly: there are three forces, he said, which the founder must use to capture the conscience, and thus provide for the happiness, of men: mystery, miracle, and authority.

Lincoln could not have better fitted these specifications had he consciously modeled himself on Rousseau's legislator or Dostoevsky's Grand Inquisitor. He knew the secret of the Grand Inquisitor: he had looked into the ark of the covenant and found it empty. And while he was by no means wholly unrelated to human nature, he was a man apart, with no real intimates—a man who, precisely as Rousseau said, "occupied" himself with the happiness of men but did not share in it, because it was only in that occupation or calling that his own happiness, the attainment of a distant glory, could be realized. Lincoln would gain his "distant glory," his authority as founder, first, by controlling events so as to make them appear inevitable, beyond the control of anyone but God—thereby providing for men's need of mystery; secondly, by interpreting events so as to imbue their mundane significance with a means of political regeneration—thereby providing for men's need of miracle; and finally, by his own death, which would perfectly exemplify the meaning of his words—thereby helping to create a sanctified Union with a universal mission, or in Dostoevsky's terms, "authority."

In attempting to control events, Lincoln usually presented himself as a passive instrument in the hands of forces over which he had no actual control. Like Washington, as quoted by Weems, who said that none of his accomplishments was due to his "personal agency," attributing them instead to the "interposition of Providence,"[65] Lincoln found in minimizing his own significance a means of explaining his presidential role. At a preinaugural flag-raising ceremony in Philadelphia, where he had made none of the necessary arrangements, he said that in the whole of that proceeding, "I was a very humble instrument."[66] Given his presidential purpose, however, such passivity was possible only because he had rejected in advance of his inauguration the possibilities of peaceful disunion and compromise.

Having resolved as early as December 1860 that national authority must be enforced in the secessionist South, that federal properties must be held or recaptured and revenues collected, Lincoln succeeded from the beginning in establishing a defensive posture: if war came, the South would have to be the aggressor and thus assume responsibility for striking the first blow.[67] As he put it in his first draft of the Inaugural Address, speaking directly to the secessionists, "In *your* hands, my dissatisfied fellow-countrymen, and not in *mine,* is the momentous issue of civil war. The government will not assail *you,* unless you *first* assail *it.* You can have no conflict, without being yourselves the aggressors." And apparently until Seward recommended a more conciliatory closing, Lincoln had intended to end the speech on a very ominous note indeed: "With *you*, and not with *me*, is the solemn question of 'Shall it be peace, or a sword?' "[68]

He returned repeatedly to this theme during the preinaugural speeches. And while proclaiming his determination to "enforce the laws" and defend the Union, Lincoln also made it clear that he was willing to use violence if he deemed it necessary. At Philadelphia he said: ". . . there is no need of blood-shed and war. . . . I am not in favor of such a course, and I may say in advance, there will be no blood shed unless it be forced upon the Government. The Government will not use force unless force is used against it."[69] The surprising thing about this statement is that just a few days before, he had called the crisis "artificial," implying that no real harm had been done. Moreover, the South had not threatened war; its position was that secession was a peaceable act, justified on both moral and constitutional grounds, and that compensation could be made for the federal properties in their possession. The provocative language Lincoln used at Philadelphia strained his defensive posture to its limits; and his words left little doubt about his course of action in the face of Southern resistance. As it turned out, even the circumstances under which the violence was initiated were carefully controlled by no one as much as Lincoln.

Much has been written about the Sumter expedition, and a review of that literature cannot be undertaken here.[70] Suffice it to say that its greatest deficiencies have been, first, the failure to recognize the extent to which Lincoln's tactics were rooted in motives of revenge for having been excluded by his constitutional fathers from political creativity and for the humiliation he suffered following his Mexican War speech; and, second, how the effects of his policy were related to his interpretation of the meaning of the war, one which followed from his long-standing belief in the functions of sacrifice.

In his Lyceum Address Lincoln called upon citizens to take up the pledge of 1776 in behalf of the Constitution in order that reverence for the laws might become the political religion of the nation. To this end, he proposed that everyone "sacrifice unceasingly upon its altars," for it was his understanding that the meaning of the Declaration of Independence resulted not so much from the self-evident nature of its truths as from the common recognition established by sacrifice in their behalf. As he put it, the evidence of sacrifice constituted a "living history," "a history bearing the indubitable testimonies of its own authenticity, in the limbs mangled, in the scars of wounds received," one that could be understood by all, the learned and the unlearned alike. There are other indications from his early years that Lincoln fully understood the political functions of sacrifice, which may suggest a way of explaining the conflicting testimony of his various clerical confessors.

Jesse Fell, founder of the Unitarian church in Bloomington and author of a campaign biography, reported to Herndon that on a variety of religious subjects, including the Atonement and "the nature and design of present and future rewards and punishments," Lincoln "held opinions utterly at variance with what are usually taught in the Church."[71] Fell concluded that Lincoln was beyond the Christian pale, but he also recognized Lincoln's religiosity.

James Smith, former pastor of the Springfield Presbyterian church attended by Mrs. Lincoln, and appointed by the president as an American consul, insisted that Lincoln had been converted as a result of reading his book, *The Christian's Defense,* which argued that the universal practice of sacrifice was proof of its divine origins and thus must be the means of divine governance. Both views might have been correct. For if Lincoln expressed the following opinions, as reported by Isaac Cogdal, he might well have been in superficial agreement with Smith although at odds with Calvinist orthodoxy of the day, especially as interpreted by a Unitarian minister. Said Cogdal of an 1859 conversation with Lincoln:

> Lincoln expressed himself in about these words: He did not nor could not believe in the endless punishment of any one of the human race. He understood . . . punishment for sin to be . . . intended for the good of the offender; hence it must cease when justice is satisfied. He added that all that was lost by the transgression of Adam was made good by the Atonement: all that was lost by the fall was made good by the sacrifice, and he added this remark, that punishment being a "provision of the gospel system," he was not sure but the world would be better off if a little more

punishment was preached by our ministers, and not so much pardon of sin.[72]

The main point here is not to make sense out of the conflicting reports of Lincoln's theological views, but to call attention to his familiarity with the redemptive and integrative functions of sacrifice. Regardless of the accuracy of the various accounts of Lincoln's conversations with the clergy, and whatever deviation from orthodoxy Lincoln expressed, there can be no doubt that he fully understood how sacrifice can create a new spiritual community—i.e., how it is possible through sacrifice to transform the discrete and isolated individual into part of a greater whole by substituting, as Rousseau put it, a partial and moral existence for the physical independence of nature from which the individual takes his life and being.

Perhaps the major issue to be considered in connection with the outbreak of armed hostilities is why Lincoln chose to make Fort Sumter rather than Fort Pickens or some other place the symbol of federal authority. The military had advised that it was not feasible to resupply Sumter, and that any attempt to do so would not only fail but provoke civil war. The majority of the cabinet was prepared to accept the evacuation of Sumter on the grounds of military necessity as preferable to provoking armed conflict. It is true that Lincoln was under considerable Republican pressure to take decisive action to protect and secure governmental properties in the secessionist states, but that did not necessarily mean it had to come at Sumter. Why then did he order a resupply attempt which seemed doomed to failure in advance when there were alternatives open to him (such as reinforcement of Pickens) which both guaranteed success and demonstrated his intent to enforce the law?

Lincoln attempted to answer this question in his message to the special session of Congress on July 4, 1861. He pointed out that reinforcements had first been ordered to land at Fort Pickens, indicating that if this had been accomplished before the provisions at Sumter were exhausted, then the latter could have been evacuated without damage to the Union cause. When he learned that his first order had not been executed, he concluded that there was no alternative but to relieve Sumter. He notified the governor of South Carolina of the resupply attempt, but said that no additional men or munitions would be sent without further notice, or unless the fort came under attack. Upon receipt of this information, Sumter was bombarded and fell even before the arrival of the provisioning expedition.[73]

Either Lincoln's memory failed him in this account or else he was dissembling: his assertion that the evacuation of Sumter was contingent upon the reinforcement of Pickens does not square with the known facts. Lincoln first solicited the advice of his cabinet on the wisdom of resupplying Sumter before he ordered the reinforcement of Pickens. A second request for advice on Sumter occurred before he knew that the Pickens order would be delayed in its execution. In other words, the decision on what to do about Sumter was made independently of the success or failure of the Pickens expedition. Five days before Lincoln heard that Pickens had not yet been reinforced, he told Seward flatly that he did "not propose to abandon Fort Sumter." Moreover, reinforcements actually did arrive at Pickens before the fall of Sumter, proving the viability of that alternative course of action had Lincoln wished to pursue it as such.[74]

Lincoln apparently gave a more candid account to his friend Orville Browning the day before his message to Congress. As Browning recorded it, Lincoln himself had "conceived the idea and proposed sending supplies, without attempting to reinforce. . . . The plan succeeded. They attacked Sumter—it fell, and thus did more service than it otherwise could."[75] Similarly, the president wrote a reassuring letter to the commander of the Sumter expedition, who was both worried about its failure and embittered by what he assumed was Lincoln's oversight in allowing the flagship for the expedition to be withdrawn from service: "You and I both anticipated that the cause of the country would be advanced by making the attempt to provision Fort-Sumter, even if it should fail; and it is no small consolation now to feel that our anticipation is justified by the result."[76]

The result of which Lincoln spoke was that the sacrifice of Sumter left him in firm control of the situation: the issue was no longer simply Southern secession but overt and violent aggression upon the United States, which meant, as Stephen Douglas put it in rallying Northern Democrats to the Union cause, that there could be no neutral ground between patriotism and treason. Lincoln could well understand the result from his own experience in attempting scrupulously to examine President Polk's justification for the Mexican War. By maneuvering the South into striking the first blow, Lincoln succeeded in re-creating the conditions which provided Polk with a rationale for his Mexican adventure, one which Lincoln had attacked on the floor of the House as "the sheerest deception," with the result that he had been branded as a traitor by his constituents. But this "Benedict Arnold" of the 7th Illinois district, this "Ranchero Spotty of one term," now sat where Polk had sat, and answered potential criticisms of his policy as Polk would have answered them. He responded with arguments rather than with facts, attempting "to prove, by telling the *truth*, what he could not prove by telling the *whole truth*. . . ." In the end, it was Lincoln, far more than Polk, who felt that ". . . the blood of this war, like the blood of Abel, [was] crying to Heaven against him."[77]

Despite his essentially passive and defensive posture during the months following the fall of Sumter Lincoln arrogated to himself unprecedented and virtually dictatorial powers as president—far exceeding those "unconstitutional" measures which the Whigs had accused Polk of taking in 1846. His message to the special session of Congress on July 4, 1861, was therefore concerned not only with explaining the circumstances surrounding the Sumter expedition, but also with seeking Congressional sanction and public support for his assertion of extraordinary powers. He asked that Congress give him the "legal means for making this contest a short, and a decisive one." The sacrifices involved would not be prohibitive: in monetary terms, less per person than the cost of the Revolutionary War. "Surely each man has as strong a motive *now*, to *preserve* our liberties, as each had *then* to *establish* them." Proclaiming that this was essentially a "People's contest," Lincoln applauded the "patriotic instinct of the plain people" and said: "They understand, without an argument, that destroying the government, which was made by Washington, means no good to them."[78]

Unfortunately for both sides, the contest did not prove to be as short as it was eventually decisive, and the Northern unity achieved after the fall of Sumter was not long-lived. Initially there was great enthusiasm for the war. Upon hearing of the attack on Sumter, Douglas abandoned his criticisms of the new administration and began organizing Democrats in support of the Union cause. Even abolitionists who had previously denounced the Constitution, in the words of Garrison, as "a covenant with death and an agreement with Hell" now supported the war for Union. Thus Lincoln had little difficulty in finding acceptance for himself as a divine instrument for saving the Union. This did not mean there was a similar willingness to accept his particular war policies as in accordance with divine will, or his leadership as divinely inspired. Even as Lincoln struggled publicly to justify his policies as divinely ordained, he privately acknowledged that there might be a discrepancy between his chosen course of action and God's will.

Lincoln's war policies were challenged almost immediately by those who saw the war as the means for abolishing slavery. As George Bancroft wrote to Lincoln in November 1861, "Civil war is the instrument of Divine Providence to root out social slavery; posterity will not be satisfied with the result, unless the consequences of the war shall effect an increase of free states."[79] Lincoln was repeatedly confronted with rival interpretations of divine will by those who favored immediate abolition, which he often answered not so much on political as on theological grounds. When called upon by groups of memorialists urging that God's blessing depended upon abolition, Lincoln responded by saying that he thought he might be an instrument in God's hands for accomplishing a great work, but that ". . . God's way of accomplishing the end which the memorialists have in view may be different from theirs." On another occasion, speaking directly to the issue of whose claims to divine authority were more credible, his own or those of his petitioners, Lincoln (with a draft of the Emancipation Proclamation in his possession) said: "I hope it will not be irreverent for me to say that if it is probable that God would reveal his will to others, on a point so connected with my duty, it might be supposed he would reveal it directly to me. . . ."[80]

Privately, Lincoln was much less certain that he had God on his side. Following the Union defeat at the second battle of Bull Run,

Lincoln directly confronted his greatest task as religious prophet in justifying the ways of God to man. In a private meditation on divine will, he wrote: "The will of God prevails. In great contests each party claims to act in accordance with the will of God. Both *may* be, and one *must* be wrong. God can not be *for*, and *against* the same thing at the same time. In the present civil war it is quite possible that God's purpose is something different from the purpose of either party—and yet the human instrumentalities, working just as they do, are of the best adaptation to effect His purpose." Then he added, "I am almost ready to say this is probably true—that God wills this contest, and wills that it shall not end yet."

If Lincoln was troubled by the presumptuousness of his self-defined role as divine instrument, he was not willing to relinquish it. To do so would be to deny either the existence or the justice of the national deity in this, the hour of the nation's greatest peril. He had no choice but to set aside his personal doubts and take up the task of articulating a theodicy which would vindicate the justice of a God who, as he put it, "could have either saved or destroyed the Union without a human contest," but who nevertheless let the contest proceed.[81] By adopting this role, he ultimately succeeded in establishing the existence of a God that was independent of his own intermediary presence.

The prophecy upon which Lincoln's authority as founder depended was that the war for the Union was wrought by God, and that its successful conclusion would be proof of divine favor. It was only by this means that Lincoln might cause the hand of God to be laid upon the Constitution with all traces of human art removed. As president, he gradually revised a theme from his preinaugural speeches that identified the cause of the Union, rather than his personal success, as being contingent upon divine assistance. This allowed him to remove all signs of his personal influence upon events, and also completed his personal identification with the Union—that identification which he had first undertaken as a young man, and which had been fully articulated during his preinaugural trip to Washington.

This can be most clearly understood in a chronological perspective. He told a group of churchmen in May 1862: "You well know, gentlemen, and the world knows, how reluctantly I accepted this issue of battle forced upon me. . . . You all may recollect that in taking up the sword thus forced into our hands this Government appealed to the prayers of the pious and the good, and declared that it placed its whole dependence upon the favor of God." A year later, Lincoln's personal role was even further diminished, and the importance of the collective cause proportionately increased: ". . . from the beginning I saw that the issues of our great struggle depended on the Divine interposition and favor. If we had that, all would be well." Within a few more months, Lincoln had removed himself from the scene altogether—presumably identifying himself with the Union cause completely: "If God be with us, we will succeed; if not, we will fail."[82]

Once again, by appearing to diminish his personal importance, Lincoln was only enhancing it. He had begun his presidency by defining himself as the instrument of the God of Washington, and in this role, he led the North into war for the Union. As the war progressed, Lincoln proceeded to abolish all evidence of his own intermediary presence, leaving the American people to face God alone—a God who worked out his will in mysterious ways by bringing down upon the nation a civil war as punishment for its collective sins, but who was also forgiving and would reward the virtuous side with victory. This was a state of rewards and punishments that did not depend upon the uncertainties of an ethereal future; it was evidence of a divine power that required no intermediary because it was an immediate presence, in this world and in this time, and terrible to behold. By 1864, with military victory possible if not imminent, Lincoln could publicly acknowledge what he had only privately admitted before, that God's will was independent of his own. By removing all traces of his personal authorship, he established the existence of a God who would give him His authority as founder.

Speaking at the Sanitary Fair in Baltimore, Lincoln said:

When the war began, three years ago, neither party, nor any man, expected it would last till now. Each looked for the end, in some way, long ere to-day. Neither did any anticipate that domestic slavery would be much affected by the war. But here we are; the

war has not ended, and slavery has been very much affected.
. . . So true is it that man proposes, and God disposes.

But we can see the past, though we may not claim to have
directed it; and seeing it, in this case, we feel more hopeful and
confident for the future.[83]

Man proposes: Lincoln proposed a short and decisive war in
which the North would seem morally blameless for defending the
Union and the Constitution would be sanctified through some
small amount of sacrifice. He proposed only to save the Union, as
he told Greeley in the famous letter of 1862, and neither to save
nor to destroy slavery. But in preserving the Union he did find it
necessary to destroy slavery—just as he had found it necessary to
resupply Sumter in order to avoid "national destruction." Since
the border states had refused to heed his appeals for compensated
emancipation, he told a Kentucky newspaper editor, he was
"driven to the alternative of either surrendering the Union and
with it, the Constitution, or of laying strong hand upon the colored
element. I chose the latter." But then he added:

> I claim not to have controlled events, but confess plainly that
> events have controlled me. Now, at the end of three years struggle
> the nation's condition is not what either party, or any man devised,
> or expected. God alone can claim it. Whither it is tending seems
> plain. If God now wills the removal of a great wrong, and wills also
> that we of the North as well as you of the South, shall pay fairly
> for our complicity in that wrong, impartial history will find therein
> new cause to attest and revere the justice and goodness of God.[84]

God disposes: Lincoln did not intend a massive and extended
war, but the war came; he did not intend to emancipate slaves, he
said, but slaves were emancipated. Thus while men can recognize
what has happened in the past, they cannot claim to have directed
it, and therein lay a source of hope and confidence for the future.
For therein lay proof, as Lincoln said later, that the Almighty has
purposes of his own—proof, that is to say, of God's independent
existence.

The discrepancies between man's proposals and God's dispos-
als were never more painfully obvious to Lincoln than in his military and political leadership. If he could control the circumstances

surrounding the outbreak of armed hostilities, as well as the timing and effective extent of emancipation, later disclaiming any such control for himself, the direction of day-to-day military operations was always beyond his reach, and control over political affairs, despite his diligent efforts, maddeningly elusive. From Lincoln's perspective, it was on the success of military operations, especially, that everything else depended. To vindicate the justice of a God who proceeded differently from his human instrumentalities was difficult but quite possible; to vindicate the justice of a God who would permit the Union cause to be destroyed on the field of battle, and, as a result, deserted at the ballot box, was unthinkable. Without military victory and political support, the Union with which Lincoln had merged his personal identity would be lost, as well as his own and the nation's chances of achieving immortality.

With Lincoln, wrote Alexander Stephens, the "Union . . . rose to the sublimity of a religious mysticism."[85] Lincoln's commitment to the "Union" was profound, but, because of the ambiguity of the term, is easily misread. As previously noted, he articulated his private views on the relationship between the Declaration of Independence and the Constitution just prior to assuming the presidency: He believed that the Constitution's purpose was to adorn and preserve the Declaration; he saw the Union as a vessel which carried liberty as its cargo. After he assumed the presidency, this order of priority, which suggested that the Union took its meaning and importance only from the Declaration of Independence, could not be publicly maintained. Slavery, after all, was still a legal part of the established constitutional order. Although Lincoln had repeatedly expressed his wish that both the institutions and the liberties of the country be perpetuated, he did not intend to say, as he almost did in Independence Hall, that the Union without the principle of the Declaration was without purpose or meaning. Nevertheless, it seems quite clear that privately the Union was of secondary importance for Lincoln, that for him the true source of American greatness was to be found in the words and deeds of 1776 rather than of 1789, that the nation's immortality depended upon the principle which "gave hope to the world for all future time." Why, then, his profound personal identification with the Union?

Lincoln's Unionism involved two distinct and contradictory commitments—the more important to the Revolution, the lesser to the Constitution—and he attempted to honor both without acknowledging the discrepancy. He executed his duty to the Union by regarding himself as having been elected president of a United States which included the secessionist states as well as all others. In his inaugural address he considered the Union to be "unbroken," and that it was his sworn duty to enforce the Constitution and its laws, which included the Fugitive Slave Law. On a practical political level, his commitment to the Constitution was reflected in his dependence upon Unionist sentiment not only among Democrats and Republicans in the North, but, as he hoped, in the border states and the South as well. Out of a combination of these considerations, Lincoln revoked the emancipation orders of generals Frémont and Hunter and urged in his first annual message to Congress that emancipation not be introduced as a war aim. He said, "I have . . . thought it proper to keep the integrity of the Union prominent as the primary object of the contest. . . ."[86]

But Lincoln's commitment to the Constitution was hedged by an important qualification. In declaiming his intent to take care that the laws would be faithfully executed in all states, he said, "Doing this I deem to be only a simple duty on my part." Then he added, "and I shall perform it . . . unless my rightful masters, the American people, shall withhold the requisite means, or, in some authoritative manner, direct the contrary."[87] As it happened, many of his "rightful masters" did direct the contrary, and the Emancipation Proclamation was seemingly thrust upon him as a strategic war measure designed to cripple the South militarily, and gain political support for his administration in Congress, among the people at large, and among nations abroad.[88] But despite the careful moderation with which Lincoln handled emancipation, it is clear after 1854, and from his preinaugural speeches, that the obligations enjoined by a union which excluded the principle of "liberty to all" could be fulfilled by him as nothing more than a "simple duty." Such a union had no "relish of salvation in it."

The union which did offer salvation was that provided by the fraternal bonds of 1776, a union which he invoked at the close of his first Inaugural Address: "The mystic chords of memory, stretching from every battlefield, and patriot grave, to every living heart and hearthstone, all over this broad land, will yet swell the chorus of the Union, when again touched, as surely they will be, by the better angels of our nature."[89] It is in those mystic chords of memory which linked the sacrifices of 1776 to the meaning of community that can be found the key to Lincoln's personal identification with the Union. For here was a human bond that triumphed over death, an enduring meaning worthy of one who dreamed dreams of Elysium.

Despite his formal obligations to the Union, Lincoln did not hesitate to justify his defense of it in revolutionary terms. Even in his 1861 annual message to Congress, after first warning against turning the war into a "violent and remorseless revolutionary struggle," he dwelt upon the importance of liberty to the Union. Couching his defense of liberty in the eighteenth-century language of classical economics, Lincoln expounded upon the labor theory of value by which workers were transformed into incipient entrepreneurs: "This is the just, and generous, and prosperous system, which opens the way to all—gives hope to all, and consequent energy, and progress, and improvement of condition to all." Since the preservation of this system within the Union would lead to continued growth and prosperity, he concluded: "The struggle of today, is not altogether for today—it is for a vast future also."[90]

In his next annual message, Lincoln discussed his concept of the Union at great length. Echoing the argument of Washington's Farewell Address, he took note of the permanence and natural unity of the land as a source of enduring commonality and community: "In all its adaptations and aptitudes, it demands union, and abhors separation." Then, as if to dramatize the difference between his Union and that of Washington, he proposed a series of amendments to the Constitution which aimed at gradual, compensated emancipation. His peroration made explicit the previous implication that his concept of the Union included the Declaration of Independence, and that, in addition, the future of world history depended upon the willingness of his generation to save the Union on that basis:

Fellow citizens, *we* cannot escape history. We of this Congress and this administration, will be remembered in spite of ourselves. No personal significance, or insignificance, can spare one or another of us. The fiery trial through which we pass, will light us down, in honor or dishonor, to the latest generation. We *say* we are for the Union. The world will not forget that we say this. We know how to save the Union. The world knows we do know how to save it. We—even *we* here—hold the power, and bear the responsibility. In *giving* freedom to the *slave*, we *assure* freedom to the *free*—honorable alike in what we give, and what we preserve. We shall nobly save, or meanly lose, the last best hope of earth.[91]

The historical theory on which Lincoln based his concept of the Union was outlined in his July 4, 1861, message to Congress. He accused the South of an "insidious debauching of the public mind" by inventing an "ingenious sophism" to justify secession, but his own theory of the origins of the Union was no less disingenuous. He believed that the Union was older than the Constitution, formed in 1774, continued in 1776, and matured by the Articles of Confederation in 1778. The purpose of the Constitution then was as stated: to form a more perfect union, not to create a new one. And since the Union preceded the states, the states never having existed outside it, the claims of state sovereignty were simply nonsensical.[92] It is not necessary here to point up the empirical flaws in this theory, which incidentally tend to sustain the Southern interpretation; it is sufficient to note only that the Union to which Lincoln referred was not that founded in 1789. In fact, the Union with which Lincoln identified himself had never existed before 1865; that it did exist thereafter was testimony to his success as a political and military leader, and, as a result, as the founder of a new political order as well.

In a comment written prior to the 1864 election, Lincoln revealed the extent to which he identified himself with his Union. Referring to the motivation behind his war policies, he said that "... the public interest and my private interest, have been perfectly parallel, because in no other way could I serve myself so well, as by truly serving the Union." As a result, he could view his re-election as considerably more than just a personal victory. While awaiting the final election returns, he told his supporters that the welfare of the country required the endorsement of his administration. "I earnestly believe," he said, "that the consequences of this day's work . . . will be to the lasting advantage, if not to the very salvation, of the country." Then he added that ". . . all who have labored today in behalf of the Union organization, have wrought for the interests of their country and the world, not only for the present, but for all future ages."[93]

No longer did Lincoln see himself simply as the instrument of the nation's majesty, as he had four years earlier; by the end of 1864, the identification between himself and the Union had become so complete that he *was* the Union. It was not, however, the Union of 1789 with which he had merged his personal identity. For Lincoln, his reelection meant that the Declaration of Independence had been readopted, that the Union had not only been saved, but saved so as to make it "forever worthy of the saving"; that the republican robe, which had been soiled and trailed in the dust, had now been washed white in both the spirit and the blood of the Revolution.

Lincoln's interpretation of the significance of his reelection was hardly an exaggeration. He had been opposed for renomination by many notables within his own party, and confronted in the election by the Democratic party candidacy of his former commanding general, George McClellan; his political prospects had seemed bleak in the early summer of 1864. His greatest liabilities were the lack of a dramatic military victory and the memory of the recent bloody battles of the Wilderness—Union casualties on May 5 and 6 alone were placed at 15,500—so that it seemed, as one embittered Radical put it, that "those who think Lincoln came down from Heaven will soon be convinced he was on his way lower down and not intended to stop here much longer."[94] But aided by Sherman's control of Atlanta, Sheridan's victories in the Shenandoah, and Grant's capture of Fort Harrison, Lincoln gained a decisive popular majority in the election, and lost but three states in the electoral college.[95] It was an outcome which attracted worldwide attention, and was so astounding to many, that Lincoln's own assessment of its significance, as saving the principle of liberty for the world, found even loftier expression elsewhere.[96] At the very least, it seems likely that had McClellan won, the Union of 1789 would have been restored in some form, and, as a result, the union of 1776 lost indefinitely.[97]

Lincoln's direct control over events which gave him the initial unity needed after Sumter to fight a war for Union, as well as an emancipation policy consistent with his contrary obligations to the Constitution and the Declaration, was not matched by a similar domination in other areas of military policy. But where direct means failed him, indirect means sufficed; where his deeds could not reach, his words sustained him. In 1862 he reportedly said, "I do not know but that God has created some one man great enough to comprehend the whole of this stupendous crisis from beginning to end, and endowed him with sufficient wisdom to manage and direct it."[98] He said he was not that man, but the record suggests otherwise. If Lincoln gained his authority in part by controlling events, so as to make them appear beyond the control of anyone but God, he also gained it by interpreting the meaning of events, so as to provide a means of political regeneration for the nation; and the two were not unrelated. He controlled events at least as much by his words as by his deeds, and it is in his words that the key to understanding his success as the founder of a new constitutional order can be discovered.

INTERPRETING EVENTS:
SACRIFICIAL DEATH AND REBIRTH

We must disenthrall our selves, and then we shall save our country.
—A. Lincoln, 1862

As Lincoln proceeded to the Capitol to assume the presidency, he repeatedly invoked the assistance of the God of Washington, the God "who had never forsaken the American people." He was inaugurated against the background of the unfinished Capitol building with the top half of its dome missing. Not far away was the uncompleted Washington Monument, its base littered with construction materials and tools.[99] Similarly, as Jefferson Davis took his oath of office on February 22, 1862, while standing near an equestrian statue of George Washington on Capitol Hill in Richmond, he said, "Acknowledging the Providence which has visibly protected the Confederacy during its brief but eventful career, to thee, O God! I trustingly commit myself, and prayerfully invoke Thy blessing on my country and its cause." A year earlier he had bid farewell to his Senate colleagues by saying, "We will invoke the God of our fathers, who delivered them from the paw of the lion, to protect us from the ravages of the bear."[100]

The phantasmagorical fears of fraternal conflict and civil war which had haunted the founding fathers, themselves the products of just such a conflict, had again become a reality. Now, as before, the warring sons would invoke and attempt to reestablish the covenant of the fathers which had provided them with a fusion of piety and politics, a theodicy which vindicated God's justice at the moment of family dissolution and fratricide. The difference this time was, as Lincoln said in his second Inaugural Address, "Both read the same Bible, and pray to the same God; each invokes His aid against the other." A dispute over the meaning of the Constitution had been transformed into a religious conflict which involved a war on heresy and hypocrisy in order to determine which side had the blessing of the national deity. It was a war which ended only with an oath, a formal recantation of heresy and pledge of allegiance to the new constitutional order.

Despite invoking the same God against one another, there were theological differences between North and South. Lincoln's religious proclamations followed very closely the form and substance of the Puritan ritual employed by the Continental Congress in 1775, which made the public confession of sins a prelude to seeking God's blessing. Jefferson Davis's were less attentive to the rigors of Puritan form, usually only seeking God's protection in time of peril, a mark of Anglican influence. But, more important, Lincoln's synthesis of secular and religious themes held out the promise of collective redemption for the nation which passed through the test of civil war. Most Southern interpreters of the war's significance focused their attention on particular persons, places, things. Northerners looked upon the war as a sacrificial cleansing of the nation, leading to spiritual rebirth. Southerners called for the protection of hearthsides and homes by the force of arms.

This Southern interpretation of the war's meaning is illustrated by the following examples. In response to the president's first call for troops after Sumter, Alexander Stephens said that Lincoln might bring his 75,000 troops against the South, but ". . . we fight for our homes, our fathers and mothers, our wives, brothers, sisters, sons and daughters, and neighbors!" He added: "God is on our side, and who shall be against us?"[101] Similarly, former West Point superintendent P. G. T. Beauregard, who resigned his commission to command troops of the Confederacy, inaugurated his service at Manassas Junction by issuing a proclamation which called upon Virginians to imitate their Revolutionary fathers "and by the purity and sanctity of your domestic firesides, to rally to the standard of your State and country." He said: "Your honor and that of your wives and daughters, your fortunes, and your lives are involved in this momentous contest."[102] Leonidas Polk, who resigned as Episcopal bishop of New Orleans to become a major general in the Confederate army, explained to a friend: "I believe most solemnly that it is for constitutional liberty, which seems to have fled to us for refuge, for our hearth-stones, and our altars that we strike. I hope I shall be supported in the work and have grace to do my duty."[103]

Focusing a justification for war on the dimension of hearth and home did not mean that Confederate leaders were any less absolute in committing themselves to their cause or any less assured of God's ultimate sanction of it than were Union leaders. Stephens, in the same speech, also said: "We can call out a million of people, if need be, and when they are cut down, we can call out another, and still another, until the last man of the South finds a bloody grave." If such words in 1861 can be discounted as prewar rhetoric, a similar statement by Jefferson Davis in 1864 cannot. Rejecting the concept of amnesty for the South, Davis reportedly said, "Amnesty, sir, applies to criminals. We have committed no crime." He went on: "The North was mad and blind, would not let us govern ourselves, and so the war came; now it must go on until the

last man of this generation falls. . . . We are fighting for independence, and that, or extermination, we *will* have."[104]

Southerners no less than Northerners found civil-war events
full of apocalyptic urgency, and committed themselves equally to
providential protection. Never failing to seek God's guidance and
favor in his speeches, Davis said at his inauguration, "We feel that
our cause is just and holy . . . [and] with a firm reliance on that
divine power which covers with its protection the just cause, we
will continue to struggle for our inherent right to freedom, independence, and self-government." If the God invoked by the Confederacy often seemed to be an Anglican presence, perhaps reflecting Davis's recent baptism into the Episcopal church,[105] the
rituals employed nevertheless honored the forms of 1776. In proclaiming a day of "humiliation, prayer, and fasting" on May 28,
1861, Davis said:

> When a people who recognize their dependence upon God, feel
> themselves to be surrounded by peril and difficulty, it becomes
> them to humble themselves under the dispensation of Divine
> Providence, to recognize his righteous government, to acknowl-
> edge his goodness in times past, and supplicate his merciful pro-
> tection for the future.
>
> The manifest proof of the divine blessing hitherto extended to
> the efforts of the people of the Confederate States of America, to
> maintain and perpetuate public liberty, individual rights, and na-
> tional independence, demand their devout and heartfelt gratitude.
> It becomes them to give public manifestation of this gratitude, and
> of their dependence upon the Judge of all the earth, and to invoke
> the continuance of his favor.[106]

As the war persisted, the language of these proclamations became more severe, reflecting the fortunes of the battlefield, and
ultimately provided a theodicy which could explain military failure.
In May 1862, Davis announced, "Recent disaster has spread gloom
over the land, and sorrow sets at the hearth-stones of our countrymen; but a people conscious of rectitude and faithfully relying on
their Father in Heaven may be cast down, but cannot be dis-
mayed." By July 5, 1863, however, this measured tone of hopeful-
ness had given way to anticipation of despair:

Had not our successes on land and sea made us self-confident and forgetful of our reliance on him; had not love of lucre eaten like a gangrene into the very heart of the land, converting too many among us into worshippers of gain and rendering them unmindful of their duty to their country, to their fellowmen and to their God —who, then, will presume to complain that we have been chastened or to despair of our just cause and the protection of our Heavenly Father?[107]

God was still just, but after the battle at Gettysburg, His justice was increasingly difficult to explain to the people of the Confederacy. Lincoln likewise wrestled with the problem of justifying the ways of God to man, but his formulation supplied what had been anticipated by Northern churchmen for more than a hundred years, a theory of atonement by which the suffering and sacrifices of the people could be linked to their salvation and redemption, a theology that joined death to collective rebirth and immortality. This theology, directly responsive to the mood of impending doom and transformation of the antebellum period, superseded American denominationalism by drawing upon Old Testament sources and apparently fulfilling New Testament prophecies. It also reunited the secular and religious orders so that participation in the war could be viewed as a religious experience.

In the two decades following the Revolution, both religious practice and church membership declined markedly. During this period only one in twenty Americans held church membership. The nineteenth century, however, opened with an explosive return to zealous religious participation, a revival movement which had its origin in New England's Second Great Awakening. The spirit of experiential faith, infused by the acceptance of "plain Gospel truths"—God's absolute sovereignty, man's total depravity, and Christ's atonement—swept the country, from the halls at Yale to the camp meeting tents in Cane Ridge, Kentucky. The chief beneficiaries of this revival movement were the Methodists, whose membership rose from less than three thousand in 1800 to more than a million in 1844, becoming the largest American church. The distinctive feature of the Methodist acceptance of plain Gospel truths was the demand for penitential conflict, the conviction of sin, and the experience of regeneration.[108]

Although Methodism, with its system of circuits and preaching stations, and its recruitment of largely untrained clergy, had its greatest appeal in the West, it also became the second-largest denomination in New England. But religious and intellectual leaders in the Northeast did not need Wesleyan theology to convince them of the need for penitential conflict, the punishment of sin, or regenerative experience. All of these themes were fully developed in the writings of Northerners, both radical and conservative in political outlook, both secular and religious in their calling. Men who could agree on nothing else could concur that civil war was good because whatever they found wrong with American society, the war could be seen as a purgative for it. Although initially there was deep division as to what the response to secession ought to be, after the fall of Sumter these differences were engulfed by enthusiasm for an apocalyptic conflict. Sober defenders of American institutions began to speak the language of John Brown; rationalistic Unitarians invoked the harsh strictures of seventeenth-century Puritanism; transcendentalist humanitarians and nonviolent abolitionists welcomed an armed crusade for Union.[109]

Francis Lieber, the conservative professor of government at Columbia University, wrote in 1860, "What we Americans stand in need of is a daily whipping like a naughty boy." It is wicked, he said, to pray for a "chastising calamity" to befall our nation; but when nations recklessly defy right, morality, and justice, ". . . God in his mercy has sometimes condescended to smite them, and to smite them hard, in order to bring them to their senses. . . ." Lieber was expressing a view more widely popularized by Charles Eliot Norton, who by the end of the 1850s had become convinced that America could be saved only by the discipline imposed by suffering. Norton saw the popular excitement following the outbreak of hostilities to be a result of people's "conservative love of order, government, and law." As a way of deepening these conservative instincts, he wrote patriotic tracts which espoused the idea of duty through sacrifice, and purification through death. For Norton there was no flinching at the prospect of death, not even at the prospect "that a million men should die on the battlefield."[110]

The idea of war as punishment and purification received support from a variety of otherwise antagonistic spokesmen. In fact, many intellectuals actually welcomed the Union defeat at the first battle of Bull Run and worried lest the war not inflict enough punishment. Following this disaster, Thoreau was reported to have been "in a state of exultation about the moral regeneration of the nation." Wendell Phillips described the defeat as the "best thing that could have happened to the North." Norton spoke of the "advantages of defeat," and Henry Bellows of the "moral necessity of the late defeat." Francis Parkman wrote, "The time may come when upheaved from its depths, fermenting and purging itself, the nation will stand at length clarified and pure in a renewed and strengthened life." Horace Bushnell seized the occasion to announce that Bull Run was God's punishment for the idolatry and sinfulness of the nation, prophesying that such suffering would bring people back to God and the church. Even Emerson seemed to welcome the loss of life as a sacrificial cleansing of the nation: ". . . one whole generation might well consent to perish, if by their fall, political liberty and clean and just life could be made sure to the generations that follow."[111]

Both radicals and conservatives could view the war as a religious conflict, and accept the notion that Lincoln was the instrument of God. The Unitarian minister Henry Bellows, who was the head of the Sanitary Commission during the war, propounded a theory of the divine right of rulers which might have come right out of seventeenth-century Massachusetts Bay: ". . . the head of a nation *is* a sacred person" who, upon taking office, is responsible not to his electorate, but to God. Similar views were put forth by Joseph T. Duryea and Horace Bushnell, and also found their way into the editorial columns of such popular magazines as *Harper's*. Bushnell went even further than Bellows toward resurrecting the Puritan theory of oligarchy: ". . . the magistrate is sovereign over the people, not they over him, having even a divine right to bind their conscience by his rule." For Bushnell, as well as for Bellows, loyalty to the state was devotion to God: "We believe that there is a relation so deep between true loyalty and religion that the loyal man will be inclined toward religion by his public devotion, and the religious man raised in the temper of his loyalty to his country, by his religious devotion."[112] By implication, disloyalty to the state became rebellion against God.

Abolitionists and transcendentalists viewed the war in a similar perspective. The intervention of divine providence made it possible for humanitarian reformers to turn away from their professed pacifism and disunionism and accept the propriety of armed conflict for Union. After the fall of Sumter, Lincoln became a divine instrument to bring about emancipation, and the war was God's way of punishing the nation for the sin of slavery. As Garrison told his followers, ". . . stand still and see the salvation of God." What he meant was more fully expressed by Louis Tappan in a pamphlet entitled "The War: Its Cause and Remedy": "Viewed in the light of Scripture and God's providence, war is the result of sin; and its remedy is repentance and reformation. God in the present calamitous rebel war, has a controversy with the people—with the whole people—North and South."[113] Some could even see in the outcome an impending millennium "wherein the distinctions of race . . . shall be obliterated, and men shall live together in the relations of Christian brotherhood."[114] But most did not look beyond emancipation as a propitiation of divine wrath, and after 1862, felt vindicated in their belief that Lincoln was indeed the providential instrument he said he was.

The origins of Lincoln's political theology, as previously noted, can be traced to the Lyceum Address. There he said that materials derived from reason and molded into general intelligence, sound morality, and reverence for the Constitution and laws would provide the means of national salvation. In his first Inaugural Address, however, he revised that list, substituting "patriotism" and "Christianity" for "sound morality," and included a source of constitutional reverence, i.e., "a firm reliance on Him, who has never yet forsaken this favored land." The implication is that for Lincoln the blending together of patriotism and Christianity would constitute a sound morality. Such a morality clearly was dependent upon the belief in the existence of the God who had never forsaken the American people. And if, as Lincoln had suggested in his "Meditation on the Divine Will," it was possible in the midst of a civil war to fear desertion by the national deity, then the establishment of that morality was dependent upon calling the people back to their sense of chosenness, anticipating and calming their anxieties about metaphysical abandonment, and securing the assurance of divine justice in spite of the hardship and travail. Except for his required annual messages to Congress, most of Lincoln's infrequent public messages and statements were devoted to this theme.

In interpreting the meaning of the war as divine punishment for the nation's sins, Lincoln was always careful to observe that such punishment was fully deserved. As he explained it: "We have been the recipients of the choicest bounties of Heaven. We have been preserved, these many years, in peace and prosperity. We have grown in numbers, wealth and power, as no nation has ever grown. But we have forgotten God." We have forgotten, he went on to say, that it was the hand of God which has been responsible for our greatness, imagining instead that America's blessings were the result of some intrinsic virtue. "It behooves us then, to humble ourselves before the offended Power, to confess our national sins, and to pray for clemency and forgiveness." To this end, he designated a Thursday in April 1863 (as he had previously set aside a Thursday in September 1861) as a "day of national humiliation, fasting and prayer" on which people were to abstain "from their ordinary secular pursuits, and to unite, at their several places of public worship and their respective homes, in keeping the day holy to the Lord, and devoted to the humble discharge of the religious duties proper to that solemn occasion."[115]

Similarly, Lincoln observed the appropriate Puritan sequel to days of humiliation, prayer, and fasting by proclaiming four separate days of "National Thanksgiving, Praise and Prayer" and issuing various other proclamations of thanksgiving and prayer. Each of these was accompanied by a commentary which acknowledged God's omnipotence and justice in the affairs of the nation, as well as his mercy and care for a penitent people.[116] These proclamations made it clear that the restoration of the Union and national authority would be the result not of superior force or military strategy but of divine favor. "It has pleased Almighty God," said Lincoln after the victory at Gettysburg, "to hearken to the supplications and prayers of an afflicted people, and to vouchsafe to the army and the navy of the United States victories on land and on sea so signal and so effective as to furnish reasonable grounds for augmented confidence that the Union of these States will be maintained, their constitution preserved, and their peace and prosperity permanently restored." A few months later, in another Thanksgiving Proclamation, Lincoln called upon his countrymen to count their many blessings even in the midst of civil war. Taking note of the peace abroad, domestic harmony outside the field of battle, the growth of industry and populations, and renewed national vigor, he said: "No human counsel hath devised nor hath any mortal hand worked out these great things. They are the gracious gifts of the Most High God, who, while dealing with us in anger for our sins, hath nevertheless remembered mercy."[117]

Lincoln's return to these Puritan rituals of the Revolution had the effect of reclaiming the covenant of 1776 and reestablishing the identity between civil and ecclesiastical orders. His formal proclamations, which reintroduced the spirit of the jeremiad by calling for public penitence, presumed the existence of a covenanted people who were being justly punished for their sins. Likewise, by ordering the observance of the Sabbath in the armed forces, Lincoln returned to a ritual of the Revolution initiated by Washington which fused together patriotic duty with service to God. Citing Washington's first General Order as his authority, Lincoln said that this "indicates the spirit in which our institutions were founded and should ever be defended: 'The General hopes and trusts that every officer and man will endeavor to live and act as becomes a Christian soldier defending the dearest rights and liberties of his country!' "[118]

Lincoln's most distinctive contribution to national ritual was his establishment of Washington's birthday as a day of patriotic celebration. Throughout his early presidential years, the twenty-second day of February held special significance for Lincoln. On February 21, 1861, he recalled having read Weems's biography of Washington, and then proceeded to give a startling synthesis of his previous preinaugural speeches which echoed the themes of the Lyceum Address. On the following day he symbolically gave up his life rather than betray his commitment to Washington's legacy. The next year, acting as commander in chief, he reserved February 22, 1862, as the effective date for "General War Order No. 1" calling for the forward movement of Union forces against the Confederates, which he obviously hoped would be an auspicious beginning for his military leadership. Less than a month later he

also designated Washington's birthday as a day of national celebration on which citizens were to assemble for a reading of "his
immortal Farewell address."[119] The following year, when February 22 fell on a Sunday, Lincoln declined an invitation to preside
over a meeting of the U.S. Christian Commission on this day
which, according to the invitation, was designed "to check distrust
and disloyalty and to restore confidence and support to the Government." He said: "The birthday of Washington, and the Christian Sabbath, co-inciding this year, and suggesting together, the
highest interests of this life, and of that to come, is most propitious
for the meeting proposed."[120] Clearly, for Lincoln, Washington's
birthday was no mere secular celebration, but both God and Washington enjoined obedience to the law.

Sometimes Lincoln was crude and heavy-handed in presenting
his theology and insisting that a system of morality based upon
patriotism and Christianity be enforced. In a comment to newspa-
perman Noah Brooks, which Lincoln billed as "The President's
last, shortest, and best speech," he wrote, ". . . in my opinion, the
religion that sets men to rebel and fight against their government
. . . is not the sort of religion upon which people can get to
heaven." In designating the first Thursday in August 1864 as a day
of prayer, Lincoln seemed to single out his Democratic opposition
in Congress for divine rebuke: he asked that God be implored not
to allow the nation to be destroyed "by obstinate adhesions to
. . . counsels which may be in conflict with his eternal purposes."[121]
But there could be no doubting Lincoln's seriousness in these
matters. After reelection, as Gideon Welles recorded it, he even
proposed to his cabinet a constitutional amendment "recognizing
the Deity in that instrument."[122] Observation of the Sabbath was
strictly enforced in the army, and clergymen in various parts of the
country were jailed and otherwise punished for failure to conform
with the required rites.[123]

If Lincoln could invoke the Old Testament covenant and insist
upon a strict performance of it, his political theology also anticipated the conventions of the New. In his 1862 annual message
to Congress, he said: "The dogmas of the quiet past, are inadequate to the stormy present. . . . As our case is new, so we must

think anew and act anew. We must disenthrall ourselves, and then we shall save our country."[124] The thralldom from which Lincoln wished to liberate the nation was that of slavery; but his interpretation of this liberating process, given the dominant cultural perspectives of the period, invited a typological understanding of its significance. Adam was in the bondage of original sin, but his descendants were freed by a process of conversion into the mystical body of Christ. Church membership in the Puritan tradition demanded an internal, experiential test of God's calling, the prototype of which was Paul's conversion on the road to Damascus. Conversion involved a liberating experience which required symbolic death and rebirth into the salvation of Christ. Lincoln's interpretation of the war's meaning also proposed that it was a test; it was a test by which the nation might be converted through blood sacrifice, suffering, and death into a new life everlasting.

Lincoln used the concept of a "test" in a strictly secular sense, but the religious connotations were inescapable. At the close of his 1862 message to Congress, he said in effect that the "fiery trial" through which the nation passed involved the test of whether it would "nobly save, or meanly lose, the last best, hope of earth." It was on the basis of this test that his hometown newspaper claimed, "Thousands of Democrats converted to freedom by the war, have, from the moment of their conversion, become his friends."[125] Lincoln made the same point more explicitly in a letter to Carl Schurz. In referring to the war dead from both parties, he said they had "seal[ed] their faith with their blood." Likewise, freed slaves who fought in the war "have demonstrated in blood their right to the ballot. . . ." Of the sacrifices of Union soldiers generally, he said they were "endeavoring to purchase with their blood and their lives the future happiness and prosperity of this country." It was through such sacrifices that the benefits of a united country could be conferred upon "our children and our children's children to a thousand years."[126]

The ultimate statement of sacrificial death and rebirth leading to immortality is to be found in the Gettysburg Address, the best-known speech in American history, which, in three short paragraphs, has provided a sacramental rite for Lincoln's political religion. It is a sacrament which has been memorized by grammar school students for generations, and thus has become so familiar to most Americans that the words have lost their meaning:

> Four score and seven years ago our fathers brought forth on this continent, a new nation, conceived in Liberty, and dedicated to the proposition that all men are created equal.
>
> Now we are engaged in a great civil war, testing whether that nation, or any nation, so conceived and so dedicated, can long endure. We are met on a great battle-field of that war. We have come to dedicate a portion of that field, as a final resting place for those who here gave their lives that that nation might live. It is altogether fitting and proper that we should do this.
>
> But, in a larger sense, we can not dedicate—we can not consecrate—we can not hallow—this ground. The brave men, living and dead, who struggled here, have consecrated it far above our poor power to add or detract. The world will little note, nor long remember what we say here, but it can never forget what they did here. It is for us the living, rather, to be dedicated here to the unfinished work which they who fought here have thus far so nobly advanced. It is rather for us to be here dedicated to the great task remaining before us—that from these honored dead we take increased devotion to that cause for which they gave the last full measure of devotion—that we here highly resolve that these dead shall not have died in vain—that this nation, under God, shall have a new birth of freedom—and that government of the people, by the people and for the people, shall not perish from the earth.[127]

At first glance, perhaps the most startling aspect of the Address is that all traces of the Union of 1789 are absent. As was his custom, Lincoln marked the beginning of the nation in 1776. However, in view of the first Inaugural Address and the letter to Greeley the previous year ("I would save the Union. I would save it the shortest way under the Constitution. The sooner the national authority can be restored; the nearer the Union will be 'the Union as it was' "[128]), one might have expected him to say that the war involved a test of the Constitution's legitimacy. But no mention is made of either the Constitution or the Union. The Civil War was a test of whether this nation, or any nation born of revolution and dedicated to revolutionary ideals, could survive. The war was not merely an internecine conflict of local interest only, but a struggle involving universal consequences: world history, and especially the history of political revolution, awaited the outcome. By implication, those who died in the war were actors on a world stage: they gave up their lives so that the revolutionary idea might survive in the United States, thus proving its viability for the world.

The occasion for the speech was the dedication of a national cemetery at Gettysburg. According to Lincoln, no mere ceremonial dedication was adequate. The men who struggled there had already consecrated the ground by their unforgettable sacrifices for the preservation of the ideals of 1776. Thus the death and suffering of the Union forces were charged with the highest significance. By their reenactment of the sacrifices of 1776, their immortality was assured; at the same time, their noble action provided an inspiring example to others so that the nation might be founded anew, and its immortality assured also.

The speech represents a perfect synthesis of religious and secular themes. Spoken against the background of the commonly accepted interpretation of the war's meaning as divine punishment for the nation's sins, Lincoln offered an interpretation which promised atonement and deliverance from sin. No mention was made of slavery, but it was clear that the legacy of the fathers was twofold: not only the Edenic promise of 1776, but the fall into the sinfulness of slavery. Since "the wages of sin is death," the war (which Lincoln always regarded as having been caused by slavery) threatened to end the life of the nation, just as it actually inflicted death upon its citizens. But the sacrifices of those who were without sin themselves, who nobly gave up their lives that the nation might live, promised to redeem the sins of the fathers. By the common recognition of their sacrifice, which was secured by Lincoln himself at Gettysburg, a new spiritual community was created in which the nation might be reborn to a life everlasting. That Lincoln was Paul before he was Christ only helped to ensure that the meaning of his own death would be properly interpreted.

The idea that sacrifice and its immediate recognition were a source of community was highly reminiscent of a theme first developed in Lincoln's Lyceum Address. There he said that the meaning of the Revolution could be read in the "living histories" of sacrifice—in the scars of war received by loved ones—which were visible to all and understood by all. But these living histories which were once pillars in the temple of liberty had crumbled away, and the temple would fall unless resupplied with other pillars hewn from the quarry of sober reason. Thus the speech was prophetic of Lincoln's role at Gettysburg: his reason presided over events on the battlefield so as to transform death and destruction into symbols of immortality, thereby supplying new living histories that could readily be understood and shared by all.

This "little speech," as Lincoln called his remarks at Gettysburg, brings to mind another theme from the Lyceum Address. There he raised the question of whether new men of talent and ambition, who would inevitably come along after the Revolutionary generation, could gratify their ruling passions simply by supporting and maintaining an edifice erected by others. His answer was once again prophetic: most certainly they cannot. And once again it was Lincoln who fulfilled his own prophecy; for by appearing to defend and maintain the Union, he was actually transforming it. By doing so, he put himself in Washington's place as father of his country.

Lincoln was always careful to emulate the style of Washington, especially his modesty and humility. During his early years, he even modeled himself on the father of his country. On his way to Washington to assume the presidency, he used the first president as the standard by which he assessed the task that lay before him. Once in office, he invoked Washington's legacy as a source of authority. Yet after 1862, Lincoln made virtually no further references to Washington—although he was presented with several occasions which seemed to demand a *pro forma* bow in Washington's direction.[129] It was as if for Lincoln Washington had suddenly ceased to exist. And in a way he had: the proclamation of his birthday as a national day of celebration signified his apotheosis, and thus his removal from the seat of authority—a place thereafter to be occupied by Lincoln himself.

The Gettysburg Address illustrates the extent of Lincoln's triumph over Washington. In his Lyceum Address, he had called upon his fellow citizens to take up the pledge of 1776 in behalf of the Constitution and its laws: "As the patriots of seventy-six did to the support of the Declaration of Independence, so to the support of the Constitution and the laws, let every American pledge his life, his property, and his sacred honor. . . ." At Gettysburg, Lincoln provided the sacramental rite by which this could be accomplished without acknowledging any discrepancy between the Declaration and the Constitution. By interpreting the war as a reenactment or a continuation of the struggle of 1776, he transformed a dispute over the meaning of the Constitution into a redemptive and sacrificial act. And by calling upon the people to dedicate themselves to this struggle, he was in effect asking them to take the pledge of 1776 in behalf of the Constitution without seeming to do so. Lincoln even succeeded in removing himself from the scene altogether ("The world will little note, nor long remember what we say here . . .") so that his words would seem to have no influence on the meaning of events. In short, where Washington tried to establish the sanctity of the Constitution through direct exhortation, Lincoln, silently and obliquely, established the means by which its sanctity could be commonly recognized. And where Washington failed, Lincoln succeeded.

A similar conclusion is warranted in regard to another aspect of the nation's civic religion. The God of Washington was a shadowy presence to be brought out on ceremonial occasions, always useful, benevolent and reassuring in a fatherly manner, shaping events indirectly, but never really doing anything in an active way. By contrast, Lincoln's God was actively and intimately involved in the affairs of the nation, a constant and omnipotent presence, granting victory in a particular battle, displaying his wrath in palpable ways, at once fearsome and forgiving. Where Washington's God commanded respect, Lincoln's exacted reverence. For where Washington simply asserted that a providential hand directed the affairs of the nation, Lincoln supplied the explicit evidence of how the hand of God made its presence known—evidence convincing enough, it would seem, to make a believer out of Lincoln himself.

In replacing the God of Washington with his own, Lincoln also considerably enlarged America's mission in the world, at least by implication. As indicated in his Farewell Address, the significance for Washington of America's providential blessing was its uniqueness, which set the nation apart as a model to be emulated by the rest of the world. For Lincoln the atonement on the field of battle at Gettysburg had immediate worldwide implications: by saving the Union on the basis of the Declaration of Independence, Union soldiers were also saving the principle which gave "hope to the world for all future time," i.e., the "promise that in due time the weights should be lifted from the shoulders of all men." Of course Lincoln cannot be held personally accountable for the subsequent uses to which his refoundation of the republic were put. Nevertheless, for the next hundred years, a regenerate people, relieved of the original sin of slavery, went forth in the world, secure in the knowledge that there was no salvation outside the church, and proceeded to refound the Union again and again in the international sphere—in the League of Nations and United Nations, in Latin America, Europe, and Asia. By winning the war on the terms that he did, Lincoln not only proved that the Union had God on its side and that emancipation had divine sanction, but he provided the ideological rationale whereby the United States could become lawgiver to the world.

DEATH AND THE RESOLUTION OF GUILT

"Who is dead in the White House?" I demanded of one of the soldiers. "The President," was his answer; "he was killed by an assassin!"
—A. Lincoln, 1865

It is among the oldest mythical truths of Western civilization that he who challenges the gods, or attempts to become as a god himself, must suffer a terrible penalty. Adam's crime against God was not merely disobedience, but eating of the tree of the knowledge of good and evil. "For God doth know that in the day ye eat thereof, then your eyes shall be opened, and ye shall be as gods, knowing good and evil." And to be as gods is to become immortal: "Behold, the man is become as one of us to know good and evil: and now, lest he put forth his hand, and take also of the tree of life, and eat, and live for ever . . .", he must be cast out of Eden.

Lincoln was well aware of the significance of this mythology. In

1854 Douglas, not always a stickler for details, suggested that popular sovereignty originated when God placed good and evil before man, asking him to choose for himself. Lincoln responded by saying that "God did not place good and evil before man, telling him to make his choice. On the contrary, he did tell him there was one tree, of the fruit of which, he should not eat, upon pain of certain death."[130] As the Lyceum Address attests, Lincoln had eaten of the forbidden fruit; and even beyond that, as his subsequent career reveals, he sought to take also from the tree of life. By attributing his wisdom to the gods, he had become as a god himself; by taking the sins of the people upon himself, and giving them in return a means of salvation, only he had to live with the knowledge of good and evil—only he knew the burdens of guilt. And by acting on his motive of revenge against constitutional fathers for having preempted the field of glory, Lincoln had become the very tyrant against whom Washington had warned in his Farewell Address, a tyrant who would preside over the destruction of the Constitution in order to gratify his own ambition. In understanding the ultimate consequences of hubris, had Lincoln also anticipated the desolation that earthly penalties might impose?

In late March 1865, with Lee's army on the verge of collapse, Grant invited Lincoln to visit his headquarters. Exhausted from previous weeks of work, which included guiding the passage of the Thirteenth Amendment through Congress, Lincoln accepted. As he anxiously awaited the news of Lee's surrender, he was joined by a party that included his wife and son, and, at his wife's invitation, a young French aristocrat. The party embarked on a tour of Richmond and Petersburg and, along the way, Confederate military prisons and Union hospital camps. When word arrived that Seward had suffered severe injuries in a carriage mishap, Lincoln started his return to Washington at once. Back on board the presidential yacht, Lincoln's mood of animated excitement of the previous days, as recorded by the Frenchman, Adolphe de Chambrun, gave way to somber reflection and meditation:

> At ten o'clock our boat steamed off. Mr. Lincoln stood a long while gazing at the hills, so animated a few days before, now dark and silent. Around us more than a hundred ships at anchor gave visible

proof of the country's maritime strength and testified to the great
tasks accomplished.

Mr. Lincoln remained absorbed in thought and pursued his
meditation long after the quickened speed had removed the lugu-
brious scene forever from our sight. [131]

A few days earlier, the evidence of what had been accomplished
was of a different sort. The Marquis de Chambrun's firsthand
account of the tour by the Lincoln party painted a picture of
destruction, carnage, hunger, and misery that was unrelieved but
for the enthusiastic greeting Lincoln received from the Negroes of
Richmond. The center of Richmond lay in complete devastation.
The people were without food, except for that provided by Union
forces. Military prisons bore unmistakable evidence of how Union
prisoners had suffered. On the trip to Petersburg, the president's
train passed by Fort Stedman, where a few days before heavy
fighting had produced 5,000 casualties. The following day, hospital camps were inspected. "God only knows all its horrors," said
de Chambrun of this review. "We passed before all the wounded
and amputated. Some had a leg cut off, some an arm. Amid this
terrible mass of agony, not a cry nor a complaint." When they
asked how the war was progressing, the president replied: "Success all along the line."[132]

As the *River Queen* steamed for Washington, D.C., Lincoln was
absorbed in dark and silent meditation. But it was not the hundred
Union ships at anchor—symbolic of his military success—which
attracted his attention, as the marquis himself acknowledged by
noting that Lincoln remained in thought long after the ships had
passed from view. His was not the meditation of the triumphant
warrior. "What I deal with is too vast for malicious dealing," he
had told an associate a few years before.[133] At Libby Prison in
Richmond, when he heard an officer who was indignant at the
apparent mistreatment of Union prisoners exclaim that Jefferson
Davis should be hanged, Lincoln replied: "Judge not, that ye be
not judged."[134] He repeated the same biblical injunction several
times upon his return to Washington when confronted with similar
views on the proper punishment for Confederate leaders. On
these occasions, however, he was said to have used the more expli-

cit pronouns employed in his second Inaugural Address: "Let us judge not that we be not judged."[135]

Headed up the Potomac for the Capitol, when conversation turned to literary subjects, Lincoln revealed something of his introspective musing, as he read aloud to the ship's company for several hours. According to de Chambrun, most of the passages he selected were from Shakespeare, especially *Macbeth.* The president had long been an admirer of this particular tragedy; telegraph operators in the War Department often noticed him carrying a worn copy of the play, and he had written to actor James Hackett in 1863, "I think nothing equals Macbeth."[136] Thus his selection of reading was not fortuitous; and, given his familiarity with the drama, neither was his choice of a particular passage for recital: "The lines after the murder of Duncan, when the new king falls a prey to moral torment, were dramatically dwelt on. Now and then he paused to expatiate on how exact a picture Shakespeare here gives of a murderer's mind when, the dark deed achieved, its perpetrator already envies his victim's calm sleep. He read the scene over twice."[137] In not judging others that he be not judged, Lincoln was offering a judgment on himself.

The scene to which de Chambrun referred opens with Lady Macbeth telling her husband not to worry himself: "Things without all remedy/ Should be without regard. What's done is done." Macbeth replies:

> We have scotch'd the snake, not killed it;
> She'll close, and be herself, whilst our poor malice
> Remains in danger of her former tooth.
> But let the frame of things disjoint, both the worlds suffer,
> Ere we will eat our meal in fear and sleep
> In the affliction of these terrible dreams
> That shake us nightly. Better be with the dead,
> Whom we, to gain our peace, have sent to peace,
> Than on the torture of the mind to lie
> In restless ecstasy.[138]

Many observers, taking note of this incident aboard the *River Queen,* have cited only the remaining portion of the speech ("Duncan is in his grave;/ After life's fitful fever he sleeps well;/ Treason has done his worst; nor steel, nor poison,/ Malice domestic, foreign levy, nothing,/ Can touch him further"), implying that somehow the South represented Macbeth in Lincoln's mind. One writer even has suggested that this reading from *Macbeth* reflected Lincoln's peace of mind: "More and more, with peace assured, his thoughts had turned to tranquil themes."[139] Such interpretations make no sense at all. Lincoln, it can be argued, had his Duncan in George Washington, but the Confederacy as Macbeth would be plausible only if the South had won the war; and there was certainly nothing tranquil about the theme of Macbeth's speech. If anything, because of the identification suggested here by Lincoln himself, the parallels between Lincoln and Macbeth are too easily drawn: both were complex and fascinating characters, capable of great goodness but driven by ambition to defy the gods; men entrapped by "necessity" in a process of violence, but who had the intelligence and sensitivity to foresee the consequences of their acts, and accepted the burdens of guilt and remorse that lesser men might have ignored. At the very least, Lincoln, like Macbeth, lived in restless ecstasy, shaken often, if not nightly, by the affliction of these terrible dreams.

A few days before the assassination, as recorded by his personal aide, Ward Hill Lamon, Lincoln told of having a dream which, he said, "has got possession of me, and, like Banquo's ghost, it will not down." In the dream, Lincoln heard "subdued sobs" downstairs in the White House, as if a number of people were weeping. He left his bed and went from room to room in search of the mourners, but saw no one until entering the East Room.

> There I met with a sickening surprise. Before me was a catafalque, on which rested a corpse wrapped in funeral vestments. Around it were stationed soldiers who were acting as guards; and there was a throng of people, some gazing mournfully upon the corpse, whose face was covered, others weeping pitifully. "Who is dead in the White House?" I demanded of one of the soldiers. "The President," was his answer; "he was killed by an assassin!"[140]

Lincoln's observers have assumed that this dream presaged his own death by assassination.[141] The dream, however, did not reveal the identity of the dead president, and, as Lamon recorded it,

Lincoln said the face of the corpse was covered. Moreover, Lincoln himself seemed specifically to rule out the possibility that he was the dead president by later telling Lamon, who was distressed by the President's disregard for his own safety,

> For a long time you have been trying to keep somebody—the Lord knows who—from killing me. Don't you see how it will turn out? In this dream it was not me, but some other fellow, that was killed. It seems that this ghostly assassin tried his hand on some one else.[142]

If not Lincoln, who was the dead president? The only other possibility suggested by the contextual evidence is that the president of Lincoln's dream was Washington, and Lincoln his ghostly assassin.

Lincoln's assertion that this dream haunted him "like Banquo's ghost" points to this conclusion. Banquo and Macbeth had been fellow generals in Duncan's army. Upon hearing of Duncan's murder, Banquo, secure in the knowledge of his own innocence and honor, says, "In the great hand of God I stand, and thence/ Against the undivulged pretence I fight/ Of treasonous malice." Macbeth, by contrast, is tormented in part because the witches who have foretold his kingship have also prophesied that Banquo's children, rather than Macbeth's, will inherit the throne. Banquo suspects that Macbeth has "play'dst most foully" for the crown, but is murdered by Macbeth's hired assassins before he can accuse Macbeth, and returns as a ghost to sit in the king's place at Macbeth's table. Staring at the silent ghost, Macbeth says, "Thou canst not say I did it; never shake/ Thy gory locks at me. . . ." Then he adds: "If . . . our graves must send/ Those that we bury back, our monuments/ Shall be the maws of kites," meaning they shall be devoured and destroyed. After the ghost and the bewildered dinner guests have left, Macbeth says of his uninvited guest, "It will have blood; they say blood will have blood."[143]

There are several intriguing aspects to Lincoln's statement that his dream of the dead president haunted him like Banquo's ghost. First of all, there is the obvious similarity between Duncan and Washington. When Macbeth is contemplating the assassination of Duncan, he considers the reasons for not going through with it. He is, after all, both Duncan's kinsman and his subject. "Besides,"

Macbeth says, "this Duncan/ Hath borne his faculties so meek, hath been/ So clear in his great office, that his virtues/ Will plead like angels. . . . And pity . . . Shall blow the horrid deed in every eye,/ That tears shall drown the wind." By comparison, Macbeth has only his "Vaulting ambition" to sustain him. Secondly, there is the inescapable implication of guilt in Lincoln's statement: by his silent accusation, Banquo reminds Macbeth of his guilt, indeed, was the ghostly personification of it. In terms of understanding Lincoln's anxieties, more importantly, Banquo is also a reminder of the witches' prophecy that it is Banquo's paternal authority, rather than Macbeth's, which is to be perpetuated. But if Lincoln, like Macbeth, feared that the monuments created by his bloody hand would not last, his anxieties must have been calmed somewhat by the other literary reference he recalled as he told about the dream of the dead president: the biblical story of Jacob's dream.

In telling Lamon and others about his dream, Lincoln said, "After it occurred, the first time I opened the Bible, strange as it may appear, it was at the twenty-eighth chapter of Genesis, which relates the wonderful dream Jacob had."[144] The wonder of Jacob's dream was that the God of Abraham and Isaac appeared to him in it and promised that Jacob's paternal line would be extended and blessed, even though he was not the legitimate heir. Born holding onto Esau's heel, Jacob had forced Esau to relinquish to him his birthright as the firstborn son, and succeeded in deceiving their father, Isaac, so that the father's blessing, rightfully Esau's, was given to Jacob instead. Jacob's dream held out the promise of immortality to Jacob and his descendants, even though Jacob lived in fear that Esau would someday seek his revenge.[145]

A thematic link between Banquo's ghost and Jacob's dream is provided not simply by guilt over acts of usurpation, but also by anxiety about legitimacy and fear that symbols of immortality might be destroyed. It was a theme which Lincoln well understood. If he could view himself as Macbeth, tortured by guilt for his crimes, he could also recall himself as Banquo, the loyal and virtuous subject. If he could conceive of himself as Jacob, the unscrupulous pretender, he could also imagine himself as Esau, the firstborn and legitimate heir. In other words, if he could see himself as his own Washington, the revolutionary son, he could also recollect his identity as Weems's Washington, upholder of virtue and constitutional order. It was the ghost of Weems's Washington who now occupied the presidential chair and who worried that his immortality might yet elude him.

This theme is also found in a recurrent dream which Lincoln had throughout his presidency, and in the hallucination, previously mentioned, which he experienced in 1860. In the latter, he saw a double image of himself reflected in a mirror. One image was lifelike, the other showed a "ghostly paleness." Lincoln had interpreted this illusion as a sign that he would be reelected, but not live to complete his second term.[146] Although it is hard to dispute the accuracy of his interpretation, it is noteworthy that these double images of himself also correspond to the two identities of Lincoln's political career. In this sense, the illusion was a striking reflection of a man divided, torn by conflicting obligations to the Declaration of Independence and the Constitution, but resolved to become the instrument of national salvation, and willing to give up his life, if necessary, to achieve that end. That his success would require the relinquishment of Weems's model he knew in advance; that it would also require his own death he had a constant foreboding.

Lincoln's recurrent dream during his presidential years, as he told his cabinet and it was reported by Gideon Welles, had him "in some singular, indescribable vessel," "moving with great rapidity towards an indefinite shore."[147] Lincoln said he had this dream "preceding nearly every great and important event of the War," and it seemed to presage military success because it had occurred just before several important Union victories. A slightly different version of the same dream was recounted by Lamon: "In this dream he saw a ship sailing away rapidly, badly damaged, and our victorious vessels in close pursuit."[148] The differences between these two accounts serve as a reminder of the metaphor Lincoln used to depict the relationship between the Constitution and the Declaration of Independence just prior to his first inauguration. At New York he said that he understood "a ship [the Constitution] to be made for the carrying and preservation of the cargo [liberty], and so long as the ship can be saved, with this cargo, it should never be abandoned."[149] Lincoln had not only saved the ship, and the cargo too, but saved it so as to make it forever worthy of the saving. And in his dream, this ship of state, with which he had merged his personal identity, was pictured especially in conjunction with anticipated military success, as carrying him rapidly toward some indefinite shore.

The ominous uncertainty of the ship's destination seems to suggest that in Lincoln's mind the military victory for which he so ardently wished was inseparably linked to the imminence of his own death. On the night before he was assassinated, as he anxiously awaited news of Johnston's surrender to Sherman, he dreamed once again of a ship on its way to an uncertain destination. A few nights before, he had dreamed of the dead president. It cannot be known for sure whether such dreams were the cause of Lincoln's insomnia, but he did often take outings alone in the middle of the night; and by his adamant refusal to accept the protection of bodyguards, he left himself open to the presumption, just as certainly as he invited an assassin's bullet, that here too the dream was the wish, that he, like Macbeth, also envied the victim's calm sleep.[150]

De Chambrun's account of Lincoln's reading from Shakespeare that day on the Potomac does not reveal what other passages he selected for recital. Perhaps among them, however, was the soliloquy by Claudius in *Hamlet* which, as Lincoln also said in his letter to actor Hackett, he thought surpassed the soliloquy by Hamlet beginning "To be or not to be . . ." In any case, it is not difficult to understand why Lincoln found Claudius's speech more compelling than Hamlet's; for where Hamlet rationally weighs the known burdens of living against the uncertain fate which lies beyond the grave, Claudius (like Macbeth) cries out in anguish born of a living hell in which there is no possible reprieve or respite:

> O, my offence is rank, it smells to heaven;
> It hath the primal eldest curse upon 't—
> A brother's murder! Pray can I not,
> Though inclination be as sharp as will.
> My stronger guilt defeats my strong intent,

And, like a man to double business bound,
I stand in pause where I shall first begin,
And both neglect. What if this cursed hand
Were thicker than itself with brother's blood,
Is there not rain enough in the sweet heavens
To wash it white as snow? Whereto serves mercy
But to confront the visage of offence?
And what's in prayer but this twofold force,
To be forestalled ere we come to fall,
Or pardon'd being down? Then I'll look up;
My fault is past. But, O, what form of prayer
Can serve my turn? "Forgive me my foul murder!"
That cannot be; since I am still possess'd
Of those effects for which I did the murder—
My crown, mine own ambition, and my queen.[151]

Apparently in a similar vein, Lincoln once said to Noah Brooks, "I have been driven many times upon my knees by the overwhelming conviction that I had nowhere else to go."[152]

Perhaps also among the selections for Lincoln's recital was the opening of *Richard III,* which he believed was often misunderstood by actors. As he once told the portraitist F. B. Carpenter, Richard was "plotting the destruction of his brothers, to make room for himself. Outwardly, the most loyal to the newly crowned king, secretly he could scarcely contain his impatience at the obstacles still in the way of his own elevation. He appears upon the stage, just after the crowning of Edward, burning with repressed hate and jealousy. The prologue is the utterance of the most intense bitterness and satire."[153] Following this exegesis, according to Carpenter, Lincoln then recited from memory Richard's opening soliloquy ("Now is the winter of our discontent . . .") with a degree of force and power which made the passage seem like a new creation to him.

Like Macbeth, the unscrupulous usurper Richard suffers from an incapacity to sleep; like Macbeth, he too is visited by visions, haunted by prophecies, consumed by ambition. Yet the anguish which Lincoln experienced as a result of waging fratricidal war in order to achieve his own "elevation" was far more complex than

these literary analogues would suggest. De Chambrun said that
after passing a length of time with Lincoln ". . . you were left with
a profound impression of poignant sadness," but that he was also
"extremely humorous":

> He willingly laughed either at what was being said or at what he
> himself was saying. Then, suddenly, he would retire into himself
> and close his eyes, while his face expressed a melancholy as inde-
> scribable as it was deep. After a few moments, as though by an
> effort of the will, he would shake off this mysterious weight and his
> generous and open disposition again reasserted itself.

In a single evening, said de Chambrun, he counted more than
twenty such alternations of mood.[154]

The lability of Lincoln's moods was invariably noted by visitors
to the White House, who were impressed with how readily his
melancholia, depression, or abstraction, as it was variously called,
gave way to manic outbursts of hilarity, humor, and storytelling.
Lincoln could be moved to tears by a frivolous romantic ballad
sung for him by Lamon, but a few minutes later be heard laughing
uproariously over a minstrel tune. He could be seen with tears
running down his cheeks while talking with a group of angry Mis-
sourians who told him that, as a consequence of their returning
home, their "blood will be on your garments"; yet a few moments
later, be seen exchanging pleasantries and engaging in "hearty
laughter" with associates. "This rapid and wonderful transition
from one extreme to the other impressed me greatly," said one
observer.[155]

Others were not so impressed. Many leading politicians, including members of his cabinet, despised Lincoln's jokes and stories; he was widely condemned for them in the press, and by 1863,
there were several Lincoln joke books available—one was entitled
Old Abe's Jokes—Fresh from Abraham's Bosom. From abroad, Lincoln
was characterized as First Magistrate and "Chief Joker of the
land."[156] Apparently Lincoln, who had used humor earlier in his
career to control his "malignant passions" of hate and revenge,
now as president employed it to mitigate the effects of having
acted upon such passions. Jokes provided a momentary relief from
the agonies of guilt and self-hatred. Lincoln seemed to make this

point on one occasion when he faced a congressman who was determined not to be put off with another anecdote. As Lincoln began to launch himself into a story, the congressman, rising to his feet, said, "Mr. President, I beg your pardon, but I didn't come this morning to hear a story." Lincoln replied: "I know how sincere you are. But if I couldn't tell these stories, I would die. Now, you sit down!" A similar conclusion was reached by Charles A. Dana in rebuking Secretary Stanton for his indignation at Lincoln's jokes. Referring to Stanton, Dana said: "He could not understand . . . that it was by the relief which these jests afforded to the strain of mind under which Lincoln had so long been living, and to the natural gloom of a melancholy and desponding temperament . . . that the safety and sanity of his intelligence were maintained and preserved."[157]

Lincoln's moods and mood changes also reflected a pattern of behavior that he had exhibited following his broken engagement to Mary Todd and his political disappointments in 1849. Associates found him to be depressed and even suicidal, but also given to outbursts of hilarity. During these periods, his behavior seemed to reflect an unresolved—perhaps unresolvable—contradiction in his attitude about death. Lincoln found the actuality of death to be intolerable. Words provided him with a way of denying the reality of death; his early poetry sublimated actual death into symbols of immortality and transformed the deadly conditions of actual social life into an Elysian community. In the process of symbolically transcending death, his words also inevitably celebrated it; the precondition of immortality is, after all, actual death. Verbal abstractions—jokes, poetry, speeches—could provide momentary relief from his anxiety, but when faced with actual prospects of death—his own political death in 1849 or his apparent fear in 1841 that he could love Mary only if she were dead—he became inconsolable. Love and death were inextricably linked in his words, implicitly expressing even a love of death, and for him that created intolerable anguish.

This anguish was horribly exaggerated by Lincoln's failure to get the short and decisive war he wanted. On the train to Gettysburg, Lincoln was quoted as telling a man whose son had died in the battle, "When I think of the sacrifice of life yet to be offered, and the hearts and homes yet to be made desolate before this dreadful war is over, my heart is like lead within me, and I feel at times like hiding in deep darkness."[158] Similarly, in 1864, his annual message to Congress proudly reported that ". . . we do not approach exhaustion in the most important branch of national resources—that of living men." The Union, he said, had "more men now than before the war began, and may, if need be, maintain the contest indefinitely." Yet a few months before, when faced with the thousands of casualties in the battles of the Wilderness, he cried, "My God! my God! I cannot bear it. I cannot bear it."[159] Again, when reviewing a number of death penalties for deserters, Lincoln could be coldly dispassionate, saying on one occasion that he would decide whether a "soldier can better serve the country dead than living"; yet he usually found some basis, often rather spurious, for granting a pardon. "Voorhees," Lincoln once said to the Indiana congressman, "doesn't it seem strange that I should be here—I, a man who couldn't cut a chicken's head off—with blood running all around me?"[160]

The miracles which Lincoln effected with his words may have offered meaningful solace to much of the nation, but they had no saving grace for him. He was not a believer in his own religion; he remained beyond the pale of his own church, inconsolable, and utterly alone in his desolation. Thus if Lincoln thought he could find dramatic analogues for himself in the tortured plight of a Claudius, a Richard, or a Macbeth, in many ways he far exceeded each of them as a tragic figure. We can only assume that Macbeth's had been a noble nature; he has surrendered his soul before the play begins. Richard's villainy is relieved only by his wit and brilliance, and Claudius hardly qualifies as a tragic character at all. By comparison, Lincoln not only played out his drama on a much grander scale, but in occupying himself with the happiness of men, presented himself as a Promethean hero larger than literature. By combining pity for all men with compassion for the guilty, he transformed his own guilt into a doctrine by which all might be forgiven: it was as if in the dark prison of Lincoln's soul the Grand Inquisitor and Jesus had met and effected their momentary reconciliation.[161]

The second Inaugural Address represents Lincoln's most com-

plete attempt at resolving the problem of his guilt. Much of the
address may be read as a direct response to his "Meditation on the
Divine Will" of 1862 in which he had struggled with the presumptuousness of his self-defined role as divine instrument:

> Neither party expected for the war, the magnitude, or the dura-
> tion, which it has already attained. Neither anticipated that the
> *cause* of the conflict might cease with or even before, the conflict
> itself should cease. Each looked for an easier triumph, and a result
> less fundamental and astounding. Both read the same Bible, and
> pray to the same God; and each invokes His aid against the other.
> It may seem strange that any men should dare to ask a just God's
> assistance in wringing their bread from the sweat of other men's
> faces; but let us judge not that we be not judged. The prayers of
> both could not be answered; that of neither has been answered
> fully. The Almighty has His own purposes.[162]

Thus did Lincoln publicly and formally, in the national ceremony of religious affirmation, acknowledge God's independent
existence. With the war virtually at its end, it at least ensured that
the God who awarded victory to the Union would not be traceable
to Lincoln's personal authorship. Privately he seemed to admit
that such an acknowledgment involved a degree of personal penitence. He wrote Thurlow Weed that he did not expect the speech
to be immediately popular: "Men are not flattered by being shown
that there has been a difference of purpose between the Almighty
and them. To deny it, however, in this case, is to deny that there
is a God governing the world. It is a truth which I thought needed
to be told; and as whatever of humiliation there is in it, falls most
directly on myself, I thought others might afford for me to tell
it."[163] The humiliation which fell directly upon Lincoln was a
result of his hubris four years earlier in claiming for himself the
status of divine spokesman. However, the remainder of the speech
suggests that Lincoln's pride now reached still greater heights:

> "Woe unto the world because of offences! for it must needs be that
> offences come; but woe to that man by whom the offence cometh!"
> If we shall suppose that American slavery is one of those offences
> which, in the providence of God, must needs come, but which,
> having continued through His appointed time, He now wills to

remove, and that he gives to both North and South, this terrible
war, as the woe due to those by whom the offence came, shall we
discern therein any departure from those divine attributes which
the believers in a Living God always ascribe to Him?[164]

Here Lincoln appears to have been simply reiterating the view
that the war was divine punishment for the national sin of slavery.
But the skeptical manner in which he phrased it, by employing a
conditional interrogative and by not explicitly counting himself
among the believers in a "Living God," suggests that his earlier
"humiliation" cannot be taken literally. He once told a group of
supporters, "I am very little inclined on any occasion to say anything unless I hope to produce some good by it."[165] Perhaps the
idea that the Almighty has His own purposes, which he thought
was a truth that "needed to be told," was uttered out of a similar
inclination. In any case, if slavery was just one of the offenses which
must needs come, were there other offenses too for which woe was
due?

The biblical context from which Lincoln selected this quotation
(Matthew 18:7) suggests a likely possibility. The chapter begins
with the disciples asking Jesus who is the greatest in the kingdom
of heaven. He replies by calling a child into their midst, saying,
"Except ye be converted, and become as little children, ye shall not
enter into the kingdom of heaven. Whosoever therefore shall humble himself as this little child, the same is greatest in the kingdom
of heaven." Then Jesus adds, "But whoso shall offend one of these
little ones which believe in me, it were better for him that a mill-
stone were hanged about his neck, and that he were drowned in
the depth of the sea." Thus the woe due the world, to which Jesus
refers in the next line, is for the offense of pride; the woe due "that
man by whom the offence cometh" is death for vitiating the humility and innocence of childlike belief. Perhaps by invoking the Gospel according to St. Matthew, Lincoln wished to signal the recantation of his former pride; yet by repeating the words of Jesus in this
context, he was also adopting for himself the role of Christ: "For
the Son of man is come to save that which was lost" (Matthew
18:11). He combined in one person what Dostoevsky separated

into two characters: Lincoln as redeemer was the one most guilty of offenses.

It was with "malice toward none and charity for all" that Lincoln proposed to bring the war on heresy and hypocrisy to an end. He proposed to end it, as he told Stanton in 1864, by the "'Christian principle of forgiveness on terms of repentance."[166] He proposed amnesty for those people of the Confederacy who would voluntarily take an oath before God to support and defend the Constitution and its laws, clemency for their civil and military officers, pardon for deserters.[167] But Lincoln's restatement of the Sermon on the Mount at the close of his Inaugural Address was not simply an act of contrition. While undoubtedly that man who shoulders the burden of a nation's guilt can appreciate more readily than most the importance of forgiveness, Lincoln seems to have known all along that for him there could be no reprieve or salvation. Yet, consummate dramatist that he was, he could at least set the stage for the final scene of the last act so that his greatest gesture of cosmic defiance, casting himself in the role of Christ, would be properly interpreted.

On Good Friday of 1865 in Ford's Theatre, Lincoln was shot by the actor John Wilkes Booth. Overshadowed by his more illustrious father and brother, the actors Junius Brutus and Edwin Booth, and dogged by his own mediocre career, he was reported to have told friends in 1863, "What a glorious opportunity there is for a man to immortalize himself by killing Lincoln!" A year later, on the occasion of his last regular stage appearance, he again reputedly said that the man who killed Lincoln would occupy a higher niche in fame than George Washington.[168] Booth won his immortality, all right; he did so by guaranteeing Lincoln his. By his death, Lincoln became the savior of the republic, the one who, by his sacrifice and atonement, redeemed the sins of the fathers and gave to the nation a new life, a life everlasting. Booth's self-justification was one Lincoln could have understood. "Our country owed all her troubles to him," wrote Booth in his diary, "and God simply made me the instrument of his punishment."[169]

4

Lincoln's Legacy:
Myth of the Eternal Return

REENACTMENT AND REFOUNDATION

We Americans are the children of the crucible.
—Theodore Roosevelt, 1917

The crowd gathered on a cold January afternoon in front of the Capitol for the inauguration of the thirty-fifth President was warmed by the eloquent rhetoric of his address. John F. Kennedy, whose personal appeal, according to the first chronicler of his presidency, lay in "the hope that he could redeem American politics by releasing American life from its various bondages to orthodoxy,"[1] spoke of rebirth and new beginnings. Yet Kennedy's remarks, delivered (but for the Twentieth Amendment) on the hundredth anniversary of Lincoln's first inauguration, were less a departure from orthodoxy than a particularly lucid rendering of it. They contained all the elements of Lincoln's political religion, stamped with a high style worthy of its founder.

Noting that the same revolutionary beliefs for which the nation's forebears fought are still at issue around the globe, i.e., "the belief that the rights of man come not from the generosity of the state but from the hand of God," Kennedy said:

> We dare not forget today that we are the heirs of that first revolution. Let the word go forth from this time and place, to friend and foe alike, that the torch has been passed to a new generation of Americans—born in this century, tempered by war, disciplined by a hard and bitter peace, proud of our ancient heritage—and unwilling to witness or permit the slow undoing of those human

rights to which this Nation has always been committed, and to which we are committed today at home and around the world.

Let every nation know, whether it wishes us well or ill, that we shall pay any price, bear any burden, meet any hardship, support any friend, oppose any foe to assure the survival and success of liberty.[2]

Here was a statement of national purpose which apparently was completely out of touch with the instrumental temper of modern technological society. Here was an expression of an old American absolutism in an age when ideology had allegedly come to an end. Perhaps for this reason it can be dismissed as just so much ceremonial cant. Yet if the science of society teaches anything, it is that the observer dismisses "mere" ritual only at his own peril; he ignores the probability that what is done consciously and rationally corresponds to something done unconsciously and irrationally, and that what is done repeatedly fuses concept and emotion into a communal meaning.

Kennedy's speech concluded as it began, with the invocation of a familiar theme:

In your hands, my fellow citizens, more than in mine, will rest the final success or failure of our course. Since this country was founded, each generation of Americans has been summoned to give testimony to its national loyalty. The graves of young Americans who answered the call to service surround the globe.

Now the trumpet summons us again . . . [to] a struggle against the common enemies of man: tyranny, poverty, disease and war itself.

Can we forge against these enemies a grand and global alliance, North and South, East and West, that can assure a more fruitful life for all mankind?

In the long history of the world, only a few generations have been granted the role of defending freedom in its hour of maximum danger. I do not shrink from this responsibility—I welcome it. . . . The energy, the faith, the devotion which we bring to this endeavor will light our country and all who serve it—and the glow from that fire can truly light the world.

And so, my fellow Americans: Ask not what your country can do for you—ask what you can do for your country.

My fellow citizens of the world, ask not what America will do
for you, but what together we can do for the freedom of man.[3]

The evidence that this was a restatement of Lincoln's political
religion does not rest only on Kennedy's call for renewed sacrifice
and devotion to the cause of freedom. It rests primarily on the fact
that for Kennedy the universality of America's mission in the world
may be simply taken for granted; it rests on his assumption that the
proof of each generation's national loyalty can be found in graves
around the world—the evidence of repeated sacrifice for the cause
of freedom. Moreover, the assumption that America's cause is the
cause of all mankind implicitly provides the rationale for the
Americanization of the world: the grand and global alliance of
North and South, East and West, is but the Union writ large and
extended to its ultimate earthly conclusion.[4]

This could be seen especially in Kennedy's reference, earlier in
the speech, to the United Nations as "our last best hope." What
for Jefferson was the world's "best hope" and for Lincoln the "last
best hope of earth" was now projected outward into the international sphere and expanded considerably. External expansion had
always been the characteristic substitute for internal renewal of
authority in the United States. The problem for Kennedy was that
according to the revised lexicon of the twentieth century, the new
union was a house divided against itself, half slave and half free.
Thus his conciliatory plea: "Let both sides unite to heed in all
corners of the earth the command of Isaiah—to 'undo the heavy
burdens . . . [and] let the oppressed go free.' " But thus also the
warning: let every nation know well that we would pay any price
to assure the survival and success of liberty.

This idea was expressed even more clearly a year later. Speaking from Independence Hall in Philadelphia on July 4, Kennedy
recalled that Hamilton, in urging the adoption of the Constitution,
had told his fellow New Yorkers to "think continentally."
"Today," said Kennedy, "Americans must learn to think intercon-
tinentally." By ourselves, he went on to say, we could not establish
justice throughout the world. "We cannot insure its domestic tran-
quillity, or provide for its common defense, or promote its general
welfare, or secure the blessings of liberty to ourselves and our

posterity. But joined with other free nations, we can do all this and more." Calling for the formation of a "more perfect union" with European allies, Kennedy said such a union "would serve as a nucleus for the eventual union of all free men, those who are now free and those who are avowing that someday they will be free." He ended the speech by quoting from Lincoln's 1861 remarks in Independence Hall, saying we "declare now our vow to do our part to lift the weights from the shoulders of all, to join other men and nations in preserving both peace and freedom. . . . 'And for the support of this Declaration, with a firm reliance on the Protection of Divine Providence, we mutually pledge to each other our lives, our Fortunes, and our sacred Honor.' "[5] Lincoln's refoundation of the Union was to be repeated in the international realm. Yet for all its cleverness, the speech probably revealed more than Kennedy intended: he would not be content simply to add to the monuments of fame erected by others; a new constitutional edifice had to be constructed which perfected the Union of 1865 still further by expanding it.

But the torch which was passed to a new generation of presidents—the first generation born in the twentieth century—did not come directly from Lincoln himself. The "sacred fire of liberty" which for Washington (in his first Inaugural Address) would illuminate only a small portion of the earth, and which by Kennedy's time had grown large enough to light the world, came most directly from flames tended by his twentieth-century predecessors: Theodore Roosevelt, Woodrow Wilson, Franklin Delano Roosevelt. But in the rarefied liturgy of the American presidency, the torch which was passed to a new generation of incumbents was kindled from flames maintained by an earlier generation and derived from the fiery trial of the Civil War. Both the first Roosevelt and Wilson, whatever their theological differences, defined their presidential purposes in Lincolnian terms, and the later Roosevelt took his presidential bearings from the legacy provided by his fallen chief, Woodrow Wilson.

"We Americans," declared Theodore Roosevelt in 1917, "are the children of the crucible."[6] What he meant was that Americans were products of the Revolution and Civil War, which in turn required, as he said as president, that " . . . we treat Americanism primarily as a matter of spirit and purpose. . . ."[7] In rallying his fellow citizens to support President Wilson's war to end all wars, he called upon the exemplary responses of Washington and Lincoln to that "crucible" as a model for his generation. "Whoever . . . attacks conscription and the draft or fails to uphold universal, obligatory, military service, is false to the teachings and lives of Washington and Lincoln." "[*T*]*hey* did not 'keep us out of war,' " Roosevelt reminded Wilson's disillusioned supporters, and the pacifist "who exalts peace above righteousness, is not only a traitor to the memory of the two greatest Americans, but has no claim to have any part . . . in the nation which one founded and the other preserved." "Let us to-day do as they did and practice what they preached," he pleaded; "let us pay with our bodies for our souls' desire!"[8]

As president, Roosevelt's soul's desire was to save a portion of the world from what he called savagery and barbarism by extending the redemptive influence of American political institutions to the Far East and Latin America. He took his authority for this enterprise directly from the "crucible" of the Civil War. Addressing war veterans on Memorial Day in 1902, Roosevelt said the occasion was a reminder of the sacrifices of those "who wagered all that life holds dear for the great prize of death in battle, who poured out their blood like water in order that the mighty national structure . . . should not crumble into meaningless ruins." It was on the success of these efforts, he said, that depended "all the future of the people on this continent, and much of the future of mankind as a whole." Thus the legacy of the Civil War was not only a reunited country and the "right of brotherhood with the men in gray"; it was also the "memory of how it was achieved." The soldiers who made good the statesmanship of Lincoln by their sacrifices, he said, had set "the standard for our efforts in the future." And for Roosevelt, the future was immediately upon him. At that very moment, he said, the U.S. army was "carrying to completion a small but peculiarly trying and difficult war in which is involved not only the honor of the flag but the triumph of civilization over forces which stand for the black chaos of savagery and barbarism."[9]

Roosevelt took his justification for pacification of the Philippines from the symbols of Civil War mythology. He responded to charges of American atrocities by reminding his listeners that similar charges had been made in the 1860s: General Grant had been called a "butcher" and Lincoln had been singled out for attack "because of his 'spirit of barbarous ferocity.'" In both periods, however, those who would attack the military were blind to the "great work of peace and freedom" being accomplished. Victory by U.S. forces, he said, was the only way of bringing cruelty to an end; for where victory has been complete, " . . . all cruelties have ceased, and the native [Filipino] is secure in his life, his liberty, and his pursuit of happiness." Moreover, the attempt to extend American influence to the shores of Asia, he argued, "should be no more a party question than the war for the Union should have been a party question." For the two highest-ranking officers in the Philippines served on opposing sides in the Civil War, but were now working together "for the welfare of the inhabitants of the Philippine Islands."[10]

If Roosevelt's interpretation of the Civil War legacy was heavy-handed, perhaps it was because he saw no conflict between duty and advantage, no discrepancy between the nation's world mission and its international strategic interests. While American sacrifice for the ideals of 1776 in both Cuba and the Philippines led to the imposition of a constitutional order modeled on that of the United States, Roosevelt was apparently not fully convinced that the regenerative effects of American institutions were inevitable and irresistible. In the Philippines the redemptive power of the U.S. mission was hedged by a separation-of-powers system which made the executive an American appointee; in Cuba, the Platt Amendment, formulated by Roosevelt's secretary of war, gave the U.S. a veto over Cuban diplomacy and fiscal relations with foreign powers, and recognized the right of American intervention "for the protection of life, property, and individual liberty."[11] But if Roosevelt hedged his bets on the American mission, there can be no gainsaying his commitment to the idea that the extension of American power served universal moral purposes:

> Our action represents a great stride forward in spreading the principles of orderly liberty throughout the world. "Our flag has

not lost its gift of benediction in its world-wide journey to [foreign] shores." We have treated the power we have gained as a solemn obligation, and have used it in the interest of mankind; and the peoples of the world . . . are better off because of the position we have assumed.[12]

Roosevelt's assumption that American purpose could serve the interests of all mankind received a loftier and more subtle treatment by one of his successors, Woodrow Wilson, who also had a fuller grasp of the mysteries which supported that purpose. In part, this was because Wilson traced his authority directly to Lincoln. Accepting Lincoln's birthplace as a national memorial, Wilson asked: "Is not this an altar upon which we may forever keep alive the vestal fire of democracy as upon a shrine at which some of the deepest and most sacred hopes of mankind may from age to age be rekindled?" The answer quite clearly was affirmative: "We are not worthy to stand here unless we ourselves be in deed and in truth real democrats and servants of mankind, ready to give our very lives for the freedom and justice and spiritual exaltation of the great nation which shelters and nurtures us."[13] Wilson would indeed prove himself worthy to stand at such an altar by his own service in attempting to join the spiritual exaltation of the nation to the reenactment of the American Revolution abroad and the refoundation of the Constitution in the international realm.

Wilson's July 4, 1914, speech in Independence Hall serves to introduce his acceptance and eventual augmentation of the Lincolnian creed. Taking note of the historic setting for his speech, Wilson told his audience that "the visible and tangible presence" of the great transaction which occurred there imposed the special obligation of "proving that we are worthy of the men who drew this great declaration." But liberty did not consist of mere declarations of the rights of man. "It consists in the translation of those declarations into definite action." The true American patriot was a man unselfish in the things that made for liberty and the rights of man; he wanted to "share them with the whole world." Following the example of 1776, it was the "dictate of patriotism to sacrifice yourself if you think that that is the path of honor and of duty," to hold out for the right even if half the world opposed you, knowing that the final judgment in both the minds of men and the tribunal of God was a moral judgment. Thus Wilson's dream for the future was that the world

> will turn to America for those moral inspirations which lie at the basis of all freedom; that the world will never fear America unless it feels that it is engaged in some enterprise which is inconsistent with the rights of humanity; and America will come into the full light of the day when all shall know that she puts human rights above all other rights and that her flag is the flag not only of America but of humanity.[14]

Throughout his presidency, Wilson invoked these themes in his public addresses. He told the Daughters of the American Revolution in 1915 that the American Revolution was a beginning, not an end, ". . . and the duty laid upon us by that beginning is the duty of bringing the things then begun to a noble triumph of completion." The completion he had in mind was nothing less than the regeneration of the world: for Wilson, "America first" meant America first and then the world. As he put it, "America has a great cause which is not confined to the American continent. It is the cause of humanity itself." Given the magnitude of the end, the principle of obligation involved would be demanding. On another occasion he said, "Loyalty means nothing unless it has at its heart the absolute principle of self-sacrifice." The purpose of American democracy was to keep alive the hopes of mankind by translating constitutions and codes of liberty into action through sacrifice and self-denial. The commands of democracy, he said, are a "compulsion" upon us.[15]

Just how this compulsion revealed itself in policy became increasingly clear. In announcing his plan for a world league, Wilson argued that its history rendered the United States peculiarly fit to "show mankind the way to liberty." American history was but a prelude to a world history in which justice and peace could prevail. He proposed that the Monroe Doctrine become the doctrine of the world, that all nations have equal rights before the law, that all governments derive their powers from the consent of the governed. Wilson frankly admitted that these were American policies and principles ("We can stand for no others"), but then he concluded by saying, "They are the principles of mankind and must prevail."[16]

The same assumptions provided the rationale for American entrance into the war when Wilson's plan for peace was ignored. The American purpose in going to war, he told Congress, was to vindicate the principles of peace and justice and to establish among free peoples of the world a "concert of purpose and action" which would ensure observance of those principles.

> To such a task we can dedicate our lives and our fortunes, everything that we are and everything that we have, with the pride of those who know that the day has come when America is privileged to spend her blood and her might for the principles that gave her birth and happiness and the peace which she has treasured. God helping her, she can do no other.[17]

In the arcane language of American political ritual, Wilson was saying in effect that the world war was but an enlarged version of the American Revolution which would lead to a new foundation of constitutional authority. The issue at stake was nothing less than the salvation of the world: "Woe be to the man or group of men that seeks to stand in our way in this day of high resolution when every principle we hold dearest is to be vindicated and made secure for the salvation of nations."[18] But Wilson was not alone in the view that American principles could save the world; nor did he alone see world history as but a variation on an American theme.

In accepting his party's nomination for president in 1932, Franklin Roosevelt took up Wilson's scepter, vowing that his indomitable spirit would continue to guide the country toward progress and justice.[19] Roosevelt's immediate concerns were domestic; it would not be long, however, before the "new deal" which he promised the American people would be promised again to the world. By adding a fourth freedom to the Jeffersonian trinity— freedom from want—Roosevelt was proposing the refoundation of the republic in time of crisis. But the consequences were not simply domestic. As he told the Democratic convention in 1936, "It is not alone a war against want and destitution and economic demoralization. It is more than that; it is a war for a survival of democracy. We are fighting to save a great and precious form of government for ourselves and for the world."[20] Within a few years the same rhetoric would be used to mobilize the nation in a foreign war of unprecedented magnitude. And like the domestic war for the survival of democracy, the call to arms around the world against the external enemies of democracy would lead to the refoundation of the Union.

The evidence of Roosevelt's acceptance of the Lincoln–Wilson creed can be found in any random sampling of his speeches. For example, his radio address to the nation in May 1941 announcing an unlimited national emergency concluded with a repetition of the pledge of 1776 in behalf of what he called a struggle to defend democracy. A few days before, he said, ". . . we are engaged in an all-out effort to perpetuate democracy in the New World by . . . aiding embattled democracy in the Old World. . . ." On the 150th anniversary of the adoption of the Bill of Rights, December 15, 1941, Roosevelt proclaimed: "We covenant with each other before all the world that, having taken up arms in defense of liberty, we will not lay them down before liberty is once again secure in the world. . . ." In designating January 1, 1942, as a day of prayer, a day "of asking forgiveness for our shortcomings of the past, of consecration to the tasks of the present, of asking God's help in days to come," Roosevelt said: "We need His guidance that this people may be humble in spirit but strong in conviction of the right; steadfast to endure sacrifice, and brave to achieve a victory of liberty and peace."[21] Similarly, in announcing the 1944 Allied invasion of Normandy, he asked the nation to join him in prayer: "Almighty God: Our sons . . . this day have set upon . . . a struggle to preserve our republic, our religion, and our civilization, and to set free a suffering humanity." Help us, he asked, "to rededicate ourselves in renewed faith in Thee in this hour of great sacrifice. . . . Lead us to the saving of our country, and with our sister nations into a world unity that will spell a sure peace . . . a peace that will let all men live in freedom, reaping the just rewards of their honest toil."[22]

A major component in Roosevelt's conception of world unity involved the application of the welfare-state programs of the New Deal to the international sphere. In the Atlantic Charter of 1941, Roosevelt and Churchill set forth principles upon which, they said, their respective countries based their "hopes for a better future for the world." Prominent among these principles was "collaboration between all nations in the economic field with the object of securing for all improved labor standards, economic advancement, and social security."[23] Throughout the war, Roosevelt often expressed the view that just as the domestic war for the survival of democracy could be won by expanding the meaning of freedom to include economic security, so too could the international war be won on that basis. As he told a United Nations economic conference in 1943, ". . . our ultimate objective can be simply stated: It is to build for ourselves, meaning for all men everywhere, a world in which each individual human being shall have the opportunity to live out his life in peace; to work productively, earning at least enough for his actual needs and those of his family; to associate with the friends of his choice; to think and worship freely. . . ."[24] The specialized agencies of the United Nations were to become an international monument, just as domestic welfare agencies were a national monument, to Roosevelt's success as founder of a new unity, a new American union.

This brief recapitulation, however, is not merely to suggest that American policymakers are bound by their culture, but to emphasize the nature of those cultural constraints. The point may be stated rather simply, though its implications are far-reaching and complex: what the language of liberalism conceals about political reality in the United States is often more important than what it reveals. While the molders of the American political tradition speak the language of modern individualism, their words acquire meaning in a context that is communal, mythical, and finally even mystical. The perpetuation of American liberalism, in short, can perhaps be best understood not so much as an ongoing tradition but as a recurrent foundation fantasy, complete with a myth of the eternal return.[25]

In the speeches of each of the presidents considered here—Kennedy, Wilson, the two Roosevelts—there is a "primitive" ontological conception: certain political action becomes real only insofar as it imitates or repeats an archetype, the act of foundation. Similarly, the repetition of paradigmatic words and gestures—especially the pledge of 1776—becomes a ritual of regeneration apparently by which historical time is periodically abolished and the world re-created: the American Revolution which leads to the foundation of constitutional authority is continuously reenacted. Lincoln established the conditions for this ontological view through his definition of the meaning of the Civil War; and just as that war could be interpreted as a reenactment of the Revolution, so too could various other wars, both cold and hot, be likewise interpreted. Just as the first reenactment of the Revolution led to the refoundation of the Union, so too would the subsequent re-enactments lead to the same culmination.

The meaning of this presidential rite of renewal is usually over-looked by studies of the presidency,[26] just as it was completely unanticipated by the founders of the Constitution. When Hamilton argued in the *Federalist* that the executive should be eligible for reelection, he expressed the fear that without such a provision, former incumbents might wander among the people "like discontented ghosts," coveting the position which they once held;[27] but he did not anticipate the equally dangerous influence of "contented" ghosts of dead presidents who had established their own legitimacy by gaining access to the Revolution and refounding the Constitution in some form. He did not anticipate such a possible danger because the founders assumed that they had done their work well enough so that no other "patriotic and respectable citizen" (as Madison described his own role at the Constitutional Convention) would be able to reshape institutions on the basis of "some informal and unauthorized propositions." Nevertheless, on the basis of the constitutionally unauthorized proposition that all men are created equal, Lincoln succeeded in reclaiming the Revolution and removing it from its paternal constraints so that, para-doxically, the legitimizing doctrine of disinherited sons in the eighteenth century was to become the basis for legitimizing a twentieth-century office which has had monarchical pretensions. Lincoln's symbolic reenactment of the Revolution provided a model of presidential action which is quite beyond liberal politics, and, in some respects, even beyond history: it established a reference point which required of his successors that they earn their legitimacy by participating in a mystical union.

Some of the mysteries of this presidential calling are illustrated by the examples previously cited. Theodore Roosevelt said that it was the duty of the "children of the crucible" to establish by force of arms the right to life, liberty, and the pursuit of happiness in the Philippines. For Wilson "the visible and tangible presence" of the act which occurred in Independence Hall imposed a duty upon his generation to repeat the primal sacrifice. The same was true of anyone who stood before the altar established by Wilson at Lincoln's birthplace: he must be willing to repeat Lincoln's own martyrdom to the cause of the nation. Kennedy simply repeated the pledge of 1776 in behalf of his own declaration of freedom, as though the words were his own, proving not that he was independent of the ritual (as he might have supposed), but that he had simply intellectualized the myth. Anyway, his seriousness could not be doubted: "We dare not forget today," he said in his inaugural, "that we are the heirs of that first revolution."

As was his inclination in many ways, Franklin Roosevelt did not honor the ritualistic forms exactly, but he kept the substance intact. Calling upon the nation to commit itself "without stint and without selfishness" to collective action for the sake of democracy, he said: "I repeat the words of the signers of the Declaration of Independence—that little band of patriots, fighting long ago against overwhelming odds, but certain, as are we, of ultimate victory."[28] The relevance of the archetype needed no further explanation; it could simply be taken for granted that the 165 years and radically changed circumstances which separated Roosevelt from the men of 1776 were of no real significance.

The eternal return in the ontology of American politics was badly flawed, however, in at least one important respect. For although the ritual itself remained substantially unchanged through time, each act of refoundation was different from the last; each re-creation of the American political cosmos was built upon previous foundations in the past. The eternal return was not an exact repetition of the archetype, not an actual reenactment of the Revolution, but a symbolic projection of it into an external sphere which led not to the internal renewal of authority, but to the enhancement of presidential power and the creation of extraconstitutional legitimacy for the incumbent. In this respect, repetition of the words of 1776 expressed the unconscious recognition that in a nation of sons who had gained their legitimacy in the covenant by committing fratricide and symbolic patricide, reestablishment of covenant authority required that the killing—both symbolic and actual—must go on forever. Thus the repeated invocation of the pledge of 1776 also expressed a profound sense of loss, a terrible and compelling nostalgia for Revolutionary authority. Ironically, perhaps this sense of loss was there from the beginning.

If the language of liberalism is of no help to the twentieth century in understanding the mythical dimensions of political reality in the United States, neither was it of much aid to the men of 1776 in understanding the experience from which the myth was derived. For there was a discrepancy between liberal language and revolutionary action that was built into the Declaration of Independence itself. This is to be found in the difference between the self-evident truths enumerated at the beginning of the document and the mutual pledge of lives, fortunes, and sacred honor which concluded it.[29] The self-evident truths provided a theory of democratic legitimacy which, *post facto,* justified revolutionary action, and therefore was of considerable usefulness in effecting the separation from Great Britain. The assertion of equality supplied what a list of grievances against the king could never supply (especially since the real grievances were against Parliament): the conclusion that monarchy itself was illegitimate. Yet the action itself was not to be understood in terms of this universalistic language. The assertion of equality was not merely a convenient tool; it was also an inconvenient source of embarrassment because of slavery.[30] It was not that the men of 1776 were world revolutionaries, as their articulation of natural rights might seem to suggest; rather, it was that they were brothers in rebellion, as their mutual pledge would seem to imply. Not equality but fraternity was the idea which captured the meaning of their action, and they had but limited ways to express it.

As Louis Hartz observed, in the history of revolution there has never been a more improbable father figure than George III.[31] Nevertheless, as the extraordinary success of Thomas Paine's attack on monarchy (in *Common Sense*) would indicate, nearly any incumbent could serve as a symbol for the hateful and fearful tyranny which American sons believed their British elders were imposing upon them. Both sides readily employed the language of primeval family conflict to characterize one another, and occasionally themselves as well. American pamphleteers saw the British as unspeakably corrupt, given to rapine and plunder, barbaric, avaricious, dissipated, and intent upon reducing the colonies to an absolute despotism. The British viewed the colonists as the promoters of a desperate conspiracy against established authority, guilty of deception and treachery: "They meant only to amuse," George III informed Parliament, "by vague expressions of attachment to the parent state and the strongest protestations of loyalty to me, whilst they were preparing for a general revolt. . . ."[32]

For all the suggestions of brotherhood in the literature of the Revolution, there was not much certainty about what it meant. Only Paine, an outsider who had not been involved in the decade of colonial disputation with the British, seemed sure enough to make explicit what had been implicit in the analyses of others: ". . . instead of gazing at each other with suspicious or doubtful curiosity," he concluded, "let each of us hold out to his neighbor the hearty hand of friendship and unite in drawing a line which, like an act of oblivion, shall bury in forgetfulness every former dissension."[33] There was not to be much guilt connected with this triumph over paternal authority, and thus not much repression either. Friendship itself, not some terrible totemistic representation, could bury the past in oblivion. And having left the past behind, America could become a refuge for liberty where world history might be begun anew, where men might live close to nature in brotherhood and benevolence: the political equivalent of a lost Eden, untainted by the original sin of hereditary monarchy.

It was a noble vision, but it did not survive except as a dream and a wish, a faint memory, an inexplicable nostalgia. The "brotherly affection" to which George Washington referred in his Farewell Address was hardly noticeable in the partisan and sectional recriminations which characterized his last years in office; it had been displaced by a paternal union which presumed that conflict rather than affection was the natural condition of brotherhood. By Lincoln's time, the fraternal bonds had become "mystic chords of memory," no longer understood and almost forgotten, certainly not viable enough to forestall further fraternal strife. By the end of the nineteenth century, all that remained of fraternal happiness was the desire to escape the repressive political and economic institutions of American capitalism, to withdraw to some idealized landscape, there to be regenerated by contact with nature which was forever receding into the past.

This propensity for flight and nostalgia, which is revealed in American literature from Cooper to Hemingway and beyond,[34] found its most forceful social and political expression in the frontier of Frederick Jackson Turner. Turner's theory of American development emphasized the extent to which the meaning of community had become identified with the land itself. "American democracy," he wrote, "is fundamentally the outcome of the experiences of the American people in dealing with the West." What he meant by this extraordinary statement is that American history was continuously being recapitulated at the edge of the frontier, that American democracy was perpetually reborn as the wilderness stripped man of his civilization and returned him in space to the primal moment. Thus when Turner said "democracy" he was really talking about community: the frontier became the "consolidatory agent" of the United States—the influence that "Americanized, liberated and fused [immigrants] into a mixed race," the place where "North and South met and mingled into a nation."[35] That Turner discovered his frontier only after the unavailability of free land in the West had become clear added a cruel irony to the nostalgia which dominated the thought of the Progressive era. For it raised the unavoidable question of how community in America could survive the passing of the frontier.[36]

Turner was not wrong in using the language of myth to describe the perpetuation of American democracy—i.e., the community. His mistake was in defining the frontier too narrowly, limiting it to the continental United States, and in not understanding that it was a myth. In Turner's frontier was to be found an expression of the foundation fantasy in a pastoral setting, an implicit microcosmic representation of the archetype, which suggested that community in America consisted of the correspondence between spatial movement and primal moment, which was continually being established, lost, and recovered in an ever-expanding cosmos. Here was a dim presentiment of how the twentieth century was to answer Turner's question on the survival of democracy: it would have to be refounded in the international realm by continuously repeating the original act.

To say the least, the language of liberalism is inadequate to explain this peculiar form of American imperialism. Nor does the Marxist critique of liberalism, which sees ideology as a mask for economic expansion, tell the whole story. For if American expansion cannot be understood in terms of a magnanimous desire to extend the benefits of liberal constitutionalism to the rest of the world, neither can it be fully understood as economic aggrandizement. Repeated efforts to refound the Union shatter the explanatory limits of both idealism and realism as categories of foreign-policy evaluation. The alternative explanation suggested here is that the outward projection of American constitutionalism can be best understood mythologically, as attempts to repeat the original act of foundation and reestablish a sense of community—refoundation attempts which betray a nostalgic longing to recapture that original moment of brotherhood. The question that remains, however, is where would it all end?

DEATH OF THE CIVIC GOD

The madman jumped into their midst and pierced them with his eyes. "Whither is God?" he cried. "I shall tell you. We have killed him—you and I."

—Friedrich Nietzsche, 1882

True, Lincoln freed the slaves—or more precisely, he declared them free in those areas of the country where he was powerless to effect their emancipation, and thereby set in motion a process that led to the passage of the Thirteenth Amendment.[37] From the perspective of a hundred years later, however, it would appear that he did more to emancipate American foreign policy than he did for American blacks. By the end of the century, the ex-slaves and their descendants found themselves in an economic and social bondage which in many ways was just as oppressive as slavery. Within the same time span, the United States, spurred by industrialization begun during the Civil War and freed from the inconvenience of extending a divided house into the international sphere, was ready to claim for itself the status of world power.

The two points are not unrelated. For just as the Civil War as atonement relieved national guilt to the extent that the problems of the freedman could easily be ignored, it also established a sanctified Union with a universal mission of bringing the blessings of freedom to other "backward" races of the world. Lincoln's political religion supplied a consummatory ethos for national institutions which linked competitive capitalism with liberal democracy, so that American political and economic expansion itself could be seen as redemptive. The proof is to be found not only in repeated attempts to refound the Union, but in the history of noncolonial imperialism as well.[38] Thus a major problem of the twentieth century was to become not how American democracy could survive the passing of the frontier, but how world frontiers could survive the passing of American democracy—not how to make the world safe for democracy, but how to make American democracy safe for the world.

The decade of the 1960s confronted this problem directly, and in so doing, celebrated the death of the civic god and proclaimed the religion moribund. The religion came to an end, as it had begun, through sacrifice and attempted refoundation—that is, by efforts to find divine legitimation through sacrifice in Southeast Asia, and by the attempted refoundation of the Constitution in Vietnam. The beginning of the end occurred when President Johnson stated the universal mission of the United States in such a way as to stand the Revolutionary ideal on its head: "When freedom is destroyed in one country, it is threatened throughout the world."[39] The *coup de grace* was delivered by the apostasy of a generation of young people who were unwilling to be cast as spear-carriers and supernumeraries in America's grand historical Passion Play, a generation who recognized that a nation willing to pay any price, bear any burden, meet any hardship, support any friend, oppose any foe to assure the survival and success of liberty no longer knew what liberty meant, and had rather dim notions of survival. The demise of the civic faith thus occurred when sacrificial death lost its miraculous redemptive quality, when external refoundation could no longer substitute for internal renewal of authority, and internal renewal was transmogrified into Richard Nixon's "New American Revolution."[40]

Nixon's various attempts to reconstruct the Constitution—from the unauthorized formation of a super-cabinet to the use of impoundment as an item veto, from his broad claims of executive privilege to his approval of the Huston plan of domestic surveillance, from his pocket veto of important legislation during a Christmas recess to his intimidation of the media, from his use of the war power to his ordering of the Watergate "cover-up"—all seem aimed at establishing rule by presidential decree.[41] In this respect, Nixon's claims to power were by no means unique; Lincoln had made assertions of power on the same order of magnitude, as had other wartime presidents. What marked Nixon's presidency as distinctive, however, is that his extraconstitutional assertions of power were utterly artless and without moral sanction of any kind. The term "naked" can be aptly applied to Nixon's use of power, for it was power without authority—power, that is to say, without the protective dress which art in combination with cultural myth can provide. Nixon's avoidance of the symbols of the civic faith in his public pronouncements perhaps reflected his own recognition that the covenant had been broken and had lost its capacity to instill unity; in any case, survey research of American attitudes during the late 1960s and early '70s clearly documents the rise of political cynicism and the loss of trust in government, politicians, and their policies. But if Jimmy Carter found himself presiding over a nation of cynics, the same research also suggests that public distrust was largely confined to particular leaders and policies, and Americans remained remarkably hopeful about the possibilities of future amelioration.[42]

It is the function of political authority, as Lincoln realized, to give hope. Hope binds society together by the promise of a continuous future and the memory of a common past, allays fears of the unknown by providing connecting links between familiar experience and the *terra incognita* of what is to come. Since there is no greater fear than of death and no greater hope than of life everlasting, Lincoln's political religion provided the basis for authority in

the United States by miraculously transforming death into symbolic immortality. By linking the defense of the Union to the sacrifices of 1776, he was allowing the mythic past to guide the nation
through the uncertain present to the unknown future in such a way
as to change the meaning of death from an end to life into a
redemptive act, the renewal of life. From this interpretation of the
meaning of the war, the Union came to embody the principle
which gave "hope to the world for all future time," i.e. the "promise that in due time the weights should be lifted from the shoulders
of all men." In this respect, Lincoln's concept of immortality both
concealed and revealed a political truth that has proved to be
significant for the twentieth century. What it concealed can be read
in the disaffection of a generation of Americans by no means
certain that the political religion could secure its own future; what
it revealed can be read in the revolutionary struggles of people
around the world seeking to gain for themselves and their posterity the political basis of hope.

The nostalgia surrounding attempts at refoundation in the
twentieth century reflects not only a loss of meaning, but a distortion of it as well. In part this distortion can be found in what
Hannah Arendt has called the identification of meaning and end,
or the semantic confusion between "in order to" and "for the sake
of."[43] This distortion was built into Lincoln's first refoundation,
and it subsequently became more severe. Where the men of 1776
took their pledge directly for the support of their declaration of
legitimacy, Lincoln's renewal of the pledge at Gettysburg placed
it in the service of an end not directly connected with the action
itself. The meaning of the Revolution in 1776 arose directly from
action; the pledge was part of the action itself and was undertaken
in order to effect freedom. In 1863, however, this meaning was twice
removed from action, since those who died at Gettysburg did so
not in order to effect their own freedom, but *for the sake of* an
abstraction—the survival of a nation conceived in liberty and dedicated to an egalitarian proposition. Likewise, since the living were
to dedicate themselves to the cause of freedom rather than to
freedom itself, this meant that their dedication was not in order to
obtain freedom's immediate effects, but for the sake of political
rebirth and immortality.

Nevertheless, the discrepancy between meaning and action produced by Lincoln's refoundation was relatively small compared to the breach which emerged in the twentieth-century attempts to repeat it. In the twentieth century, there was hardly any connection whatsoever between the actions undertaken by the presidents considered here and the meaning which they ascribed to them. Indeed, the meaning of their words can only be understood in mythical terms as the attempt, whether deliberate or not, to emulate Lincoln and reestablish the covenant of 1776, the effect of which was not the renewal of constitutional authority, but the expansion of presidential power. Moreover, if war can abolish institutions of tyranny such as slavery, the history of the twentieth century would seem to indicate that neither war nor any other kind of external liberation can establish the conditions of freedom, especially when modern military technology is the means to that end. And when national hope depends upon meaningless death, then political authority rests upon a delusion.

It is a long and tortuous route by which Thomas Paine's assumption that the cause of America was the cause of all mankind became a justification for killing peasants in Southeast Asia. However, the hope which America symbolized for Paine—the promise of a new beginning for mankind—was not itself lost with the loss of the American Revolution. Frantz Fanon, for example, in calling upon Africans to turn their backs on Europe and the United States, proposed a third beginning for mankind: "It is a question of the Third World starting a new history of Man. . . ." Proclaiming the spiritual death of the western world, Fanon said: "For Europe, for ourselves and for humanity, comrades, we must turn over a new leaf, we must work out new concepts, and try to set afoot a new man."[44] It is in this business of inventing new men, the business of founding, that Lincoln's concept of immortality may provide further insight into the twentieth century. For if his political religion concealed a betrayal of the Revolution, it also revealed the way in which revolution was to make itself known to much of the world.

By providing the revolutionary hero missing from 1776, Lincoln also fulfilled the classic role of founder: his own unhappy consciousness gave impetus to his preoccupation with the happiness of men, so that a personal death anxiety became transformed into a symbolic immortality for the nation.[45] Lincoln's political religion may thus be viewed as a prototype of the political religions which have formed the bases of legitimacy in many new nations of the third world.[46] And while such an interpretation of Lincoln's founding may not be flattering to the conception Americans have of themselves as nonideological pragmatists, this kind of comparison does suggest that they are not wrong in seeing world history as a variation on an American theme—not wrong, but right for the wrong reasons. For the political and economic development of the United States has not been due to the Revolution of 1776, which has not always been understood very clearly, but to its culmination in 1865, which has hardly been understood at all. Thus, in attempting to export the events of 1776 as a model for development around the world, the United States has failed to recognize that other new nations have been following its own model of 1865; in opposing, out of a compulsion for liberal democracy, consummatory ideologies as the basis for modernization, the United States has failed to see that its own democracy has rested upon just such an ideology.

At the present time, however, this ideology has lost its capacity to instill domestic unity and purpose. And if those observers who see a new Malthusian specter of scarcity haunting the world are correct—or even partially correct—the challenge to political authority to guarantee the future has never been greater. But a crisis of authority, as Lincoln realized, is both an opportunity and a danger; the death of God still means that everything is permitted. If new men and women of ambition are to gratify their ruling passions by establishing authority anew, they will recognize, as Lincoln said in 1862, that the dogmas of the past are inadequate for the present: "We must disenthrall our selves, and then we shall save our country."

Address Before the Young Men's
Lyceum of Springfield, Illinois

JANUARY 27, 1838

THE PERPETUATION OF OUR
POLITICAL INSTITUTIONS

As a subject for the remarks of the evening, *the perpetuation of our political institutions,* is selected.

In the great journal of things happening under the sun, we, the American People, find our account running, under date of the nineteenth century of the Christian era. We find ourselves in the peaceful possession, of the fairest portion of the earth, as regards extent of territory, fertility of soil, and salubrity of climate. We find ourselves under the government of a system of political institutions, conducing more essentially to the ends of civil and religious liberty, than any of which the history of former times tells us. We, when mounting the stage of existence, found ourselves the legal inheritors of these fundamental blessings. We toiled not in the acquirement or establishment of them—they are a legacy bequeathed us, by a *once* hardy, brave, and patriotic, but *now* lamented and departed race of ancestors. Their's was the task (and nobly they performed it) to possess themselves, and through themselves, us, of this goodly land; and to uprear upon its hills and its valleys, a political edifice of liberty and equal rights; 'tis ours only, to transmit these, the former, unprofaned by the foot of an invader; the latter, undecayed by the lapse of time, and untorn by [usurpation—to the latest generation that fate shall permit the world to know. This task of gratitude to our fathers, justice to] ourselves, duty to posterity, and love for our species in general, all imperatively require us faithfully to perform.

How, then, shall we perform it? At what point shall we expect the approach of danger? By what means shall we fortify against it? Shall we expect some transatlantic military giant, to step the Ocean, and crush us at a blow? Never! All the armies of Europe, Asia and Africa combined, with all the treasure of the earth (our own excepted) in their military chest; with a Buonaparte for a commander, could not by force, take a drink from the Ohio, or make a track on the Blue Ridge, in a trial of a thousand years.

At what point then is the approach of danger to be expected? I answer, if it ever reach us, it must spring up amongst us. It cannot come from abroad. If destruction be our lot, we must ourselves be its author and finisher. As a nation of freemen, we must live through all time, or die by suicide.

I hope I am over wary; but if I am not, there is, even now, something of ill-omen amongst us. I mean the increasing disregard for law which pervades the country; the growing disposition to substitute the wild and furious passions, in lieu of the sober judgement of Courts; and the worse than savage mobs, for the executive ministers of justice. This disposition is awfully fearful in any community; and that it now exists in ours, though grating to our feelings to admit, it would be a violation of truth, and an insult to our intelligence, to deny. Accounts of outrages committed by mobs, form the every-day news of the times. They have pervaded the country, from New England to Louisiana;—they are neither peculiar to the eternal snows of the former, nor the burning suns of the latter;—they are not the creature of climate—neither are they confined to the slave-holding, or the non-slaveholding States. Alike, they spring up among the pleasure hunting masters of Southern slaves, and the order loving citizens of the land of steady habits. Whatever, then, their cause may be, it is common to the whole country.

It would be tedious, as well as useless, to recount the horrors of all of them. Those happening in the State of Mississippi, and at St. Louis, are, perhaps, the most dangerous in example, and revolting to humanity. In the Mississippi case, they first commenced by hanging the regular gamblers: a set of men, certainly not following for a livelihood, a very useful, or very honest occupation; but one which, so far from being forbidden by the laws, was actually licensed by an act of the Legislature, passed but a single year before. Next, negroes, suspected of conspiring to raise an insurrection, were caught up and hanged in all parts of the State: then, white men, supposed to be leagued with the negroes; and finally, strangers, from neighboring States, going thither on business, were, in many instances, subjected to the same fate. Thus went on this process of hanging, from gamblers to negroes, from negroes to white citizens, and from these to strangers; till, dead men were seen literally dangling from the boughs of trees upon every road side; and in numbers almost sufficient, to rival the native Spanish moss of the country, as a drapery of the forest.

Turn, then, to that horror-striking scene at St. Louis. A single victim was only sacrificed there. His story is very short; and is, perhaps, the most highly tragic, of any thing of its length, that has ever been witnessed in real life. A mulatto man, by the name of McIntosh, was seized in the street, dragged to the suburbs of the city, chained to a tree, and actually burned to death; and all within a single hour from the time he had been a freeman, attending to his own business, and at peace with the world.

Such are the effects of mob law; and such are the scenes, becoming more and more frequent in this land so lately famed for love of law and order; and the stories of which, have even now grown too familiar, to attract any thing more, than an idle remark.

But you are, perhaps, ready to ask, "What has this to do with the perpetuation of our political institutions?" I answer, it has much to do with it. Its direct consequences are, comparatively speaking, but a small evil; and much of its danger consists, in the proneness of our minds, to regard its direct, as its only consequences. Abstractly considered, the hanging of the gamblers at Vicksburg, was of but little consequence. They constitute a portion of population, that is worse than useless in a [ny community; and their death, if no perni]cious example be set by it, is never matter of reasonable regret with any one. If they were annually swept, from the stage of existence, by the plague or small pox, honest men would, perhaps, be much profited, by the operation. Similar too, is the correct reasoning, in regard to the burning of the negro at St. Louis. He had forfeited his life, by the perpetration of an outrageous murder, upon one of the most worthy and respectable citizens of the city; and had he not died as he did, he must have died by the sentence of the law, in a very short time afterwards. As to him alone, it was as well the way it was, as it could otherwise have been. But the example in either case, was fearful. When men take it in their heads to day, to hang gamblers, or burn murderers, they should recollect, that, in the confusion usually attending such transactions, they will be as likely to hang or burn some one, who is neither a gambler nor a murderer [as] one who is; and that, acting upon the [exam]ple they set, the mob of to-morrow, may, an[d] probably will, hang or burn some of them, [by th]e very same mistake. And not only so; the innocent, those who have ever set their faces against violations of law in every shape, alike with the guilty, fall victims to the ravages of mob law; and thus it goes on, step by step, till all the walls erected for the defence of the persons and property of individuals, are trodden down, and disregarded. But all this even, is not the full extent of the evil. By such examples, by instances of the perpetrators of such acts going unpunished, the lawless in spirit, are encouraged to become lawless in practice; and having been used to no restraint, but dread of punishment, they thus become, absolutely unrestrained. Having ever regarded Government as their deadliest bane, they make a jubilee of the suspension of its operations; and pray for nothing so much, as its total annihilation. While, on the other hand, good men, men who love tranquility, who desire to abide by the laws, and enjoy their benefits, who would gladly spill their blood in the defence of their country; seeing their property destroyed; their families insulted, and their lives endangered; their persons injured; and seeing nothing in prospect that forebodes a change for the better; become tired of, and disgusted with, a Government that offers them no protection; and are not much averse to a change in which they imagine they have nothing to lose. Thus, then, by the operation of this mobocratic spirit, which all must admit, is now abroad in the land, the strongest bulwark of any Government, and particularly of those constituted like ours, may effectually be broken down and destroyed—I mean the *attachment* of the People. Whenever this effect shall be produced among us; whenever the vicious portion of population shall be permitted to gather in bands of hundreds and thousands, and burn churches, ravage and rob provision stores, throw printing presses into rivers, shoot editors, and hang and burn obnoxious persons at pleasure, and with impunity; depend on it, this Government cannot last. By such things, the feelings of the best citizens will become more or less alienated from it; and thus it will be left without friends, or with too few, and those few too weak, to make their friendship effectual. At such a time and under such circumstances, men of sufficient tal[ent and ambition will not be want]ing to seize [the opportunity, strike the blow, and overturn that fair fabric], which for the last half century, has been the fondest hope, of the lovers of freedom, throughout the world.

I know the American People are *much* attached to their Government; —I know they would suffer *much* for its sake;—I know they would endure evils long and patiently, before they would ever think of exchanging it for another. Yet, notwithstanding all this, if the laws be continually despised and disregarded, if their rights to be secure in their persons and property, are held by no better tenure than the caprice of a mob, the alienation of their affections from the Government is the natural consequence; and to that, sooner or later, it must come.

Here then, is one point at which danger may be expected.

The question recurs "how shall we fortify against it?" The answer is simple. Let every American, every lover of liberty, every well wisher to his posterity, swear by the blood of the Revolution, never to violate in the least particular, the laws of the country; and never to tolerate their violation by others. As the patriots of seventy-six did to the support of the

Declaration of Independence, so to the support of the Constitution and Laws, let every American pledge his life, his property, and his sacred honor;—let every man remember that to violate the law, is to trample on the blood of his father, and to tear the character [charter?] of his own, and his children's liberty. Let reverence for the laws, be breathed by every American mother, to the lisping babe, that prattles on her lap—let it be taught in schools, in seminaries, and in colleges;—let it be written in Primmers, spelling books, and in Almanacs;—let it be preached from the pulpit, proclaimed in legislative halls, and enforced in courts of justice. And, in short, let it become the *political religion* of the nation; and let the old and the young, the rich and the poor, the grave and the gay, of all sexes and tongues, and colors and conditions, sacrifice unceasingly upon its altars.

While ever a state of feeling, such as this, shall universally, or even, very generally prevail throughout the nation, vain will be every effort, and fruitless every attempt, to subvert our national freedom.

When I so pressingly urge a strict observance of all the laws, let me not be understood as saying there are no bad laws, nor that grievances may not arise, for the redress of which, no legal provisions have been made. I mean to say no such thing. But I do mean to say, that, although bad laws, if they exist, should be repealed as soon as possible, still while they continue in force, for the sake of example, they should be religiously observed. So also in unprovided cases. If such arise, let proper legal provisions be made for them with the least possible delay; but, till then, let them if not too intolerable, be borne with.

There is no grievance that is a fit object of redress by mob law. In any case that arises, as for instance, the promulgation of abolitionism, one of two positions is necessarily true; that is, the thing is right within itself, and therefore deserves the protection of all law and all good citizens; or, it is wrong, and therefore proper to be prohibited by legal enactments; and in neither case, is the interposition of mob law, either necessary, justifiable, or excusable.

But, it may be asked, why suppose danger to our political institutions? Have we not preserved them for more than fifty years? And why may we not for fifty times as long?

We hope there is no *sufficient* reason. We hope all dangers may be overcome; but to conclude that no danger may ever arise, would itself be extremely dangerous. There are now, and will hereafter be, many causes, dangerous in their tendency, which have not existed heretofore; and which are not too insignificant to merit attention. That our government should have been maintained in its original form from its establishment until now, is not much to be wondered at. It had many props to support it through that period, which now are decayed, and crumbled away. Through that period, it was felt by all, to be an undecided experiment; now, it is understood to be a successful one. Then, all that sought celebrity and fame, and distinction, expected to find them in the success of that experiment. Their *all* was staked upon it;—their destiny was *inseparably* linked with it. Their ambition aspired to display before an admiring world, a practical demonstration of the truth of a proposition, which had hitherto been considered, at best no better, than problematical; namely, *the capability of a people to govern themselves.* If they succeeded, they were to be immortalized; their names were to be transferred to counties and cities, and rivers and mountains; and to be revered and sung, and toasted through all time. If they failed, they were to be called knaves and fools, and fanatics for a fleeting hour; then to sink and be forgotten. They succeeded. The experiment is successful; and thousands have won their deathless names in making it so. But the game is caught; and I believe it is true, that with the catching, end the pleasures of the chase. This field of glory is harvested, and the crop is already appropriated. But new reapers will arise, and *they,* too, will seek a field. It is to deny, what the history of the world tells us is true, to suppose that men of ambition and talents will not continue to spring up amongst us. And, when they do, they will as naturally seek the gratification of their ruling passion, as others have so done before them. The question then, is, can that gratification be found in supporting and maintaining an edifice that has been erected by others? Most certainly it cannot. Many great and good men sufficiently qualified for any task they should undertake, may ever be found, whose ambition would aspire to nothing beyond a seat in Congress, a gubernatorial or a presidential chair; *but such belong not to the family of the lion, or the tribe of the eagle* [.] What! think you these places would satisfy an Alexander, a Caesar, or a Napoleon? Never! Towering genius disdains a beaten path. It seeks regions hitherto unexplored. It sees *no distinction* in adding story to story, upon the monuments of fame, erected to the memory of others. It *denies* that it is glory enough to serve under any chief. It *scorns* to tread in the footsteps of *any* predecessor, however illustrious. It thirsts and burns for distinction; and, if possible, it will have it, whether at the expense of emancipating slaves, or enslaving freemen. Is it unreasonable then to expect, that some man possessed of the loftiest genius, coupled with ambition sufficient to push it to its utmost stretch, will at some time, spring up among us? And when such a one does, it will require the people to be united with each other, attached to the government and laws, and generally intelligent, to successfully frustrate his designs.

Distinction will be his paramount object; and although he would as willingly, perhaps more so, acquire it by doing good as harm; yet, that opportunity being past, and nothing left to be done in the way of building up, he would set boldly to the task of pulling down.

Here then, is a probable case, highly dangerous, and such a one as could not have well existed heretofore.

Another reason which *once was;* but which, to the same extent, is *now no more,* has done much in maintaining our institutions thus far. I mean the powerful influence which the interesting scenes of the revolution had upon the *passions* of the people as distinguished from their judgment. By this influence, the jealousy, envy, and avarice, incident to our nature, and so common to a state of peace, prosperity, and conscious strength, were, for the time, in a great measure smothered and rendered inactive; while the deep rooted principles of *hate,* and the powerful motive of *revenge,* instead of being turned against each other, were directed exclusively against the British nation. And thus, from the force of circumstances, the basest principles of our nature, were either made to lie dormant, or to become the active agents in the advancement of the noblest of cause[s?] —that of establishing and maintaining civil and religious liberty.

But this state of feeling *must fade, is fading, has faded,* with the circumstances that produced it.

I do not mean to say, that the scenes of the revolution *are now* or *ever will be* entirely forgotten; but that like every thing else, they must fade upon the memory of the world, and grow more and more dim by the lapse of time. In history, we hope, they will be read of, and recounted, so long as the bible shall be read;—but even granting that they will, their influence *cannot be* what it heretofore has been. Even then, they *cannot be* so universally known, nor so vividly felt, as they were by the generation just gone to rest. At the close of that struggle, nearly every adult male had been a participator in some of its scenes. The consequence was, that of those scenes, in the form of a husband, a father, a son or a brother, a *living history was* to be found in every family—a history bearing the indubitable testimonies of its own authenticity, in the limbs mangled, in the scars of wounds received, in the midst of the very scenes related—a history, too, that could be read and understood alike by all, the wise and the ignorant, the learned and the unlearned. But *those* histories are gone. They *can* be read no more forever. They *were* a fortress of strength; but, what invading foemen could *never do,* the silent artillery of time *has done;* the levelling of its walls. They are gone. They *were* a forest of giant oaks; but the all-resistless hurricane has swept over them, and left only, here and there, a lonely trunk, despoiled of its verdure, shorn of its foliage; unshading and unshaded, to murmur in a few more gentle breezes, and to combat with its mutilated limbs, a few more ruder storms, then to sink, and be no more.

They *were* the pillars of the temple of liberty; and now, that they have crumbled away, that temple must fall, unless we, their descendants, supply their places with other pillars, hewn from the solid quarry of sober reason. Passion has helped us; but can do so no more. It will in future be our enemy. Reason, cold, calculating, unimpassioned reason, must furnish all the materials for our future support and defence. Let those [materials] be moulded into *general intelligence, [sound] morality* and, in particular, *a reverence for the constitution and laws;* and, that we improved to the last; that we remained free to the last; that we revered his name to the last; [tha]t, during his long sleep, we permitted no hostile foot to pass over or desecrate [his] resting place; shall be that which to le[arn the last] trump shall awaken our WASH[INGTON].

[Upon these] let the proud fabric of freedom r[est, as the] rock of its basis; and as truly as has been said of the only greater institution, *"the gates of hell shall not prevail against it."*

Notes

INTRODUCTION

1. G. S. Boritt, *Lincoln and the Economics of the American Dream* (Memphis, 1978), 298–9.

2. John T. Morse, Jr., *Abraham Lincoln* (Boston, 1893), 33.

3. William H. Herndon and Jesse Weik, *Herndon's Life of Lincoln*, ed. Paul M. Angle (Cleveland, 1947), xxxix.

4. Woodrow Wilson, *The New Democracy, Presidential Messages, Addresses and Other Papers,* ed. Ray Stannard Baker and William E. Dodd (New York, 1926), II, 295.

5. Edmund Wilson, *Patriotic Gore* (New York, 1966), 123. This essay was originally published in Wilson's previous book *Eight Essays* (New York, 1954).

6. Mason Locke Weems, *The Life of Washington,* ed. Marcus Cunliffe (Cambridge, Mass., 1962). The influence of Weems on Lincoln has also been studied, apparently independently of my own work, by George B. Forgie, *Patricide in the House Divided* (New York, 1979); but his interpretations are substantially different from mine. See Dwight G. Anderson, "The Quest for Immortality: Abraham Lincoln and the Founding of Political Authority in America" (unpublished Ph.D dissertation, University of California at Berkeley, 1972), ch. 1. See also Michael Paul Rogin, *Fathers and Children: Andrew Jackson and the Subjugation of the American Indian* (New York, 1975), 36–7.

7. Many of my conclusions about Lincoln's political religion have been anticipated by Garry Wills, *Inventing America: Jefferson's Declaration of Independence* (New York, 1978), Prologue. Another treatment of this subject is provided by Glen E. Thurow, *Abraham Lincoln and American Political Religion* (Albany, N.Y., 1976). Thurow's perspective on Lincoln's political religion, however, is diametrically opposed to the one developed here. He contends that Lincoln did not seek "to foster religious beliefs in order to support political institutions" (p. xii).

8. A detailed discussion of twentieth-century historiography is neither necessary nor appropriate here, but a few titles will illustrate the dominant

influences to which I refer: Charles A. Beard, *An Economic Interpretation of the Constitution* (New York, 1913) is the classic work of the Progressive school. Daniel Bell, *The End of Ideology* (Glencoe, Ill., 1959), and Seymour Martin Lipset, *Political Man* (Garden City, N.J., 1960), are representative of pluralist social science, and together with Daniel Boorstin, *The Genius of American Politics* (Chicago, 1953), and Louis Hartz, *The Liberal Tradition in America* (New York, 1955), illustrate the various assumptions of the consensus interpretation. A critique of this school of thought is provided by John Higham, "The Cult of the 'American Consensus': Homogenizing our History," *Commentary* 27 (Feb. 1959), 93–100, and Michael Paul Rogin, *The Intellectuals and McCarthy* (Cambridge, Mass., 1967), chs. 1 and 2. On violence and rebellion, see Richard E. Rubenstein, *Rebels in Eden: Mass Political Violence in the United States* (Boston, 1970).

9. This interpretive perspective was first suggested to me by Edwin G. Burrows and Michael Wallace, "The American Revolution: The Ideology and Psychology of National Liberation," *Perspectives in American History* 6 (1972), 167–307. See also Rogin, *Fathers and Children;* Winthrop Jordan, "Familial Politics: Thomas Paine and the Killing of the King, 1776," *Journal of American History* 60 (Sept. 1973), 294–309; and Forgie.

10. Richard Neustadt, *Presidential Power* (New York, 1960). For an alternative view, see Clinton Rossiter, *The American Presidency* (New York, 1960).

11. F. G. Hutchins, "Presidential Autocracy in America," *The Presidency Reappraised,* eds. Rexford G. Tugwell and Thomas E. Cronin (Santa Barbara, Calif., 1974), 35–55.

12. Richard M. Pious, *The American Presidency* (New York, 1979). See also Arthur M. Schlesinger, Jr., *The Imperial Presidency* (Boston, 1973), 8–10.

13. Roy P. Basler, ed., *The Collected Works of Abraham Lincoln* (New Brunswick, 1953), V, 535. (Hereafter cited as *Collected Works.*)

14. Sigmund Freud, *Moses and Monotheism* (New York, 1939); Erik Erikson, *Young Man Luther* (New York, 1958).

15. This is perhaps less a revision of Freud than it is an emphasis on his later work. It first came to my attention in Robert Jay Lifton, *Death in Life: Survivors of Hiroshima* (New York, 1967), ch. 6 and pp. 481–2. See also Norman O. Brown, *Life Against Death: The Psychoanalytical Meaning of History* (New York, 1959), 118; and Ernest Becker, *The Denial of Death* (New York, 1973), 36.

CHAPTER 1

1. *Collected Works,* IV, 235.

2. Mason Locke Weems, *The Life of Washington,* ed. Marcus Cunliffe (Cambridge, Mass., 1962), 140–1.

3. *Collected Works,* IV, 235–6. According to contemporary sources, Lincoln borrowed a copy of Weems's *Washington* from a neighbor at age fifteen, and then paid for it by a day or two of labor after it had become damaged by rain. He read this and the few other books available to him repeatedly, often memorizing word for word parts that pleased him. One source reported that Lincoln read Weems at age twenty, suggesting the likelihood that he continued to read the book over a period of several years. See Albert J. Beveridge, *Abraham Lincoln 1809–1858* (Boston, 1928), I, 75–7.

4. *Collected Works,* IV, 236.

5. *Ibid.,* 192.

6. *Ibid.,* 204.

7. Daniel J. Boorstin, *The Americans: The National Experience* (New York, 1965), 340. This account of Weems is based upon Boorstin, pp. 340–5, and Marcus Cunliffe's "Introduction" to Weems's *Life of Washington,* ix–lxii.

8. Cunliffe, xiv, xv.

9. Weems, 55–7, 140 (italics deleted).

10. Boorstin, 343.

11. Cunliffe, xviii–xix.

12. The following summary is taken from Weems, 58–128. All quotations, unless otherwise noted, are from his text.

13. *Collected Works,* IV, 235.

14. Edwin G. Burrows and Michael Wallace, "The American Revolution: The Ideology and Psychology of National Liberation," *Perspectives in American History* 6 (1972), 167–307. See also Michael Paul Rogin, *Fathers and Children: Andrew Jackson and the Subjugation of the American Indian* (New York, 1975), 19–37.

15. Bernard Bailyn, *The Ideological Origins of the American Revolution* (Cambridge, Mass., 1967), 34–54. (The quote is from p. 35.) See also the same author's *The Origins of American Politics* (New York, 1968), 3–59.

16. Bailyn, *Origins of American Politics,* 39.

17. *Ibid.,* 66–106.

18. Bailyn, *Ideological Origins,* 125.

19. The following examples illustrate the similarities: The town of Farmington, Connecticut, resolved in 1774 that "the present ministry, being instigated by the devil and led by their wicked and corrupt hearts, have a design . . . to enslave us forever," and that "those pimps and parasites who dared to advise their masters to such detestable measures be held in utter abhorence. . . ." Similarly, handbills in Philadelphia warned that a "corrupt and prostituted ministry are pointing their de-

structive machines against the sacred liberties of the Americans, [attempt-ing] . . . by every artifice to enslave the American colonies and plunder them of their property and, what is more, their birthright, *liberty.*" One explanation for this policy was that the ministry had exhausted its re-sources for patronage and spoils in Britain and thus was looking for a pretext to drain America as well: "America was the only remaining spot to which their oppression and extortion had not fully reached, and they considered her as a fallow field from which a large income might be drawn." The ministry wished "to see America in arms . . . because it furnished them with a pretense for declaring us rebels; and persons con-quered under that character forfeit their all. . . ." Another explanation supports Weems exactly: soldiers returning from the French and Indian War conveyed "a very exalted idea of the riches of this country" to the ministry, suggesting new sources of patronage by which they might bribe Parliament. Still another thought that Great Britain was on the brink of ruin due to ministerial depravity: "The insatiable avarice or worse ambi-tion of corrupt ministers intent on spreading that corruption through America by which they govern absolutely in Great Britain, brought the British empire to the brink of ruin, armed . . . subject against subject, the parent against the child, ready to add unnatural murders to the horrors of civil war." By 1775 it was decided in the second Continental Congress that only armed resistance could induce the king to "forbid a licentious ministry any longer to riot in the ruins of the rights of mankind." *Ibid.,* 125–6, 128, 129, 131.

20. Merrill Jensen, ed., *Tracts of the American Revolution* (Indianapolis, 1967), 276, 257.

21. *Ibid.,* 47, 58.

22. *Ibid.,* 61–2.

23. *Ibid.,* 77.

24. *Ibid.,* 114, 120.

25. *Ibid.,* 172, 176.

26. Gordon S. Wood, *The Creation of the American Republic* (Chapel Hill, 1969), 76.

27. *Ibid.,* 74.

28. *Ibid.,* 106, 74.

29. *Ibid.,* 79, 80, 82.

30. James Thomas Flexner, *George Washington: The Forge of Experience (1732–1775)* (Boston, 1965), 112, 121, 147, 160, 170–6.

31. "Within a very short time, Americans developed an ideological attachment to republicanism. . . . What is puzzling is the reason for the sudden and virtually complete revolution in attitude." Cecelia M. Kenyon,

"Republicanism and Radicalism in the American Revolution: An Old-Fashioned Interpretation," *William and Mary Quarterly* 19 (1962), 166–7. See also Wood, 92–3, and Winthrop D. Jordan, "Familial Politics: Thomas Paine and the Killing of the King, 1776," *Journal of American History* 60 (Sept., 1973), 294–309.

32. Thomas Paine, *Common Sense and Other Political Writings* (Indianapolis, 1953), 21, 27.

33. Jensen, 374.

34. Wood, 53–65.

35. Jordan, 299.

36. Wood, 475–7.

37. Weems, 172, 187, 191.

38. *Ibid.*, 209, 211, 215–16.

39. *Ibid.*, 214.

40. Dexter Perkins, *The American Approach to Foreign Policy* (Cambridge, Mass., 1955), 11.

41. In 1792, Washington, contemplating withdrawal from public life, sent Madison certain suggestions and asked him to put them into the form of an address, which he did. In 1796 Washington sent to Hamilton the draft by Madison, together with additional paragraphs of his own, and asked him to "redress" it. Hamilton's draft was again revised by Washington and was published September 17, 1796, as the Farewell Address. See Gaillord Hunt, ed., *The Writings of James Madison* (New York, 1906), VI, 106–10, and Henry Cabot Lodge, *The Works of Alexander Hamilton* (New York, 1886), VII, 143.

42. James D. Richardson, ed., *Messages and Papers of the Presidents* (Washington, D.C., 1899), I, 214.

43. See Chapter Three, Section 1, for a discussion of covenant theology and the Revolution.

44. John Adams, *The Works of John Adams* (Boston, 1851), III, 452n.

45. *Ibid.*, IV, 290.

46. Richardson, I, 215.

47. Wood, 101–3.

48. Richardson, I, 215–16.

49. Norman Jacobson, "Political Science and Political Education," *American Political Science Review* 57 (Sept. 1963), 561–70.

50. Wood, 428.

51. Samuel Flagg Bemis, "Washington's Farewell Address: A Foreign Policy of Independence," *American Historical Review* 39 (Jan. 1934), 262–3.

52. Clinton Rossiter, ed., *The Federalist Papers* (New York, 1961), No. 11, 91. (Hereafter cited as *Federalist.*)

53. *Ibid.,* No. 12, 90–1.
54. *Ibid.,* Nos. 6 and 7, 56–9, 60–5.
55. *Ibid.,* No. 8, 68.
56. *Ibid.,* 70–1.
57. Max Farrand, ed., *The Records of the Federal Convention* (New Haven, 1937), I, 133.
58. On the latter point, see Martin Diamond, "What the Framers Meant by Federalism," *A Nation of States,* ed. Robert A. Goldwin (Chicago, 1964), 24–42.
59. Farrand, 133, 134.
60. *Ibid.,* 136.
61. Wood, 487–8.
62. *Ibid.,* 490–5, 500–2.
63. Richardson, 216.
64. Wood, 476.
65. *Ibid.,* 477 (italics deleted).
66. *Ibid.,* 475.
67. *Ibid,* 476.
68. *Ibid.,* 477, 478 (italics deleted).
69. *Federalist,* No. 3, 43.
70. Richardson, 218–19.
71. *Federalist,* No. 10, 83–4.
72. Richardson, 220.
73. Wood, 565–87.
74. Adams, *Works,* IV, 221.
75. Zoltán Haraszti, *John Adams and the Prophets of Progress* (Cambridge, Mass., 1952), 62–3.
76. Hannah Arendt, *Between Past and Future* (New York, 1963), 128–34.
77. Adams, *Works,* VI, 9.
78. *Ibid.,* 281 (italics deleted).
79. Richardson, 220.
80. *Ibid.*
81. *Federalist,* No. 49, 315.
82. *Ibid.*
83. *Ibid.,* No. 1, 36–7.
84. This perspective on the Philadelphia Convention is developed by Hannah Arendt, *On Revolution* (New York, 1963), who argues that it was the Constitution which cheated Americans of knowledge of their Revolution, while the convention was a major event in that Revolution.
85. *Federalist,* No. 39, 243 and No. 40, 251.
86. *Ibid.,* No. 40, 252–3.

87. As quoted by Max Farrand, *The Framing of the Constitution of the United States* (New Haven, 1913), 61–2.

88. Richardson, II, 219.

89. The Missouri Compromise, the Compromise of 1850, and finally the Kansas–Nebraska Act of 1854 were all decisions which aimed at keeping the Union together. The complication is that while the presence of the Western land made compromise possible, the acquisition of it made compromise necessary, and increasingly difficult to achieve. But as an indication of how closely related territorial expansion was to avoidance of constitutional crisis, many Northerners believed, even after secession occurred, that the Union could be restored on the basis of Manifest Destiny. See Allan Nevins, *The War for the Union* (New York, 1959), I, 19–24.

90. *Collected Works,* IV, 235–6.

91. Weems, 217.

92. *Ibid.,* 172–224 *passim.*

93. *Ibid.,* 221.

94. *Ibid.,* 221–4.

95. Boorstin, 342.

CHAPTER 2

1. The following account is based upon Paul M. Angle's introduction to William H. Herndon and Jesse Weik, *Herndon's Life of Lincoln* (Cleveland, 1947); and David Donald, *Lincoln's Herndon* (New York, 1948), 206, 212–16, 236–8, 256–7, 271–82.

2. Josiah Holland, *Life of Abraham Lincoln* (Springfield, Mass., 1866).

3. Herndon and Weik, 355.

4. Ward Hill Lamon, *Life of Abraham Lincoln* (Boston, 1872), 487–504.

5. *Ibid.,* 498.

6. Donald, 359.

7. *Collected Works,* I, 382.

8. Richard N. Current, *The Lincoln Nobody Knows* (New York, 1958), 62.

9. F. B. Carpenter, *Six Months at the White House* (New York, 1867), 189.

10. William J. Wolf, *The Almost Chosen People* (New York, 1959), 143.

11. I am indebted to Norman Jacobson for this interpretive perspective on the Lyceum Address. See his "Lincoln's Abraham," *Helderberg Review* 1 (Spring 1971), 13–23.

12. The Lyceum Address appears in *Collected Works,* I, 108–16. All quotations, unless otherwise noted, are from that speech. See Appendix for the complete text.

13. In this interpretation of the significance of Lovejoy's death, I have

followed Basler in *ibid.*, 111, and Harry V. Jaffa, *Crisis of a House Divided* (Garden City, New York, 1959), 196–9. Jaffa is one of the few Lincoln scholars to take the Lyceum Address seriously, though his interpretation differs from my own. In general, he is so intent upon vindicating Lincoln as a moral philosopher and a virtuous man that he sometimes ignores Lincoln's words in favor of the implications he can read into them. This is particularly true of his handling of the Temperance Address (see below). On the Lyceum Address, Jaffa rejects Edmund Wilson's suggestion that Lincoln projected himself into the role of tyrant, preferring instead to see this as simply a matter of Lincoln "thinking of the passions of the rival factions at Alton, Illinois, and of the politicians who would seek votes without regard to the instrinsic rightness or wrongness of the methods or the goals of the men in the mobs" (p. 224).

14. *Collected Works,* I, 273.

15. Adams, *Works,* IV, 292–3.

16. After describing the horrible consequences of civil war, Weems then assures his reader: "But, O ye favoured countrymen of Washington! your republic is not lost yet; yet there is hope. The arm that wrought your political salvation is still stretched out to save . . ." (p. 222). From what follows it is not clear whether that arm belongs to God or to Washington; but in either case, the means of political salvation is quite clear; observe the advice of the Farewell Address.

17. *Collected Works,* II, 499–500.

18. Herndon and Weik, 152.

19. Edmund Wilson, *Patriotic Gore* (New York, 1966), 130. Another writer to attempt an analysis of the Lyceum Address is George B. Forgie, in *Patricide in the House Divided* (New York, 1979), 55–87. He relates it to the general theme of "ambition in the post-heroic age." Forgie's work is an illustration of why psycho-history is so widely held in disrepute. He argues that Lincoln created the tyrant out of "undesirable wishes he could not recognize in himself," which "he expelled and then reified . . . into the image of the bad son." In a footnote he explains, "Psychoanalysts call this operation 'projection' " (p. 86). Actually, however, it is Forgie's projection rather than Lincoln's that is the relevant factor in this interpretation. For not only does Forgie ignore Lincoln's explicit statement of identification with those who might become tyrant ("and I believe it is true . . ."), it is hardly bold to assume that he may also have been unconsciously hostile to Lincoln's actual words, because his central thesis is that Stephen A. Douglas is the "bad son" of the Lyceum Address whom Lincoln symbolically killed in the 1850s. This preposterous conclusion, to be considered more fully below, would seem to be a monumental case of

intellectual regression in service of the professional ego (to alter slightly a characterization Forgie applies to Lincoln).

20. Mason Locke Weems, *The Life of Washington,* ed. Marcus Cunliffe (Cambridge, Mass., 1962), 221.

21. It is noteworthy that Weems ends his book on the same theme: Other governments, following the example of the United States set in pursuance of Washington's advice, shall likewise become transformed. "Thus, step by step progressing in virtue, the world will ripen for glory, till the great hour of her dissolution being come, the ready archangel shall lift his trumpet and sound her knell" (p. 224).

22. Herndon and Weik, 304.

23. Norman O. Brown, *Life Against Death; The Psychoanalytical Meaning of History* (New York, 1959), 118.

24. Ernest Becker, The *Denial of Death* (New York, 1973), 36.

25. Erik Erikson, *Young Man Luther: A Study in Psychoanalysis and History* (New York, 1958), 83. See also Robert Jay Lifton, *Revolutionary Immortality* (New York, 1968) for a treatment of this theme in connection with the Chinese cultural revolution; and, by the same author, *Death in Life: Survivors of Hiroshima* (New York, 1967).

26. Herndon and Weik, 354.

27. *Collected Works,* I, 48, 139

28. *Ibid.,* 265, 280.

29. In 1863 Lincoln wrote to Shakespearean actor James Hackett, "I think nothing equals Macbeth." *Ibid.,* VI, 392. The passage referred to here is: "Tomorrow and tomorrow and tomorrow/ Creeps in this petty pace, from day to day,/ To the last syllable of recorded time,/ And all our yesterdays have lighted fools/ The way to dusty death. Out, out, brief candle!/Life's but a walking shadow, a poor player/That struts and frets his hour upon the stage/ And then is heard no more: it is a tale/ Told by an idiot, full of sound and fury,/ Signifying nothing."

30. *Collected Works,* I, 1.

31. *Ibid.,* 378. Lincoln quoted from this poem in his eulogy of Zachary Taylor (*ibid.,* II, 90) and privately at the White House. See Carpenter, 60.

32. *Collected Works,* II, 90.

33. *Ibid.,* 89.

34. *Ibid.,* III, 482.

35. *Ibid.,* II, 90.

36. *Ibid.,* 123.

37. Albert J. Beveridge, *Abraham Lincoln, 1809–1858* (Boston, 1928), I, 15n.

38. *Collected Works,* I, 456, 459.

39. *Ibid.,* II, 97. (The word "sparrow" may have had a double meaning for Lincoln in this context. His mother's aunt and uncle, who lived with the Lincolns in Indiana, were named Sparrow.)

40. *Ibid.,* IV, 169.

41. *Ibid.,* I, 378.

42. Beveridge, I, 57.

43. *Ibid.,* 51, 54n.

44. *Ibid.,* 66, 68.

45. *Collected Works,* I, 384.

46. Alexis de Tocqueville, *Democracy in America,* ed. Phillip Bradley (New York, 1945), II, 105–6.

47. *Collected Works,* I, 282.

48. Beveridge, I, 288–97.

49. *Ibid.,* 314, 315.

50. *Ibid.*

51. *Collected Works,* I, 229.

52. *Ibid.,* 228.

53. Beveridge, I, 150.

54. *Collected Works,* I, 265, 267–8.

55. *Ibid.,* 268.

56. *Ibid.,* 367.

57. *Ibid.,* 369–70.

58. *Ibid.,* 387–9.

59. *Ibid.,* III, 203–4.

60. *Ibid.,* I, 165.

61. *Ibid.,* II, 514.

62. *Ibid.,* III, 547.

63. *Ibid.,* II, 122.

64. *Ibid.,* 132.

65. *Ibid.,* 482.

66. *Ibid.,* III, 27.

67. *Ibid.,* II, 547.

68. *Ibid.,* III, 334.

69. Both James G. Randall, *Lincoln the President* (New York, 1945), and Harry V. Jaffa, *op. cit.,* for example, are in substantial agreement on these points. Randall, however, sees no essential difference between the positions adopted by Lincoln and Douglas during the debates, since events proved popular sovereignty a workable formula for keeping slavery out of the territories—first in Kansas, then in Dakota, Nevada, and Colorado (I, 126, 129–31). This leads to the implication that the Civil War was a "needless war." Jaffa, on the other hand, finds the differences between

Lincoln and Douglas to be of the highest significance, involving the future of free government in the United States, which leads to the implication that the Civil War was fully justified on moral grounds (pp. 27, 340, *passim*). Both interpretations fail to recognize that Lincoln was motivated by much more than a desire for office, or a desire to establish a moral principle. As indicated here, and demonstrated more fully in the next section, Lincoln derived his principles from his ambitions, rather than vice versa, and his ambitions went far beyond officeholding.

70. *Collected Works*, III, 367.

71. *Ibid.*, 436.

72. Republicans were badly divided on the issue of slavery in 1858. When Douglas broke ranks with the Buchanan administration's attempt to force slavery into Kansas, it put Republicans in a quandary. On the one hand, they wanted to support Douglas as a way of defeating Buchanan's policy, but on the other, they were loath to admit that territories could approve slavery, as "popular sovereignty" would require. Nevertheless, all ninety-two Republican Congressmen voted for the Crittenden bill, which provided for a referendum on the Lecompton (slave) constitution of Kansas. Some radicals, including Seward, even wanted to endorse Douglas against Lincoln in the Senate contest. See Eric Foner, *Free Soil, Free Labor, Free Men* (London, 1970), 130–2. In short, with the exception of Salmon Chase, no one, besides Lincoln, defined Republican principles very clearly and consistently, and Lincoln was more concerned with his immortality than with his principles. See also Don E. Fehrenbacher, *Prelude to Greatness* (Stanford, Calif., 1962), who discusses the rather incoherent and fragmentary beginnings of the Republican party and then concludes that when Lincoln finally joined the Republicans, "he adopted their name, but they accepted a platform that was closer to his way of thinking" (p. 35).

73. *Collected Works*, I, 420–2.

74. Beveridge, I, 424n.

75. The speech appears in *Collected Works*, I, 431–43.

76. *Ibid.*, 347.

77. Beveridge, I, 381.

78. *Collected Works*, I, 431.

79. *Ibid.*, 420.

80. *Ibid.*, 430.

81. *Ibid.*, 439.

82. *Ibid.*, 446–7.

83. Weems reported that Washington as a youth would attempt to prevent fights among his fellow students. "If he could not disarm their

savage passions by his arguments, he would instantly go to the master, and inform him of their barbarous intentions" (p. 19). The boys, understandably, were often angry at this.

84. *Ibid.*, 5.
85. *Collected Works*, I, 8.
86. Michael Paul Rogin, *Fathers and Children: Andrew Jackson and the Subjugation of the American Indian* (New York, 1975), 53.
87. *Collected Works*, I, 274.
88. Weems, 191.
89. *Collected Works*, I, 278.
90. *Ibid.*, 279.
91. *Ibid.*, 275.
92. Beveridge, I, 329–30.
93. *Collected Works*, I, 279.
94. *Ibid.*, 178–9.
95. Weems, 135 (italics deleted).
96. Beveridge, I, 428.
97. *Ibid.*, 430–2, 432n. Debate among historians about the actual political effects of Lincoln's Mexican War speech has tended to obscure the more important issue of how Lincoln personally responded to these attacks. Once again, Herndon is at the center of the controversy and has succeeded in defining the terms of the debate. In an 1887 letter, Herndon claimed that when Lincoln returned home from Congress in 1849, he was "politically dead," an assertion which owed its credibility largely to the fact that the Whigs lost their safe 7th District seat to Democratic candidate Harris in 1848. However, as a recent study points out, Harris was a war hero running against a weak Whig candidate (Logan), and even then only managed to win by 106 votes. Moreover, Whig candidate Taylor carried the district by a wide margin in the presidential contest, and apparently Logan's defeat did not diminish Lincoln's standing among Illinois Whigs, who urged him to seek reelection to Congress in 1850—an election won by Whig candidate Yates. See Paul Findley, *A. Lincoln: The Crucible of Congress* (New York, 1979), 212–16. Findley attributes the widespread acceptance of Herndon's assumption that Lincoln's antiwar stance was politically ruinous to the influence of Beveridge, who, as an American missionist, "had no use for war critics," and thus "dignified the Herndon myth" (p. 217). Although Findley is correct that Beveridge seems to blame Lincoln for Logan's defeat, his assertion that Beveridge simply "dignified the Herndon myth" is unwarranted, and even depends in part on his misquoting of Beveridge. Findley writes, "Although all solid historical evidence was to the contrary, Beveridge concluded that Lincoln *'knew*

his fortunes were ended forever' " (p. 217, italics added). Actually Beveridge's conclusion is that Lincoln *"thought* his *political* fortunes were ended forever," a conclusion about Lincoln's state of mind rather than the objective reality, which Beveridge then substantiates by presenting a picture of Lincoln's psychological devastation in the face of his perceived political failure (Beveridge, I, 493, and ch. IX). Beveridge's account thus helps to provide an explanation of why Lincoln did not seek political office in 1850 and immediately thereafter, despite the urging of his Whig colleagues. Findley, however, has no explanation for Lincoln's political moratorium in the early 1850s, despite his fully documented conclusion that Lincoln remained a viable candidate. Another factor which would help explain Lincoln's refusal to seek public office for five years was the narrow range of minor offices available to him. See Fehrenbacher, 20–1. Given the magnitude of Lincoln's ambition, such limited opportunities must have contributed to his personal sense of failure.

98. *Collected Works,* I, 467–8, 474.

99. Beveridge, I, 442, 493.

100. *Ibid.,* 498.

101. *Ibid.,* 553, 555.

102. *Ibid.,* 499, 529–35.

103. *Ibid.,* I, 465–6.

104. *Ibid.,* 499–500; *Collected Works,* II, 15–16.

105. Beveridge, I, 523–4.

106. *Ibid.,* 507, 521–4.

107. *Ibid.,* 524n, 524, 506n.

108. *Ibid.,* 525n.

109. *Ibid.,* 520.

110. *Ibid.*

111. *Collected Works,* II, 249 (italics added). Forgie overlooks this transformation in Lincoln's identity, arguing that Lincoln's career was one of "lifelong filiopiety" (p. 85). It is apparently this misapprehension, in addition to his failure to recognize the political distinctions between 1776 and 1789, which leads Forgie to the bizarre conclusion that Lincoln projected his own "unacceptable" wishes onto a "mythical patricidal figure" (Douglas) whom he then had to kill "in order to save the fathers' work" (p. 250). In fact, so devoted is Forgie to this notion that he even suggests that the fratricidal guilt which Lincoln experienced at the end of the Civil War was due to his having symbolically killed Douglas in the 1850s, as though the 600,000 actual victims of fratricide were of no significance by comparison (p. 247). But Forgie's conclusion is correct in one sense: "The bad son of the Lyceum Address prophecy had at last appeared to make his assault

upon the fathers' institutions" (p. 262). It's just that Forgie has misidentified the son.

112. *Collected Works,* I, 488.

113. *Ibid.,* II, 249, 275–6.

114. *Ibid.,* 385.

115. *Ibid.,* 406.

116. *Ibid.*

117. *Ibid.,* III, 324.

118. *Ibid.,* II, 407.

119. Staughton Lynd, "The Abolitionist Critique of the United States Constitution," *The Antislavery Vanguard,* ed., Martin Duberman (Princeton, N. J., 1965), 230–5.

120. *Collected Works,* III, 315.

121. *Ibid.,* II, 255. See also *Federalist* No. 1, 33–4.

122. Foner, 8–9.

123. *Collected Works,* II, 263–4.

124. *Ibid.,* 404.

125. Beveridge, II, 379, 398–9, 446.

126. *Ibid.,* 545.

127. In a private note of 1856, Lincoln specifically made the connection between his ambition and the cause of the "oppressed." Comparing himself with Douglas, Lincoln wrote that he had first become acquainted with Douglas twenty-two years before. "Even then, we were both ambitious; I, perhaps, quite as much so as he. With *me,* the race of ambition has been a failure—a flat failure; with *him* it has been one of splendid success. His name fills the nation; and is not unknown, even, in foreign lands. I affect no contempt for the high eminence he has reached." One might expect that Lincoln was about to give Douglas a polite accolade for having bettered him in the race of ambition. Not so. His next words dwell on what might have been had his ambitions been realized: "So reached, that the oppressed of my species, might have shared with me in the elevation, I would rather stand on that eminence, than wear the richest crown that ever pressed a monarch's brow." *Collected Works,* II, 382–3.

128. *Ibid.,* III, 95.

129. *Ibid.,* II, 275, 274.

130. Foner, 205, 215.

131. Beveridge, II, 574. Lincoln's obvious reference here was to Matthew 12:25: "Every kingdom divided against itself is brought to desolation; and every city or house divided against itself shall not stand." The possible influence of the house mentioned in George Washington's mother's dream should not be overlooked, however: ". . . if well kept

together, it will last for ever, but if you take it apart, you will make the house ten thousand times worse than it was before." Weems, 57.

132. Foner, 213.

133. *Collected Works,* III, 334.

134. *Ibid.,* II, 506.

135. *Ibid.,* 265.

136. *Ibid.,* 270, 276.

137. *Ibid.,* IV, 168–9.

138. *Ibid.,* 193–4.

139. *Ibid.,* 91.

140. Washington also defined himself as an instrument of a higher purpose. Referring to his military and political career, he said: "I feel that nothing is due to my personal agency." Weems, 183 (italics deleted).

141. Woodrow Wilson, *The New Democracy, Presidential Messages, Addresses and Other Papers,* eds. Ray Stannard Baker and William E. Dodd (New York, 1926), II, 295.

142. Current, 78.

143. *Collected Works,* IV, 162 (italics added).

144. *Ibid.,* 260. The final draft of the address also maintained this same impartiality by using the phrase "on your side of the North, and yours of the South."

145. Ward Hill Lamon, *Recollections of Lincoln* (Washington, D. C., 1911), 112–13.

146. *Collected Works,* IV, 215, 216, 220.

147. *Ibid.,* 226. See also 228, 236, 238.

148. *Ibid.,* 261.

149. *Ibid.,* 199, 204, 220–1, 226. It is noteworthy that Weems quoted Washington to the same effect: "My diffidence in my own abilities was superseded by a confidence in the rectitude of our cause and the patronage of Heaven" (p. 182; italics deleted).

150. *Collected Works,* III, 204, 443.

151. *Ibid.,* 95; II, 498; III, 488.

152. *Ibid.,* I, 289.

153. *Ibid.,* III, 410.

154. *Ibid.,* IV, 236.

155. *Ibid.,* 197.

156. *Ibid.,* 260. See also 270, 207, 221.

157. *Ibid.,* 160–1, 169.

158. *Ibid.,* 265.

159. *Ibid.,* 210, 221, 231.

160. *Ibid.,* 233.

161. *Ibid.*, 239.

162. *Ibid.*, 240. Lincoln's allusion here was probably to the warning he had received that an assassination attempt would be made as his train passed through Baltimore.

163. *Ibid.*, 241. That Lincoln was not merely worried about having revealed an assassination plot is suggested by the fact that he reiterated his willingness to die.

CHAPTER 3

1. *Collected Works,* VIII, 406n.

2. *Ibid.*, IV, 482.

3. In the formulation of what follows, I am especially indebted to Perry Miller, "From the Covenant to the Revival," *The Shaping of American Religion,* eds. James Ward Smith and A. Leland Jamison (Princeton, N. J., 1961), 322–69.

4. *Ibid.*, 322–7. Quote is from p. 322.

5. Michael Walzer, *The Revolution of the Saints* (New York, 1974), 10, 295–6.

6. *Ibid.*, 166–71. Quote is from p. 167.

7. Perry Miller, *Errand into the Wilderness* (New York, 1964), 48–9, 90–1.

8. Edmund S. Morgan, ed., *Puritan Political Ideas* (Indianapolis, 1965), 91–3.

9. Walzer, 48.

10. Miller has called the revision of the covenant "shamelessly pragmatic" (*Errand into the Wilderness,* 88). Daniel J. Boorstin presents an alternative view in *The Americans: The Colonial Experience* (New York, 1964), pt. I.

11. Robert N. Bellah, *The Broken Covenant* (New York, 1975), 10–12.

12. Sidney Mead, *The Lively Experiment* (New York, 1963), 78.

13. Conrad Cherry, ed., *God's New Israel* (Englewood Cliffs, N. J., 1971), 55–60.

14. Sydney E. Ahlstrom, *A Religious History of the American People* (New York, 1975), I, 361, 425–6.

15. Gordon S. Wood, *The Creation of the American Republic* (Chapel Hill, 1969), 114.

16. Miller, "From the Covenant to the Revival," *op. cit.,* 342.

17. *Ibid.*, 330, 328.

18. Cherry, 81.

19. Bernard Bailyn, *The Ideological Origins of the American Revolution* (Cambridge, Mass., 1967), 154.

20. Cushing Strout, *The New Heavens and New Earth* (New York, 1974), 66.

21. Cherry, 84–5.

22. Miller, "From the Covenant to the Revival," 333, 327; and Strout, 67–8.

23. As quoted by Strout, 67–8.

24. Robert N. Bellah, "Civil Religion in America," *Daedalus* 96 (Winter 1967), 8n. See also Cherry, 65.

25. Wood, 393–429; Miller, "From the Covenant to the Revival," 346–50.

26. Wood, 428.

27. Bellah states that God is mentioned or referred to in all inaugural addresses except Washington's second, and that the word "God" does not appear until Monroe's second. "Civil Religion in America," 7n.

28. James D. Richardson, ed., *Messages and Papers of the Presidents* (Washington, D.C., 1899), I, 52–3.

29. *Ibid.,* 64.

30. Ahlstrom, I, 617, 469–614 *passim;* Mead, 35, 36, 65, 66; Strout, 98–9.

31. Miller, "From the Covenant to the Revival," 357.

32. Richardson, 322–3, 381–2.

33. Boorstin, *The Americans: The National Experience* (New York, 1965), 307–25, offers an excellent discussion of the declamatory literature of the period.

34. Ahlstrom, I, 462.

35. Miller, "From the Covenant to the Revival," 357.

36. *Ibid.,* 358–9.

37. John William Ward, *Andrew Jackson: Symbol for an Age* (New York, 1962), 107–8, 109.

38. Joseph L. Blau, ed., *Social Theories of Jacksonian Democracy* (Indianapolis, 1954), 30, 31.

39. This literature is discussed by Boorstin, *The Americans: The National Experience,* 356–62.

40. *Ibid.,* 374–5.

41. *Collected Works,* III, 357.

42. Henry Nash Smith, *Virgin Land* (Cambridge, Mass., 1950), 165–72.

43. William H. Pease and Jane H. Pease, ed., *The Antislavery Argument* (Indianapolis, 1965), 130, 179–81.

44. Bailyn, 245, 243.

45. George M. Fredrickson, *The Inner Civil War* (New York, 1965), 7.

46. Miller, "From the Covenant to the Revival," 367–8.

47. Edmund Wilson, *Patriotic Gore* (New York, 1966), 88.

48. Francis Grierson, *The Valley of Shadows* (Boston, 1909), 1.

49. Wilson, 5, 32.

50. Mead, 144.

51. Albert J. Beveridge, *Abraham Lincoln, 1809–1858* (Boston, 1928), II, 422.

52. Ahlstrom, II, 101–3; Ernest Lee Tuveson, *The Redeemer Nation* (Chicago, 1968), 77–8, 84, 190–1, 192–6; Beveridge, II, 489, 490–1.

53. Stephen B. Oates, *To Purge This Land with Blood* (New York, 1970), 245.

54. *Ibid.*, 222, 229–30.

55. *Ibid.*, 291.

56. *Ibid.*, 351.

57. Fredrickson, 36–7, 38, 41–3, 40.

58. As quoted by S. E. Morison and H. S. Commager, *The Growth of the American Republic* (New York, 1956), I, 634.

59. Wilson, 92–4.

60. *Ibid.*, 95.

61. Allan Nevins, ed., *The Messages and Papers of Jefferson Davis and the Confederacy* (New York, 1966), I, 103.

62. *Collected Works*, VIII, 318n.

63. Jean Jacques Rousseau, *The Social Contract and Discourses*, ed. G. D. H. Cole (New York, 1950), 38, 40–1.

64. *Ibid.*, 37–8.

65. Mason Locke Weems, *The Life of Washington*, ed. Marcus Cunliffe (Cambridge, Mass., 1962), 182–3.

66. *Collected Works*, IV, 245.

67. Kenneth M. Stampp, *And the War Came* (Baton Rouge, La., 1950), 184–9.

68. *Collected Works*, IV, 261.

69. *Ibid.*, 240–1.

70. The best of these interpretations are as follows: James G. Randall, *Lincoln the President* (New York, 1945), I, 311–50, and David M. Potter, *Lincoln and His Party in the Secession Crisis* (New Haven, 1942), reject the view that Lincoln deliberately goaded the South into firing the first shot. They maintain that he was forced by events to undertake the Sumter expedition since there was no time to reinforce and secure Fort Pickens, and that he wished only to preserve the status quo in Charleston Harbor by an unprovocative resupply of provisions. Stampp, *op. cit.*, however, argues that Lincoln's purpose was to preserve the Union by a "strategy of defense" which aimed at neither war nor peace *per se*, but which risked

the possibility of war. Stampp points out, furthermore, that debate over the wisdom of supplying Sumter occurred only after Lincoln thought the reinforcement of Pickens would be successful (p. 283). Indeed, Stampp's evidence seems to support the conclusion of Richard N. Current, *Lincoln and the First Shot* (New York, 1963), that Lincoln maneuvered the South into the position of either having to accept defeat or initiate violence, and he did so with the expectation that hostilities were probable.

71. William H. Herndon and Jesse Weik, *Herndon's Life of Lincoln,* ed. Paul M. Angle (Cleveland, 1947), 351.

72. As quoted by William J. Wolf, *The Almost Chosen People* (New York, 1959), 104.

73. *Collected Works,* IV, 424–5.

74. This interpretation follows Stampp, 282–6. See also *Collected Works,* IV, 284–5, 316–18. It is interesting to note that Lincoln's refusal to abandon Fort Sumter corresponds to an incident reported by Weems. In his account of the Revolution, Weems denigrates Charles Lee for wanting to abandon the fort in Charleston harbor, and warmly praises General Moultrie for refusing to do so. Weems, 76–7.

75. As quoted by Current, 181.

76. *Collected Works,* IV, 351. Nothing said here is meant to imply that Lincoln alone must bear the responsibility for the outbreak of hostilities. The South too needed a decisive event which would mobilize opinion and bring Virginia into the Confederacy. Thus the Confederate Congress adopted on February 15 a resolution to the effect that Sumter and Pickens should be taken by either force or negotiation, and Davis instructed South Carolina officials not to permit resupply of Sumter. Current, 138–48.

77. *Collected Works,* I, 432, 439.

78. *Ibid.,* IV, 431–2, 438–9.

79. *Ibid.,* V, 26n.

80. *Ibid.,* 279, 420. See also p. 478.

81. *Ibid.,* 403–4.

82. *Ibid.,* 212; VI, 244, 531. By 1864, Lincoln had diminished his personal role so far that he could mark the beginning of the war with the firing on the *Star of the West* which had occurred during the Buchanan administration. *Ibid.,* VIII, 1.

83. *Ibid.,* VII, 301.

84. *Ibid.,* 282.

85. As quoted by Wilson, 422.

86. *Collected Works,* V, 49.

87. *Ibid.,* IV, 265.

88. Nevins, *The War for the Union* (New York, 1959), II, 163.

89. *Collected Works,* IV, 271.

90. *Ibid.,* V, 52, 53.

91. *Ibid.,* 537.

92. *Ibid.,* IV, 433–5, 265.

93. *Ibid.,* VIII, 1, 96.

94. Allan Nevins, *War for the Union,* IV, 108.

95. *Ibid.,* 40.

96. The worldwide response to Lincoln's reelection is reported in Carl Sandburg, *Abraham Lincoln: The War Years* (New York, 1940), III, 576–86.

97. Nevins, *War for the Union,* IV, 98.

98. As quoted by Sandburg, II, 238–9.

99. Nevins, *War for the Union,* I, 137.

100. Sandburg, I, 479, 14.

101. *Ibid.,* 225.

102. *Ibid.,* 294.

103. Ahlstrom, II, 116.

104. Sandburg, I, 225; III, 165.

105. Nevins, *War for the Union,* II, 108.

106. Nevins, *Messages and Papers of Jefferson Davis and the Confederacy,* I, 22, 103.

107. *Ibid.,* 228, 328.

108. Ahlstrom, I, 442, 506, 530, 400.

109. This account is based upon Fredrickson.

110. As quoted by Fredrickson, 48, 47, 69, 74.

111. *Ibid.,* 73–81 *passim.*

112. *Ibid.,* 136–9.

113. Frank Freidel, ed., *Union Pamphlets of the Civil War* (Cambridge, Mass., 1967), I, 102.

114. Fredrickson, 82.

115. *Collected Works,* VI, 156. See also IV, 482.

116. *Ibid.,* V, 32, 185–6; VI, 332–3, 496–7; VII, 431–2; VIII, 55–6.

117. *Ibid.,* VI, 332, 496–7.

118. *Ibid.,* V, 498.

119. *Ibid.,* III, 136.

120. *Ibid.,* VI, 114.

121. *Ibid.,* VIII, 155; VII, 431.

122. Gideon Welles, *The Diary of Gideon Welles* (Boston, 1911), II, 190.

123. Sandburg, II, 3, 156–7.

124. *Collected Works,* V, 537.

125. Sandburg, III, 392–3.

126. *Collected Works,* V, 510; VII, 101; V, 438, 450. Lincoln expressed

similar views in the famous Bixby letter (VIII, 116–17) and in his remarks to Union soldiers mustering out after their terms of service (VII, 512, 528).

127. *Ibid.*, VII, 23.

128. *Ibid.*, V, 388.

129. On two separate occasions, for example, Lincoln was presented with canes made from the arch under which Washington passed in Trenton on his way to assume the presidency. One of these presentations was made before a public gathering. Yet on neither occasion did Lincoln make any direct comment about Washington. *Ibid.*, VII, 397n, 458n. The only exceptions to Lincoln's silence about Washington after 1862, as recorded in the *Collected Works*, were in 1863, when Washington's birthday fell on the Sabbath, and the same year when he pardoned a policeman convicted of beating demonstrators following a reading of the Farewell Address the previous year. *Ibid.*, V, 498; VI, 106.

130. *Ibid.*, II, 278.

131. Adolphe de Chambrun, *Impressions of Lincoln and the Civil War* (New York, 1952), 83.

132. *Ibid.*, 75–9.

133. *Collected Works*, V, 346

134. Benjamin P. Thomas, *Abraham Lincoln* (New York, 1952), 512.

135. De Chambrun, 85.

136. David Homer Bates, *Lincoln and the Telegraph Office* (New York, 1907), 223; *Collected Works*, VI, 392.

137. De Chambrun, 83.

138. *Macbeth*, III, iii.

139. Thomas, 514.

140. Ward Hill Lamon, *Recollections of Abraham Lincoln* (Washington, D. C., 1911), 116–17.

141. Wilson, 128–9, for example, makes this assumption; but it is apparently made on the basis of a misunderstanding of the exact words Lincoln used in recounting his dream. Wilson quotes the voices in Lincoln's dream as saying: "Lincoln is dead." Lamon, incidentally, claimed detailed accuracy for his version of the dream: "I give it as nearly in his own words as I can, from notes which I made immediately after its recital." Lamon, 114.

142. *Ibid.*, 117–18.

143. *Macbeth*, III, iii.

144. Lamon, 115.

145. Genesis 28:12–17; 32:11.

146. Lamon, 112–13.

147. Welles, II, 282.

148. Lamon, 118.

149. *Collected Works,* IV, 233.

150. That Lincoln's dream of the dead president was a cause of insomnia is reported by Lamon: "In conversations with me he referred to it [the dream] afterward, closing one with this quotation from 'Hamlet': 'To sleep; perchance to dream! ay, *there's the rub!'* with a strong accent on the last three words" (p. 117). That he also had a suicidal disregard for his own safety is reported by a number of sources, including Lamon. Perhaps the most obvious example of this was Lincoln's two-mile walk through Richmond on April 4, 1865, which was witnessed by thousands of Confederate citizens, a trek which he undertook without the benefit of a military escort. (Sandburg, IV, 176–8). That Lincoln was not unaware of the danger of assassination is suggested by the fact that he kept an envelope in his desk marked "Assassination" in which he placed threatening letters and other relevant material (Sandburg, IV, 135).

151. *Hamlet,* III, iii. Lincoln also recited this soliloquy to Carpenter, *op. cit.,* 50.

152. As quoted by Wolf, 125.

153. Carpenter, 51.

154. De Chambrun, 100.

155. Sandburg, I, 596; II, 406. Many other similar incidents are reported by Sandburg in his account of the war years.

156. *Ibid.,* III, 311, 301.

157. As quoted in *ibid.,* 305, 565.

158. *Ibid.,* II, 463.

159. *Collected Works,* VIII, 150–1; and as quoted by Sandburg, III, 47.

160. As quoted in Sandburg, III, 525.

161. Dostoevsky's story, as Hannah Arendt has written, "contrasts the mute compassion of Jesus with the eloquent pity of the Inquisitor." After listening silently to the Inquisitor's speech, in which he claims to have provided for the happiness of men by abolishing freedom and giving men what they really want—mystery, miracle, and authority—Jesus responds simply with a gesture of compassion and forgiveness, a kiss. Hannah Arendt, *On Revolution* (New York, 1963), 80–1.

162. *Collected Works,* VIII, 332–3.

163. *Ibid.,* 356.

164. *Ibid.,* 333.

165. *Ibid.,* V, 358.

166. *Ibid.,* VII, 169.

167. Regarding the oath of allegiance to his reconstituted Union,

Lincoln insisted that it be voluntary and that it be a test of faith. "There must be a test by which to separate the opposing elements, so as to build only from the sound; and that test is a sufficiently liberal one, which accepts as sound whoever will make a sworn recantation of his former unsoundness." *Ibid.*, VII, 51. Only the saved, in other words, were to be accepted into Lincoln's Union.

168. Lloyd Lewis, *Myths After Lincoln* (New York, 1957), 155.

169. As quoted by Sandburg, IV, 402. Booth, incidentally, was present at the hanging of John Brown in 1859, and considered him a hero though he hated Brown's cause. Afterward, Booth sent his sister a spear which he said belonged to Brown with "Major Washington to J. Wilkes Booth" inscribed on the handle. Sandburg, 312.

CHAPTER 4

1. Arthur M. Schlesinger, Jr., *A Thousand Days* (New York, 1965), 114.

2. Edmond S. Ions, ed., *The Politics of John F. Kennedy* (New York, 1967), 49–50.

3. *Ibid.*, 51–2.

4. I am indebted to Norman Jacobson for suggesting to me that twentieth-century presidents might be viewed as attempting to refound the Constitution in the international sphere.

5. Ions, 117–18.

6. Theodore Roosevelt, *The Foes of Our Own Household* (New York, 1917), 58.

7. Theodore Roosevelt, *The Works of Theodore Roosevelt: Presidential Addresses and State Papers* (New York, 1913), I, 38.

8. Roosevelt, *Foes of Our Own Household*, 86, 57 (italics deleted).

9. Roosevelt, *Works*, I, 57, 58, 59.

10. *Ibid.*, 63, 67.

11. S. E. Morison and H. S. Commager, *The Growth of the American Republic* (New York, 1956), II, 344.

12. Roosevelt, *Works*, III, 90–1.

13. Woodrow Wilson, *The New Democracy, Presidential Messages, Addresses and Other Papers*, eds. Ray Stannard Baker and William E. Dodd (New York, 1926), II, 296–7.

14. *Ibid.*, I, 225–34.

15. *Ibid.*, 400; II, 251, 296.

16. *Ibid.*, II, 414.

17. Woodrow Wilson, *War and Peace: The Public Papers of Woodrow Wilson*, eds. Ray Stannard Baker and William E. Dodd (New York, 1927), I, 16.

18. *Ibid.*, 67.

19. Samuel I. Rosenman, ed., *The Public Papers and Addresses of Franklin D. Roosevelt* (New York, 1932–50), I, 648.

20. *Ibid.*, V, 235–6.

21. *Ibid.*, X, 194, 139, 556–7, 594.

22. *Ibid.*, XIII, 152–3.

23. *Ibid.*, X, 314–15.

24. *Ibid.*, XII, 241.

25. The term "myth of the eternal return" is taken from Mircea Eliade, *Cosmos and History* (New York, 1959).

26. Most studies of presidential psychology concentrate on individual psychology. For example, see James David Barber, *The Presidential Character* (Englewood Cliffs, N. J., 1977). This would seem to be a necessary but insufficient basis for understanding the subject. F. G. Hutchins, "Presidential Autocracy in America," *The Presidency Reappraised,* eds. Rexford G. Tugwell and Thomas E. Cronin (Santa Barbara, Calif., 1974), 35–55, recognizes the influence of a president's predecessors in defining the presidential role. Hutchins argues that a president must "safeguard his legitimacy by identifying himself with his precursors."

27. *Federalist,* No. 72, 438.

28. Rosenman, X, 194.

29. Hannah Arendt, *On Revolution* (New York, 1963), 175–7. She describes this discrepancy as a difference between two types of social-contract theory.

30. Bernard Bailyn, *The Ideological Origins of the American Revolution* (Cambridge, Mass., 1967), 232–46.

31. Louis Hartz, *The Liberal Tradition in America* (New York, 1955), 71. Hartz recognized that the American Revolution posed "the unusual problem of a fatherless tribe."

32. Bailyn, 153.

33. Thomas Paine, *Common Sense and Other Political Writings* (Indianapolis, 1953), 52.

34. See Wright Morris, *The Territory Ahead* (New York, 1958) and Leo Marx, *The Machine in the Garden* (New York, 1967).

35. Frederick Jackson Turner, *The Frontier in American History* (New York, 1920), 266, 22–9.

36. For a discussion of nostalgia in Progressive thought, see David Noble, *The Paradox of Progressive Thought* (Minneapolis, 1958). William A. Williams has demonstrated the connection between Turner's frontier thesis and expansionist foreign policy. See his *The Tragedy of American Diplomacy* (New York, 1962) and "The Frontier Thesis and American Foreign Policy," *Pacific Historical Review* 24 (Nov. 1955), 379–95.

37. Lincoln issued the Emancipation Proclamation as a war measure on the basis of his power as commander in chief, and it applied only to those states or portions of states in actual rebellion against the United States.

38. Williams, *Tragedy of American Diplomacy*, chs. 2 and 3.

39. San Francisco *Chronicle*, March 10, 1967. Johnson's attempt to refound the Constitution in South Vietnam also included some of his "Great Society" programs. At Honolulu in 1966, the United States pledged itself to "the principle of the self-determination of peoples and of government by the consent of the governed." The same statement also declared, "We have helped and we will help [the Vietnamese] to stabilize the economy, to increase the production of goods, to spread the light of education and stamp out disease." As quoted by Frances FitzGerald, *Fire in the Lake* (Boston, 1972), 233. In addition, Johnson thought that a development program for the Mekong River, along the lines of the TVA, could be used as a bargaining point in negotiations with the North Vietnamese. See Doris Kearns, *Lyndon Johnson and the American Dream* (New York, 1976), 278–81.

40. Nixon outlined his plan for a "New American Revolution" in his 1971 State of the Union address. He has said that his purpose was to diffuse power and return it to the people. See *R.N.: The Memoirs of Richard Nixon* (New York, 1978), 533. The revolution he actually effected, however, concentrated power in the presidency. See Arthur M. Schlesinger, Jr., *The Imperial Presidency* (Boston, 1973), 252.

41. Schlesinger, *Imperial Presidency*, ch. 8, *passim.*

42. Trust in the government in Washington, D.C., to do what is right "always or most of the time" declined from 76 percent in 1964 to 53.5 percent in 1970. See Arthur H. Miller, "Political Issues and Trust in Government: 1964–1970," *American Political Science Review* 68 (Sept. 1974), 951–72. Distrust of government rose sharply from 1972 to 1976. See data supplied by the Survey Research Center, University of Michigan, as cited by James Q. Wilson, *American Government: Institutions and Policies* (Lexington, Mass., 1980), 90. However, the increase in cynicism has apparently been largely directed at particular officials and policies rather than the system itself. See Jack Citrin, "Comment: The Political Relevance of Trust in Government," *American Political Science Review* 68 (Sept. 1974), 973–88.

43. Hannah Arendt, *Between Past and Future* (New York, 1963), 78–9.

44. Frantz Fanon, *The Wretched of the Earth* (New York, 1966), 255.

45. Hartz, 46, notes that a "hero is missing from the revolutionary literature of America," i.e. the legislator who lays the foundations of society. Weems's Washington provided Lincoln with a model which meets

the requirements set by Rousseau's conception of the legislator's "happiness"—the attainment of a distant glory. Weems said that Washington achieved his happiness by the "imitation of God in benevolent and useful life." Washington, he said, found his happiness in providing for the happiness of others. Weems, 128, 126. It would appear that the same is true of Lincoln.

46. David Apter, *The Politics of Modernization* (Chicago, 1965), 266–313.

Index

A Note About the Author

Dwight G. Anderson was born in Miles City, Montana, in 1938. He received a B.A. from the University of Montana and an M.A. and Ph.D. from the University of California, Berkeley. Since 1969, he has taught political science at San Diego State University.

A Note on the Type

This book was set, by computer-driven cathode-ray tube, in Baskerville. Linotype Baskerville is a facsimile cutting from type cast from the original matrices of a face designed by John Baskerville. The original face was the forerunner of the "modern" group of type faces.

John Baskerville (1706–1775) of Birmingham, England, a writing master with a special renown for cutting inscriptions in stone, began experimenting about 1750 with punch-cutting and making typographical material. His types, at first criticized as unnecessarily slender, delicate, and feminine, in time were recognized as both distinct and elegant.

Composed by The Haddon Craftsmen, Inc.,
Allentown, Pennsylvania

Printed and bound by R. R. Donnelly & Sons,
Harrisonburg, Virginia

Typography by Joe Marc Freedman